4TH AND GOAL EVERY DAY

ALABAMA'S RELENTLESS PURSUIT OF PERFECTION

PHIL SAVAGE

AND

RAY GLIER

Preface by
Nick Saban

Foreword by
Rece Davis

St. Martin's Press

New York

www.stmartins.com

Designed by Omar Chapa

The Library of Congress Cataloging-in-Publication Data is available upon request.

ISBN 978-1-250-13080-8 (hardcover)
ISBN 978-1-250-13081-5 (ebook)

Our books may be purchased in bulk for promotional, educational, or business use. Please contact your local bookseller or the Macmillan Corporate and Premium Sales Department at 1-800-221-7945, extension 5442, or by email at MacmillanSpecialMarkets@macmillan.com.

10 9 8 7 6 5 4 3 2

To Dorothy, Honor, and Ever

CONTENTS

PREFACE

In 2009, when Mal Moore approached me with the idea of Phil Savage becoming our radio color analyst, I could not have given him a higher recommendation.

Going back to our days on Bill Belichick's first staff in Cleveland, I knew the kind of work ethic, loyalty, and attention to detail he would bring to the job.

Through his experiences as a coach, scout, and general manager in the NFL, Phil has not only been an asset to the radio broadcasts, but he has also become a trusted part of our organization.

I am positive that this book will give football fans everywhere a unique perspective on our program, but even more, a true picture of what makes Alabama football so special.

—Nick Saban

FOREWORD

I don't remember exactly what brand of radio it was, but I was glued to it. I was a five-year-old in Guin, Alabama, and that black box with a silver antenna connected me to the Crimson Tide.

It was September 10, 1971, a Friday night. The Marion County High School Red Raiders had won their game, and now Alabama had a game on the West Coast against Southern California. Bedtime was negotiable for something epic, and Alabama football was always epic.

I lay on the floor, eyes fixed on that radio, maybe thinking that if I stared just a little harder, I'd actually be able to see the players move across my radio dial.

This was the first game of the wishbone era under Bear Bryant. Throughout the game, I would run to my mom and dad to earnestly report what John Forney, the voice of the Tide, had said on the air:

"Johnny Musso shook off two guys in the backfield."

I'd proclaim it as if I'd seen it myself. I guess I was practicing for a future career, but at that moment, I was certain I was destined to follow in the cleat marks of my favorite players, Musso and quarterback Terry Davis. Alabama upset the Trojans that night. It is my first memory of Alabama football.

I won my first bet that season, too. My babysitter, Mrs. Linda Aldridge, was a die-hard Auburn fan. Behind eventual Heisman Trophy winner Pat Sullivan, she was sure the Tigers would prevail when the two met in the Iron Bowl in a clash of unbeatens. Her confidence and teasing fueled my defense of the Crimson Tide. She goaded me into a wager, an agreement I immediately regretted when it occurred to me that I didn't have any money. Asking my parents was a risk. Gambling of any sort was frowned upon in the Davis household.

Turns out it was the stone-cold lock of the week. The Tide rolled 31–7, and Mrs. Aldridge graciously had the handsome sum of thirty-five cents ready for me upon my arrival at her doorstep Monday morning. The emotional investment and reward were far more exhilarating.

Two years later, my parents took me to Tuscaloosa for the first time. The first college game I ever saw in person, Alabama beat Virginia Tech, 77–6. College football in general and Alabama in particular had a near mystical quality. The players were larger-than-life. Whatever is bigger than that is what Coach Bryant was.

When I go into Bryant-Denny today, with crowds of more than one hundred thousand fans, the luxury suites, and the high-tech video board, the scene bears virtually no resemblance to the fifty-eight-thousand-seat bandbox I first walked into in 1973. That magical first trip as a seven-year-old never seems far away. I suspect my perspective is similar to that of a lot of kids growing up in Alabama. Football and church were the cornerstones of life. Hopefully, not in that order, though admittedly the lines got blurred from time to time.

My parents constantly reminded me that it was just a game. Crying over losses wasn't allowed. That made it necessary to pretend to take a late bath on New Year's Eve 1973 to properly mourn—alone in the bathroom—Alabama's one-point Sugar Bowl loss to Notre Dame. Mom and Dad figured I was allowed a few tears on that one. Perspective needed constant monitoring, but my emotional tie with the Crimson Tide was unmistakably deep and meaningful.

Alabama rarely lost when I was a kid, which is very much as it is in this era. What I didn't realize is that it wasn't nearly as easy as the Crimson Tide made it look then. That cold, hard truth became evident shortly after my enrollment at the University of Alabama. The first game I watched from the student section as a freshman in 1984 was against Boston College. Doug Flutie turned in a virtuoso performance leading the Eagles from a 31–14 deficit to a 38–31 win. Flutie went on to win the Heisman. The Tide went on to its first losing season in a quarter of a century.

Winning titles wasn't a birthright the way most of us thought, and nothing underscored that like the ubertalented 1986 team. A squad with Cornelius Bennett, Derrick Thomas, Jon Hand, Bobby Humphrey, Mike Shula, and Howard Cross didn't win the SEC. They didn't even win the state championship, losing to Auburn in the Iron Bowl. Alabama played in the Sun Bowl. The lesson: winning titles doesn't just happen.

Broadcasters have to take a step back from their childhood and student allegiances. It's the only way to do the job well. You owe that to your audience. I've never believed that means you automatically become a cynic or disavow that you ever rooted for a team. It just demands that you be fair in your judgments. Broadcasters also get opportunities to look through unique windows and hopefully gain insight into what makes people interesting or successful, people such as Nick Saban.

I first met him in 1994. I was working at WJRT-TV in Flint, Michigan, and was just three months from leaving for ESPN. Nick was the guy Michigan State hired to replace George Perles.

I don't remember any of the questions I asked him, but I know it had nothing to do with the Process. I do recall that while he wasn't the polished speaker you see now, he did have a commanding presence in the room.

While Nick started to build his college résumé at Michigan State, Alabama football largely floundered for much of the 1990s and early 2000s, except for a brief run in the Gene Stallings era. The program was plagued by ill-advised coaching hires, NCAA sanctions, and a permeating sense of entitlement that kept Alabama bound by tradition rather than building on it.

While one of the storied programs in the sport, for much of my early years in the studio hosting college football for ESPN, Alabama was an afterthought. The Tide wasn't a must-see on the list of highlights for the show. When Alabama was discussed, it was usually about what expectations should be considered realistic and whether the school was a dinosaur whose dreams of a return to glory were remote at best or delusional at worst. For the record, I never bought that line of thinking, but it was commonplace among many of my colleagues to think Alabama was finished as a powerhouse.

I first met Phil Savage in 2005. It was in the press box at Williams-Brice Stadium in Columbia, South Carolina, for Steve Spurrier's debut as the Gamecocks' head coach. Phil had just become general manager of the Cleveland Browns. His keen eye for talent was well established in football circles. We are talking about the guy who, as a member of the Ravens front office, strongly advocated drafting Ray Lewis and Ed Reed. Seems easy now, but both of those picks were in the latter stages of the first round. As Browns GM, he grabbed offensive lineman Joe Thomas, who is still working on a Hall of Fame career.

Phil and I chatted about players, Spurrier's return to college football, and home, which for both of us is Alabama. Home for Phil is also pretty much anywhere there's football. He's worked side by side with such coaching luminaries as Nick Saban and Bill Belichick, legendary offensive minds such as Homer Smith, and immensely respected coaches such as Iowa's Kirk Ferentz.

Phil earned the respect and trust of all of those coaches, among many others. Phil never acts as if he's the smartest guy in the room, though often he is. He listens intently and evaluates what he hears. Yet he never just parrots back what somebody tells him. He has strong opinions. That's why he is so well respected by the coaches and players I mentioned earlier. This broadcaster feels the same way about him.

Phil's relationship with Nick Saban dates back to the time when they both worked for the Browns. Saban isn't inclined to trust yes-men or people who take shortcuts. He knows that Phil has an acute understanding of what it takes to build a successful football organization. Phil can deliver unique insight into Saban's Process, which has delivered what I believe is the greatest dynasty in college football history.

Just as it was when I was a kid watching Bear Bryant's teams, winning isn't nearly as easy Nick Saban's Crimson Tide makes it look. Winning is hard. Winning consistently is the domain of the elite. Building, maintaining, and expanding a dynasty such as Alabama's is incomparable in modern football. But Saban has done it by following his well-known mantra: the Process.

Of all the championships, trophies, and accolades that have piled up under Saban at Alabama, the most remarkable to me is this:

> Since the start of the 2008 season, Alabama has played in exactly three regular-season games in which it had been eliminated from the national title chase.

Three! Do you realize how incredible that is? Can you fully comprehend the ridiculous level of consistency that takes? No off days. No season-wrecking upsets.

I don't know if I was the first person to come up with that stat, but I remember when I shared it with Saban. He was at ESPN headquarters for a preseason interview, and he didn't know it. Nick isn't one to look back and revel in past glory, not even for a second, but the look on his face showed that even he was amazed by that stunning level of excellence.

During the 2016 season, it was if an unofficial criterion to be included in the College Football Playoff was whether a team would provide the toughest matchup for Alabama. Forget the team's résumé. Do they have the secret sauce to give Alabama fits? Who can do what Johnny Manziel did? When you think about it, it's the ultimate compliment. Just over a decade ago, Alabama was supposedly as outdated as a rotary phone. Now it's the streaming device no one else can keep up with.

How does Saban do it? The Process is brilliant in its simplicity. If you simply execute what's important at the moment to the best of your ability, without undue regard for the outcome, your chances of ultimately getting the result you want increase exponentially. It sounds great, until you actually have to chase worry about winning or pressure or outside expectations out of your mind. Now, try to get more than one hundred players to do it, not to mention an entire coaching and administrative staff.

See the challenge? I think the genius is in the flexibility. From my vantage point, this hasn't been merely a step-by-step get-rich-quick scheme. It's an entirely different mental approach. It's training the mind, not just robotically following a formula. It's finding joy and fulfillment in the moment rather than awaiting the outcome.

No one can give more unique insight into how Saban has turned this from mantra to methodology than Phil Savage. Not only has Phil had a front-row ticket, he's had a backstage pass to the dynasty. His relationship with Saban, his knowledge of the game and ability to communicate, are evident in his work on the Crimson Tide radio network and in his work with us at ESPN.

4th and Goal Every Day. Will you get the touchdown? I know this: to get the score, I'd trust Phil Savage to call that play.

—*Rece Davis*

INTRODUCTION

MY CLOSE-UP OF 4TH AND GOAL

I am often asked, not exactly in these words, "What is the essential element of the Alabama football program that makes it so successful?"

The curious want a deeper peek inside, a revelation, the inscription on the walls of the Crimson Tide mind-set, the secret handshake. They want me to tie it all together and help explain for them why Alabama stays in close pursuit of a national championship year after year.

My answer comes from what a Crimson Tide assistant coach told me several years ago:

"You know how it is around here, Phil. It's fourth and goal every day."

So sit there for a minute and take that in: 4th and goal. That moment in a game has an edge: you either score a touchdown or give up the ball. Picture it. Players straining, coaches exhorting, a roiling sideline of emotion because you are not taking the cheaper three points with a field goal. You are going for it.

So, in other words, my answer is, Alabama goes for it.

This book is my view of Alabama football, and not an opinion from anyone or any place else. It is a view from the radio booth where I am the color analyst for the Crimson Tide Sports Network. It is a view from the sidelines where I evaluate prospects for the Reese's Senior Bowl as executive director. I am a student of the game and this is my thesis of the Saban Era, if you will, but also a look at my background in football and why the game is the national pastime of my state and how all of this ties into the most dominant decade in modern college football history.

My simple conclusion is that Alabama wins more than anyone else because it is 4th and goal to these people in Crimson every practice, every meeting, every game, every day. Do not underestimate the power of that mind-set.

I'm sure that 4th and goal inside the Alabama football facility can mean pressure that is overwhelming some days. But I also know there are more days when working there is not overwhelming, but fulfilling.

You are on the top shelf of college football at Alabama. You signed up for the Crimson Tide because football is important to you and you wanted the privilege of having a seat on this train.

It would be a letdown for an ambitious assistant coach or player-personnel staffer to come into Coach Nick Saban's program to see even a single minute of a given hour wasted. No one walks away from Alabama football saying, "Is that it? What's the big deal?"

Sure, the Crimson Tide can be corrupted by complacency—it happened in 2010—but it does not happen often. Your ambition is usually rewarded, not by merely wins, but by knowing the Alabama culture has made you dig deep to find resources inside yourself. Coach Saban sets that tone of doing "extra."

The Crimson Tide is not infallible. It can run up against a sensational quarterback such as Clemson's Deshaun Watson and crafty play-callers such as Tigers' coach Dabo Swinney. The Tide can lose to a Heisman Trophy winner such as Cam Newton, as well as a near–Heisman winner in Watson.

Still, four national championships in eight seasons in this era of college football is remarkable. Nick's record at Alabama in ten seasons is 119-19. When you put it all together—national titles (4), conference titles (5), NFL draft picks, and graduation rate—Alabama has the best college football program in the Football Bowl Subdivision, formerly known as Division I-A.

I mentioned at the start of this chapter how Alabama is in close pursuit of the national championship season after season. The Crimson Tide has played just three regular-season games since 2008 when it has been eliminated from national title contention. Think about the downturns at other programs and realize Alabama is the only program that has been to the College Football Playoff all three years of its existence. Think about the way-too-early 2017 polls where Alabama is no. 1 and national champion Clemson is no. 13 (CBS) because Watson and a host of other Tigers will have departed the program. That poll is perception more than fact, but you see the point. Alabama's talent level across offense, defense, and special teams sticks to a standard.

The Alabama system is even more intriguing because it has roots that go back to the Dallas Cowboys of the 1960s. Dallas player-personnel director Gil Brandt and head coach Tom Landry first used "computer analytics" in the mid-1960s to build a perennial NFL playoff team. Brandt passed that study off to Bill Belichick, and his friend Nick Saban.

Here are some things in the book that will help you better understand Alabama's success:

- The "analytics" behind Alabama's recruiting.
- The development of players once they are on campus.
- The devotion, and the discipline, not to waver from football fundamentals.

- Coach Saban's own intense film study of opponents and recruiting prospects.
- The successful execution of complementary football: offense, defense, and special teams.
- How Coach Nick Saban binds it all together in a perfect marriage.

I am close to the program. Some days I am really close, such as inside the building and on the practice field. It is remarkable to see how Alabama has thrived when so many other college programs are digging just as furiously as the Tide and don't even have one national championship. Alabama, if you were paying attention the last ten years, is five or six plays from having six of the eight national titles awarded from 2009 to 2016.

The difference, of course, is that no one else has Nick Saban.

Consider this one statistic. Saban took over the program in 2007. Just one member of his original on-field staff—running backs coach Burton Burns—was still with him during the 2016 season. Saban has won five national championships—four at Alabama and one at LSU—and he's done it with different coaching staffs. Bobby Bowden lost key assistant coaches at Florida State and the Seminoles faded. Urban Meyer's staff at Florida turned over, and the Gators fizzled after four seasons. Pete Carroll could not sustain Southern California's success after he lost several noteworthy assistant coaches.

Nick hires really good assistant coaches and then, when they move on to promotions or the NFL, he finds replacements that are just as smart, ambitious, and driven to succeed. When an assistant coach receives a phone call from Nick Saban, most run to Tuscaloosa for an opportunity to witness first-hand what it takes to construct, maintain, and continuously improve the most thorough program in the country.

For 2017, the Tide offensive staff has undergone another series of changes with Brian Daboll as the new coordinator arriving from the New England Patriots. Brent Key (offensive line), Mike Locksley (wide receivers), and Joe Pannunzio (tight ends and special teams) will join the aforementioned Burns (running backs) to round out that side of the football.

On defense, Jeremy Pruitt returns for his second season as the defensive coordinator and his staff remains intact with Karl Dunbar (defensive line), Tosh Lupoi (linebackers), and Derrick Ansley (defensive backs) all staying in place.

In my view, despite having some outstanding assistant coaches over his career, Nick Saban is the common denominator and the primary linkage between the success enjoyed at MSU, LSU, and now at Alabama.

I visited the Bama program in the spring of 2009 after I had been fired as general manager of the Cleveland Browns. I saw the diligence from the top down, which is how you achieve consistency. I saw players who were ranked as five-star prospects in high school being developed from the ground up with an intense focus on the fundamentals, another hallmark of Saban's program.

What was going on in 2009 looked similar to what was going on in 1991 when I first worked for Saban with the "original" Cleveland Browns. There was devotion to every detail.

Saban is all about the details, just like the legendary UCLA basketball coach, John Wooden. Bill Walton said that when he was a freshman at UCLA, Wooden sat the players down in the locker room and instructed them how to put their socks on correctly because it would prevent blisters. Saban is a master of the minuscule, like Wooden, and like another coach I worked for, Bill Belichick.

My first NFL job was in Cleveland with Belichick, who was the head coach. His defensive coordinator was Nick Saban, who was my boss. I was twenty-five years old and the defensive assistant, or what is now referred to as the quality-control coach.

Under these two men, I learned how to pay attention to every nuanced detail that is required to win in professional football.

After four difficult seasons as GM in Cleveland (2005–8), it was rejuvenating to come home and watch this strict adherence to detail in Tuscaloosa. Alabama coaches and players practiced in 2009 with an expectation of winning. They were focused on improving, and they practiced with an urgency to rebuild a football powerhouse.

The urgency was there in 2009, and it was still that way after the 2016 season. Daily urgency is core to Saban's mission at Alabama.

There is also an urgency around fundamentals. I walked out for a spring Alabama practice in 2009 and saw a freshman defensive lineman being schooled in fundamentals by assistant coach Bo Davis, as if this kid had never before played the game. The explosiveness of this "No. 57" in one-on-ones was incredible, but he was not being permitted to win with raw talent. He was being taught every detail in stance, strike, and hand usage.

After practice, I asked a staffer, "Who is that number 57? He's the most explosive lineman you have." It was Marcell Dareus, who morphed from a support role in September 2009 to BCS National Championship Game MVP by January. Dareus became the third pick in the 2011 NFL draft and later signed a deal for $103 million, with $63 million guaranteed by 2015. It was the snap in those hips and the powerful hands, along with practice intensity, that led to his becoming a millionaire.

On my ride home to Fairhope, Alabama, after that practice, it hit me. I'd been here before. My family has majored in 4th and goal.

My grandfather was murdered in 1941 at the iron ore mine where he worked in Overton, Alabama. He left a widow and three small children, one of whom was my father. They survived.

My father, Big Sav, nearly died on a football field in 1954 when his body, neck to toe, cramped and his uniform had to be sheared off with a razor blade.

My brother Joe Savage survived a blood clot on his brain, a result of a ninth-grade football drill, and now he rescues young girls in Eastern Europe from being sold into the sex-trafficking industry.

My wife, Dorothy, was a teenager when she lost her mother to cancer. Dot then grinded her way through college with her future on the line.

Me, I was a nearsighted and benched senior quarterback at Murphy High School in Mobile. I had one offer to play college football. That's it. Who knows if my life would have turned to football if not for that one chance to play at Sewanee, the University of the South.

Think about your life and your own miniseries filled with 4th and goals. We all have them.

They have them every day in Tuscaloosa in the meeting rooms, in the weight room, and on the practice field.

So when I got a chance to audition for color analyst with the Crimson Tide Sports Network on April 18, 2009, I treated that A-Day game as a priority, because I know how important Alabama football is to the fans.

Replacing legendary quarterback Kenny "the Snake" Stabler as analyst was not going to be easy. My job that Saturday was to sit next to play-by-play man Eli Gold—for a game that did not count in the record books—and back up Eli's play calls with expert X's and O's. It might as well have been the College Football Playoff for me because I prepared for that game as if it were win or go home.

My own mother, Carol Savage, sent the extra-man pressure, saying, "I hope you know what you're doing. I loved listening to Snake."

I showed up to the booth with ten pages of notes—for a spring game!—and a three-deep depth chart. My brother quizzed me over the phone when I was driving up to Tuscaloosa by asking me, "Okay, who's the third-string left tackle?"

Three weeks later, I had the job.

For Dot and me, it was as if we had hit the lottery. We celebrated as if I had just gotten my first job. We jumped up and down like little kids. We didn't know if it would be for more than one year, but being part of Alabama football again would give me another football season and maybe heal some of the scars from being fired by the Cleveland Browns.

The people in Mobile and Fairhope and the state of Alabama think my radio job is the coolest job in the world. They look at me and say, "This is a lot better than being an NFL general manager, isn't it?"

Here is what I understood about this new role. I knew I could not bring the rambunctious personality of the Snake to the broadcasts, so I needed to play to my strength, which was film study. The plan was to pour myself into watching the opponent, dissect its personnel, and try to figure out how the opponent might strategize against Alabama.

Coach Homer Smith, my mentor, told me, "You are going to have a platform to teach football."

One afternoon, he tried to explain to his wife why I could be pretty good at this new radio position: "These announcers are always saying, 'They have too many men in the box.' What is the box? The box is undefined. Phil can teach the game to a farmer on his tractor, or a grandmother on the porch, or a banker who is in his car."

I took that to heart. That's what initiated my film study of Virginia Tech in 2009. To this day, Troy Finney and Daniel Lyerly, who handle the videotape for Alabama, will send me flash drives of opponents so I can do my own film work.

In my regular-season debut in 2009, Alabama beat Virginia Tech in the Georgia Dome in Atlanta. At the end of the postgame show, Eli looked at me and said, "Well, we won; I guess we'll bring you back next week."

The team went 14-0 and won a national championship in 2009. We started 5-0 in 2010 before losing to South Carolina.

During those nineteen consecutive victories, I told people, "I'm not sure if I'm any good, but we keep winning, so they keep bringing me back."

Now, eight seasons later and going into 2017, I am one of only three people connected to Alabama football who can stand in the public square and talk about the Bama program without censor. Nick Saban and Eli Gold are the others.

For everyone else inside Alabama athletics, Coach Saban is the one voice. It keeps the message uniform and it relieves other people within the football program of the burden of choosing their words carefully.

Saban handles the distractions that can come from abrupt news flashes. He manages the tedious questions of Alabama's place in all that is college football. Everyone else—coaches, players, personnel staff—can focus on the task at hand, which is winning games, because Saban's force of will slams the window on any sideshows. He has the playbook and the experience to manage a crisis.

I have some advantages in this job. I was an assistant coach in the SEC (1987–89) and the Pac-10 (1990). I was an assistant coach, scout, player-personnel director, and general manager while in the National Football League for twenty years. I have a degree of credibility when it comes to the film room, the practice field, and game day.

I have one other advantage. I worked for Nick Saban. I met him my first day in the NFL with the Browns in 1991. You could tell right away this guy was smart, driven, and competitive.

My indoctrination on film study came from Nick and Belichick. I watched so much tape in 1991 I developed calluses on my elbows from sitting in a wooden-armed desk chair for hours. My family did not hear from me for months, so my mother sent my brother up from Mobile to make sure I was okay.

Twenty-five years later I am the executive director of the Reese's Senior Bowl. Scouting is my primary role in what is the most important college all-star game, as far as the NFL is concerned. The Reese's Senior Bowl is an NFL predraft event, and the league counts on us to help it identify Sunday players.

My NFL experience prepared me for the Senior Bowl and trained me to analyze Alabama football. I was the college scouting director for the Baltimore Ravens' first Super Bowl championship (2000) and spent fourteen years working with Alabama legend and NFL great Ozzie Newsome. I became an NFL general manager when I was thirty-nine. I was the ultimate authority for a franchise in deciding who could play and who couldn't, and who was going to be on the team and who wasn't.

Now, I stand right here in the intersection between you and this modern-day Alabama football dynasty. My eyes to your ears, me watching from the radio booth and sideline and you listening over your radio.

When I became a scout in 1994, veteran NFL talent evaluators Dom Anile, Ernie Plank, and Ron Marciniak sharpened my eyes. They saw things no one else could see, which is how they made careers in pro football. I have also learned player-evaluation skills from many other friends in coaching and scouting, too many to name here. Alabama fans are the beneficiaries. In this book you will learn about training the eyes for player evaluations.

I take seriously the job of analyzing Alabama football. I want to "win" at being a color analyst because of the culture at Bama, and also because of how much I owe the university. Alabama gave me a chance to get back into football after my being let go by the Browns. Serving the fans and the program is a payback of sorts for me.

When you are an exiled GM, it is tough to find work. People don't understand that coaches get recycled, but GMs usually do not. Only two second-chance GMs were in the NFL at the start of the 2016 season.

I had gone from graduate assistant at Alabama in 1987 to general manager in the NFL—GA to GM. I was deposed by the Browns on December 28, 2008. I was knocked down and then picked back up by the same school that gave me my first job in 1987.

This job with the Crimson Tide network is not casual work for me, not with a fan base as attentive as the Bama Nation. I made a commitment in June 2009 to study film of Alabama's opponent and have a grasp of the schemes, tendencies, and personnel of the Tigers and Vols and Gators, and whoever else was on the schedule.

Maybe that's why my film-study notes of each Alabama opponent—every game for eight seasons—find their way into the Alabama scouting report each week. I e-mail my notes every Sunday night or Monday morning to Linda Leoni, the administrative aide to Coach Saban.

You should know a little something about Linda Leoni. She is, after all, the gatekeeper for Nick Saban.

She served as Bill Belichick's administrative assistant when he was the Browns' head coach (1991–95). Then she moved to the New York Jets with Bill Parcells before he retired the first time. From there,

Linda went to the Fiesta Bowl and stayed nine years to be closer to her ailing mother.

When I became the Browns' general manager in January 2005, she called and said, "Little Philly Savage has gone from GA to GM, I want to come home and work for you." As a native of Cleveland and a previous Browns employee, she would, I knew, be a trusted ally.

I wasn't the only who thought Linda was an asset.

I was terminated by the Browns on the final Sunday of the 2008 season. Linda was fired on Monday. Three weeks later, Nick Saban called me as I was driving across the Mobile causeway to a Senior Bowl practice. "Hey, boy, you'll be a'ight. But where's Linda?"

Nick hired her in spring 2009. A few months later, I was brought on as the radio color analyst.

After spending that 2009 summer studying film of Virginia Tech, I decided—on a lark—to share my notes on the Hokies with just one person before I shared them with the fans on Saturday: Nick Saban. I thought, what the heck, maybe something in there can help.

So ten days before Alabama played Virginia Tech in the Georgia Dome, I called Linda and told her I was e-mailing a ten-page scouting report complete with stats, and an overview on the Tech program. There would be notes on offense, defense, and special teams.

"Bathroom reading for Nick," I told Linda. I didn't think any more about it. It was just a courtesy.

On September 5, 2009, the Crimson Tide came from behind to defeat the Hokies, 34–24, with offense, defense, and special teams—complementary football, all three phases working together. Alabama was off to its first national championship under Saban.

Believe me, I did not think for a moment my report had anything to do with the Tech win. If I were that brash, I would have e-mailed my notes on the next opponent, Florida International, the day after the Virginia Tech game. Instead, Dot and I flew to New York on Sunday to spend a few days in the city. She's a musical-theater singer and we had bought a studio apartment during my time with the Browns so she could stay there for her auditions.

Around 10:00 a.m. Monday, September 7, my cell phone rang. I didn't look at it. Then it rang again, and then a third time. I walked over, looked down, and there were three missed calls from Linda Leoni. When she calls multiple times within seconds, that means something is up, a 911. I called her back.

"Philly, where are your notes? Nicky wants to know if you have that report."

"Wait, he read my notes?"

"Yes, Philly, he reads them. It was the first thing on top of his weekly scouting notebook."

I don't know what Dot and I had planned that morning in New York, but it had to wait. I had watched all the film of FIU, so now I just needed to clean up some details on my report. I asked Linda to give me forty-five minutes and I would e-mail them to her.

My report is generic compared to what Nick's staff provides him each week. His behind-the-scenes staff and his assistant coaches put together a comprehensive rundown complete with diagrams, pictures, and full descriptions of what a given opponent does on offense and defense.

My notes are an abridged version that Nick can breeze through and then use to talk to the media each Monday. Some scouting nuggets are in there, I'm sure. The notes could also be one of those superstitions that leak into the sports world when things are going well. Alabama wins and I send the notes.

I know one thing. I don't want my phone to ring on Monday morning again, so I have religiously sent them every week, for 111 consecutive games.

You will find examples of my notes later in this book.

Alabama is 100-11 since I started my film study, writing my notes, and bringing the X's and O's into your home where the radio is turned up and the TV volume is turned down. It is my eyes to your ears in the barn in Clanton where your radio hangs from a rusty nail. It is my eyes to your ears if you are driving I-5 in Northern California, or I-75 in Lexington, Kentucky., listening to Bama football on SiriusXM.

If you are in Bryant-Denny Stadium, tucked down in a corner near the end zone, and you didn't see a block that led to a big play, I saw it, and I can tell you all about it in your radio earpiece. The scout's job is to see what you don't see.

If you know Nick Saban, you know another set of eyes on an opponent is always welcome. There is no self-complacency with him, no ego when it comes to looking for an edge to win a game. You got something, let's hear it, is how Nick thinks.

This is what you should understand about the Alabama football program:

You can say all you want about Alabama's Signing Day success and the talent of the prospects that pull the Crimson jerseys over their heads, but two essential ingredients to the program go along with the talent:

blocking and tackling fundamentals
intentional, individualized player development

Alabama is always portrayed as the bully, the Goliath that just runs over your team. The Crimson Tide, in just about every game it plays, has the bigger, faster, and stronger players. I understand that. NFL scouts have labeled Bama the thirty-third NFL franchise. That abundance of talent causes resentment across college football.

Natural ability is on the roster, to be sure, but one dimension is often overlooked and never compromised regardless of opponent: preparation. The Crimson Tide can get outplayed (rarely) and can get outcoached (still more rarely), but it does not get outhustled in the film room or on the practice field. I try to put as much into my video study as the Alabama staff puts into its film study, no matter who the opponent is.

This book is going to be about some of the things that happened in plain sight from 2009 to 2016, right there on film available to everyone. You would have seen these tips yourself if you looked closely or had spent thirty years acquiring a scout's eye. Grab the clicker and hit FORWARD, then hit BACK, then FORWARD again, and then STOP. Write down some observations and do it over and over.

The secret of Saban is right there as you manage the cowboy remote and look at a given play again and again and again. As you make your way through this book, you will sharpen your eye and see Alabama's essential elements, not secret ingredients. Alabama has a playbook with more than X's and O's inside. The playbook is recruiting to strength and conditioning to development to academics to game plans. It will be laid out for you in these pages.

I'll apologize now if Nick Saban comes off as too virtuous in this book to suit you. This isn't about him as saint and savior. No, this book is about his program and how he built it from my perspective of having worked with him twenty-five years ago, and now, calling the Crimson Tide games on radio for the past eight seasons.

I admire and marvel over the man's competitive drive, his reservoir of energy, and his willingness to adapt to the ever-changing landscape of the game. I respect more his love for his wife and his compassion for people that is not often seen.

What you should take away from this book is that Saban and the Crimson Tide's way of doing business on the practice field is unmatched elsewhere in the sport, pro or college. Behind those green privacy screens hanging on the fences surrounding Alabama's three outdoor practice fields is a steadfast belief that fundamentals and being prepared are as important as skill.

The good scout sees more than you see. It's been my job for almost thirty years to see more than the fan sees. It's what I do for a living. I look at body types, assess athletic ability, determine explosiveness, and then forecast what a player can become at the NFL level. I study schemes, evaluate coaches, and figure out who is going to be the next rising star in the business.

I started playing this game when I was six years old. I have been coached by the keenest minds in the game on and off the field. I grew up around the tribalism of Alabama football. I was one of those runts who gave 110 percent, just as Nick Saban demands of his players. My family history prepared me.

Now it's your turn to read what I have seen in the last eight seasons, and what I have experienced in the last fifty-two years. Please, after you, let's get started.

1
AMERICA'S TEAM SEEDS A DYNASTY

THE COWBOYS AND THE CRIMSON TIDE

In spring 1977, the Dallas Cowboys held a staff meeting to decide which of the two premier college running backs they would draft: the University of Pittsburgh's Tony Dorsett, or the University of Southern California's Ricky Bell. Dorsett was a shifty runner at five feet eleven, 192 pounds, and was the 1976 Heisman Trophy winner. Bell was a 225-pound thumper and the 1976 Heisman Trophy runner-up.

The Cowboys had acquired Seattle's pick in the draft, no. 2 overall, contingent on Dorsett's being available, but now there was a debate in the organization.

Veteran scout Red Hickey preferred the Cowboys draft Bell instead of Dorsett.

Gil Brandt, the director of player personnel, wanted Dorsett.

Tom Landry, the legendary Dallas head coach, was not going to halt the wrangling between trusted scouts. He just looked at Brandt and said, "Gil, what does the Book say? Read the numbers."

Brandt flipped open a binder with reports on each college prospect the Cowboys scouted.

The Book had computer-generated data on Bell and Dorsett. The

Cowboys had relied on the formula for fourteen years to draft college players. When you stood two players side by side, the Cowboys were confident the formula—the Book, as Landry called it—could predict a player's NFL success, or failure, based on his physical and mental characteristics.

"Coach, the book says Ricky Bell has no chance to be an All-Pro. He has a five percent chance of being a Pro Bowler, a sixty-two percent chance of being a starter on a championship team," Brandt said.

"Dorsett has a ninety percent chance of being an All-Pro, a hundred percent chance of being a Pro Bowler."

Hickey was familiar with the Book. He quickly waved a white flag: "Tom, I bow to the machine."

The Cowboys, it turned out, did not have to decide between the two running backs because Tampa Bay, coached by former USC head coach John McKay, took Bell with the first pick of the 1977 draft. The Cowboys gleefully took Dorsett with the second pick.

Bell, as the Book predicted, did not make All-Pro. He led the Bucs to their first playoff win in franchise history in 1979 with 1,263 yards, and he was, by all accounts, a terrific person. But Bell was out of football by 1982 with various ailments. He died tragically of heart illness when he was twenty-nine years old.

Dorsett was NFL Offensive Rookie of the Year in 1977, and was All-Pro in 1981. He was selected for the Pro Bowl four times. Dorsett is a member of the Pro Football Hall of Fame.

What does all this have to do with Alabama football?

In October 2015, I heard this comment from Arkansas coach Bret Bielema about the Alabama defensive line: "They all look the same. I swear there's a machine that just creates them."

I thought to myself, "If only Bret knew the rest of the story."

So here is the rest of the story and a significant reason why Alabama has a uniform-looking team. The Crimson Tide players are perfectly suited for each position.

The Dallas Book/Machine that trumped a veteran scout in the Cowboys' 1977 draft room—Dorsett over Bell—was a scouting guide produced by an IBM 360 computer between 1962 and 1965. The computer was housed in a building along Page Mill Road, on the southern perimeter of the Stanford University campus. It was on the northern edge of what is now called Silicon Valley.

The Cowboys started working on this data approach to the draft in 1960, their first season in the National Football League. Tex Schramm, the Dallas general manager, had worked for CBS Sports at the 1960 Winter Olympics and marveled over IBM technology that had put computer chips in skis to measure time splits over snow.

Brandt said he and Schramm and Landry started talking in 1961 about using a computer to help them draft college football players. They wanted to develop an anchor system so the scout in California would evaluate a player the same way as a scout in Florida. The right tackle in California would be a carbon copy of the right tackle in Florida. If you drafted either college player, you got the same guy.

The Book was a matrix: the ideal height/weight/speed for each position, the critical factors that a player needed to play each position, and the personal characteristics of the player, such as competitiveness. The Cowboys would assign a college player number grades for each of these categories, then feed the data into a computer and ask for the probabilities of success of that player.

Data analytics in football started with the Cowboys in the sixties. Be patient, I'm getting to Bama.

In 1962, Brandt said the Cowboys paid college coaching staffs $100 each to fill out a survey of the characteristics a coach would want in the ideal football player, position by position. Jerry Claiborne, a former assistant coach under Paul "Bear" Bryant and the head coach at Virginia Tech, was one of the coaches who filled out a survey, Brandt said.

Landry and Brandt asked college coaches to take the survey because they certainly couldn't ask NFL coaches such as Vince Lombardi of the Green Bay Packers what he thought the Cowboys should look for in a college player.

"Sure, Landry, your defensive end needs to be five feet eight, 155 pounds," Lombardi might say. "You need those fast guys who can move around and get in the way of our fullback Jim Taylor."

The Cowboys used the surveys of college coaches to help them scout and evaluate players because they were trying to determine two things: What did the ideal football player, by position, look like based on height, weight, and speed and certain other physical characteristics? What were the probabilities of his success in the NFL?

"All we wanted them to do was tell us 'What is a good football player?' and from that we came up with nine characteristics," Brandt said. "We later reduced it to five characteristics."

The measurables of height/weight/speed were collated along with a Dallas scout's sleuthing of a college player's background, such as arrests or suspensions or coachability, and the specifics of playing a position, such as a runningback's "ability to run inside." There was also a way to grade a player's frame, and the likelihood he could add some bulk, as well as a grade for overall athletic ability. Scouts paid close attention to competitiveness, which is a critical factor in evaluating a linebacker, for instance.

Never, ever could a scout say, "I have a hunch about this guy," Brandt said. Everything was assigned a number. There was no numeric rating for a "hunch."

During the college football season of 1963, Dallas scouts fanned out across the country to get the height, weight, and speed of players, no matter where these players went to school and, in some cases, no matter what sport they played. It could be basketball. Brandt said Dallas had five former college basketball players on its first Super Bowl champion. He said the Cowboys scoured the historically black colleges and universities (HBCU) from Texas to Delaware.

Brandt said the Cowboys in late winter, early spring 1964 started feeding data on players into a computer. The computer could not read names, so each player was assigned a number. The player's school was assigned a number.

That IBM computer sat three feet off the ground and was twelve feet long. This computer was less powerful than today's laptop. The

Cowboys' programmers first used punch cards (think hanging chads) to input data.

They had a mastermind, Salem Qureishi, a computer programmer and statistician. He didn't know football, but he understood what the goal was and created a system to get there. Brandt said Qureishi helped fashion the survey that was sent out to college coaches asking them to list the characteristics of an ideal football player.

"He didn't know if a football was pumped or stuffed," Brandt said, "but he made something very complex simple for us to understand. It was complicated, like taking the side off the Panama Canal. 'Garbage in, garbage out,' he would say. He made it so we could understand."

The Cowboys were still working out the bugs in 1964, but they used enough of the system to pick two cornerstone players, one on offense, one on defense. Bob Hayes, a sprinter at Florida A&M, an HBCU, was a seventh-round pick, and became a star wide receiver. Mel Renfro of Oregon became an All-Pro defensive back.

Scouts started to buy in and understood their "hunches" and "inside information" would be left outside the draft room and not be made part of the calculations. "We had a grading system, and you had to use it," Brandt said. "You don't want somebody saying, 'I've been doing this thirty-five years and I've got a gut feeling about this guy.'

"It was all data. We needed people thinking alike so we could figure out the eighty percent in the middle. A housewife could pick the top player, and we could pick the worst player. It was all the other players we wanted to be sure of."

The computerized system not only found good players, it rejected players. That was half the battle. Sorting. It goes on in college recruiting every day. Names are deleted from digital files.

But, back to the Cowboys.

The Book, or the Machine, along with the scouts who worked for Brandt and Landry, were responsible for twenty consecutive winning seasons. It was analytics in an era before jeans were designer and computers were personal. The player either had the goods, per the Book, or he didn't.

The Cowboys won two Super Bowls and 13 division championships using this computer-driven scouting system. In 1992, Brandt flew to Berea, Ohio, to the Cleveland Browns headquarters and shared the Cowboys' computerized system of drafting players.

The Cleveland head coach was Bill Belichick.

The defensive coordinator was Nick Saban.

I was the defensive quality control coach—in essence, Saban's assistant.

Belichick has five Super Bowl championships as head coach of the New England Patriots. The Baltimore Ravens used the Dallas system as their foundation when I was the college scouting director in Baltimore—after the Browns had left Cleveland. That system helped us build a Super Bowl champion in 2000, and the Ravens won the world title again in 2012 with the same philosophy in place.

It was this data system that Brandt explained to Belichick and Michael Lombardi, his personnel director at the time, in Berea fifteen years after Dorsett was drafted. Saban was running the Browns defense, and he sat in on some of those meetings with Brandt.

In our predraft preparation, Saban would also fly around the country and work out college players individually, and number grades were incorporated into those workouts. During those early years in 1991 and '92, all of us with the Browns started hearing about "height/weight/speed, critical factors, and position specifics." This was the Cowboys' system.

Saban adopted this methodical approach and adapted the system for his use as head coach at Michigan State, LSU, and Alabama. He kept modifying it as he saw the game evolving. Do you see now? Nick's recruiting is a scientific brainchild derived from Dallas in the 1960s.

The Dallas Cowboys in the 1960s were the early seeds to the Process.

In chapter 2 of this book I will explain more how Alabama has made the system fit its needs.

Of course, this scouting system is not all there is to Nick Saban's way of doing business. Not by a long shot. Some things are wholly owned by Saban, such as his brand of player development, scouting the opposition, strength and conditioning, the teaching of fundamentals, game plans, in-game adjustments, and off-field duties that keep the organization humming.

Still, this system developed by the Cowboys has been crucial to Alabama's success the last decade. Here's why. The Crimson Tide does not simply try to haul in the twenty-five best recruits every year on the gut instincts of its recruiters. Bama builds its team with data based on the ideal characteristics, position by position, of a college player, just as Dallas did with the draft. This data, which is mixed with grades on character, helps Alabama's player-personnel staff narrow down their recruiting list. When you start with thousands of names, it saves time, and time is the only completely fair thing across the college landscape.

This is one of the key reasons why Alabama trucks on a winning path even after changes on the coaching staff. Assistant coaches, no matter what area of the country they are in, must abide by the data-driven recruiting system, just as the Dallas Cowboys scouts were told to do in the sixties, seventies, and eighties. The Alabama assistant coach cannot act on a hunch. It's why the Alabama program has so much consistency, even though it has only one assistant coach, Burton Burns, remaining from the original staff.

Here is something else. The Cowboys did not assign a "draft round" to a player's capability. They drafted based on physical data and a strong, unbiased view of a player's talent and personality. They never ranked players by what round the player should be drafted.

Does that sound familiar to you? How often have you heard Saban say he abhors the terms *four-* and *five-star recruits*? Like the Cowboys, the Crimson Tide has a philosophy of recruiting from the inside out, rather than outside in.

Bill Belichick would tell us scouts, "Never grade prospects by rounds, just tell me what you think the player is and what he can do for us in the future; we will decide where to draft him."

It was one of the hallmarks of Brandt's tutoring in Berea, Ohio, in the late spring and summer of 1992. The team decides a player's value, no one else. Brandt hammered that home each visit.

The former Cowboys executive, still one of the most revered people in the NFL, was picked up at the Cleveland airport each time by a young member of the Browns' player-personnel staff, Jim Schwartz, who would later become the head coach of the Detroit Lions. Schwartz is currently the defensive coordinator of the Philadelphia Eagles.

Brandt laid out the Cowboys system in Belichick's office, which had a short table extending from the front of his desk. Michael Lombardi was there, too, as the top personnel man in the building along with Dom Anile the scouting director. Ron Marciniak, a veteran scout who came from the Cowboys, had some input and would talk with Belichick, sometimes while the Browns coach rode his stationary bike or used the treadmill.

It became apparent early on the Browns wanted a big, fast, strong team. The motto was "Big people beat up little people."

Brandt recommended that Belichick and Lombardi add "letters" to the numeric grades, which served as "red flags" regarding a physical deficiency or intangible concern. A letter would appear in front of the final number grade if the player had a physical issue that had to be discussed further, such as B for "lack of bulk." A letter after the number grade would note a player's intangibles, such as C for "character." A lowercase c might mean the character flaw was something that could be managed.

Their whole goal was to find "clean" prospects, guys with no letters. Alabama does that today in its recruiting room.

You're not going to bat 1.000. Even a great coach can make mistakes without the proper guidelines. Nick doesn't make many mistakes now because (1) he has learned from his mistakes and (2) he has his system in place that keeps Alabama from taking too many chances on high school kids who are "outliers" to the formula.

I was on the coaching-staff side and not part of the inside look at the Cowboys' system when Brandt started coming to Berea in spring

1992. I would hear bits and pieces of the implementation of the Book, but mostly I broke down the opponent tapes, helped Saban with the defensive backs, and ran the scout teams.

But, in the fall of 1992, I got a chance to see what the fuss was about with this new grading system.

Belichick told me the Browns were in the market for defensive backs for the 1993 draft. He wanted me to be with the coaching staff Monday through Thursday, then to go scout college players on Friday and Saturday. I would join up with the team Saturday night, or Sunday morning, for the Browns' game that week.

All the Cleveland scouts had a notebook with the height/weight/speed chart, and you would refer to that every single night when you went back to your hotel and started writing your report on players. Back then, it was all handwritten by scouts and then put into a computer.

At the top of those reports, as the most important thing, they had the critical factors: athletic ability, strength/explosion, size, speed, and competitiveness. The next page of the reports were the individual traits by position that I'm sure were developed by Gil and the polling of the college coaches from thirty years before—those were the position specifics.

We would fill in the size box and the speed box. We would also put in some verbiage, then write our summary and give the prospect a final grade.

The Browns tried to limit mistakes in the draft by eliminating players from consideration using the computer system, just like the Cowboys. That was the beauty of the Book. You could start with a thousand college prospects, but the matrix of height/weight/speed immediately eliminated players and saved time.

If they weren't big enough or fast enough, they were crossed off the list. Despite some exceptions, a player who did not have the physical characteristics the team wanted position by position found little mercy. You better believe this is a hallmark of Alabama recruiting.

The grading scale went from 5.0 (reject) to 8.0 (the best ever at his position). In eighteen years of scouting, I gave one 8.0, to University of Michigan defensive back Charles Woodson, a future Hall of Famer.

A Pro Bowl–level NFL starter was 7.0–7.5. The 6.0–6.9 category was for a prospect who had varying degrees of the traits needed to be a potential starter.

The 5.7–5.9 prospects were deemed "make it" prospects, with 5.9 being a quality backup for the Browns, and 5.7 being a backup for another team. Anyone graded 5.6 or lower was seen as an undrafted free-agent candidate.

The 7.0 and above was a player who could create mismatches, a difference maker. Two landing spots were for players with a lot of upside, with traits that could be developed: 6.5 and 6.0. The 6.5 was reserved for the raw-ability prospect who had rare physical attributes. The 6.0 guy could flash the skill, but had little consistency in performance and did not have as much potential.

These number grades were on the second page of the scouting report with position-specific boxes, and you could grade from a 3 to a 7. A 7 was a top-of-the-line talent, a player who showed elite skill with a flair. A 6 was a player who consistently displayed the factor or specific, but without the wow factor.

A 5 was dead average, a flat line.

What is tricky about the system is that a player who rated a 4 could actually be tied closely to a player who was a 6. You all know the phrase that describes a 4: diamond in the rough. Look at Jamey Mosley, the brother of former Tide star linebacker C. J. Mosley. Jamey is six feet five, 228 pounds, but he was a walk-on because he lacked strength and needed more physical development to set the edge of the defense against a tight end, as an example. Jamey needs to fill out, get stronger, learn the schemes, and then apply his athletic ability to the outside linebacker position.

You look at a player such as Jamey Mosley and he just wasn't ready to be a scholarship player at Alabama. He was a classic 4.

But . . . Saban saw the makings of a player. He saw some potential of what Jamey could be . . . a 6. This is how the 4 and the 6 are tied together. The 6 is a six-foot-five, 228-pound player who is strong enough and aware enough of responsibilities. Mosley was eventually given a scholarship in August 2016 because Saban saw he was on his way to being a 6.

Here is where Belichick and Lombardi and Saban earned their money with the Browns. They believed that a 4 was actually better than a 5 because a 4 could turn into a 6 with proper coaching and training. They felt a 5 could only go so far, but a 4 might convert to a 6 with the right attitude and work ethic.

That has always been a debate in draft rooms across the NFL: Are you better off taking the known 5 versus the unknown 4 who might elevate? Saban has done this well at Alabama.

Here is the substance of the one-system approach:

All you had to do, Lombardi said, was look at the various draft "war rooms" on NFL draft night to see the potential for mistakes. These rooms were crowded with scouts and personnel men, people with opinions on players. It was not crowded in the New England Patriots' draft room, which was run by Belichick. There was not a multitude of decision makers inside that room. It was a small group of people. The decision maker was the system.

This scouting system is at the core of Saban's Alabama success.

Here are some examples of the Process working along the game plan first laid out in the Dallas system, then practiced in Cleveland and carried to Michigan State and LSU and Alabama.

Ed Stinson (2009–13), out of South Florida (Homestead), was not a blockbuster recruit for Alabama. He was 240 pounds and as a Jack linebacker was redshirted his freshmen year. Stinson had not been exposed to rigorous weight-training or nutrition programs. The Jack linebacker is a pass-rush specialist in the 3-4, but he also has to be able to drop into zone coverage or cover man-to-man.

Stinson had big hips and a big frame and long arms. He could add weight. The first year at Alabama he added fifteen pounds, then another twenty. Stinson became a 280-pound defensive lineman and an NFL prospect. In the Dallas/Cleveland system, he was a 4 who became a 6.

Stinson's development was significant because he was part of Nick Saban's third recruiting class and a South Florida signee. Saban, I'm told, was given the "high hat" by some Miami-area high school coaches because of his departure from the Dolphins, so Stinson represented a breakthrough in a fertile recruiting area for assistant coach Bobby Williams.

Remember, stellar wide receivers Amari Cooper and Calvin Ridley came out of South Florida. Stinson was a living testimony to high school coaches in that area that Saban was worth doing business with and would develop their players.

Center Ryan Kelly (2011–15), who is from West Chester, Ohio, was not offered a scholarship by Jim Tressel's staff at Ohio State, according to most reports. Kelly had offers, but again, he was not a five-star by most schools' standards. He was light for an SEC offensive lineman, but Alabama linebacker coach Sal Sunseri, who recruited Kelly, saw a 4 who could become a 6. Saban signed off on it.

Kelly was redshirted and like a lot of other players who needed to be bulked up, he was given protein shakes after every weight-lifting workout. Peanut-butter bars and other snacks were stuffed into his backpack. Players walk around a lot on campus and burn calories so the "protein bar" run by nutritionist Amy Bragg is always open.

Here was the other thing about a 4 becoming a 6. Sunseri and the Alabama staff looked at Kelly's pedigree. His dad was a big man. More than that, the family work ethic was passed down to Ryan. He had no letters for character or grade issues. Far from it. Kelly was nicknamed A-plus throughout the facility.

So while a 4 in the Cleveland system was in many cases associated with inconsistency, for Stinson and Kelly it was about size and trying to find a specific position for each of them at Bama.

Belichick would say, "We would rather have a player who grades out at all fours that we can turn into sixes than somebody that we give fives to across the board, to the point where all we're doing is practicing our coaching, and he's never really going to get any better."

Belichick and the Patriots will often draft a player no one figured would go as high as picked, and the player will stick in the league and succeed. When this happens, I am convinced the Book inspired the pick. This was a proverbial 4 whom the Patriots thought they could turn into a 6.

The system anchors Alabama when it is recruiting a high school prospect. There are exact definitions for a player who fits the Crimson Tide system, and the definitions help assistant coaches avoid the hype around a player, the imperfect four- and five-star TV recruiting labeling. How many times does the call come in to a football office from a town in Alabama: "Hey, you need to look at this guy. He's a four-star, at least"?

The Book has created some ill will toward Tuscaloosa over the local four-stars' not being signed. Alabama football had a twenty-year run where Coach Paul "Bear" Bryant's shadow loomed over recruiting, and over most everything else. A succession of coaches were engulfed in the Bear legacy. There was pressure to take some high school players who were pretty good, but without the talent the Southeastern Conference demanded.

Saban arrived and said it was going to be his way of recruiting and development, or nothing. He respected Coach Bryant, but the player decisions were going to be unforgiving and "the friend of the program" would have a harder time getting a high school favorite a scholarship. The Dallas system would not permit it; Saban would not allow it.

I knew how strong willed Nick is, and I knew the Alabama fan base was just as strong willed. Nick was certainly going to take heed of the legacy of Coach Bryant, but Nick was going to the University of Alabama with his own ideas of how things were going to be done, and it was going to be the Saban way, or the highway. He was going to implement things with a system, and everyone would bend to his system, or he would be out of there.

That first season saw some growing pains. Alabama lost to LSU, which started a four-game losing streak. The Tide finished 7-6.

Coach Saban did not get indecisive and wobbly. He stuck with the grading/recruiting system and did not yield to pressure. It's been that way for ten seasons.

For example, Billy Neighbors was a key player for Bear Bryant's 1961 national championship team. His son, Wes Neighbors, was a terrific player for Alabama in the 1980s.

One grandson of Billy Neighbors, Wes, played defensive back for Alabama. Another grandson, Connor, a high school fullback, was not offered a scholarship by Alabama. The Crimson Tide, in its system, does not make much use of a fullback. Connor went to LSU, causing some grumbling because there was no room for the offspring of a legend.

Some feelings have been hurt along the way, I'm sure, because some people across the state had used connections in the Bryant coaching tree to get a player on the Alabama team. When Saban arrived, that did not happen much. Alabama said we're going to recruit and sign our own players, and whom we offer one of those twenty-five scholarships to is cut-and-dried. The player who was offered a scholarship twenty years ago might be an invited walk-on now.

Alabama might get some intelligence on a high school linebacker from Foley, Alabama, who makes fifteen tackles a game. But the player's incredible competitiveness could be trumped by his size: five-eleven, 210 pounds. The Crimson Tide will take a phone call from the friend of the program to discuss the upside and ruggedness of this competitive linebacker, but Bama will get its own eyes on the player, either through tape, a summer camp, or at the player's high school games, and decide for itself.

The Dallas/Bama system cuts through what I call "the fog of confusion."

You are working from inside your building rather than from what a mock draft or a media pundit is saying about a player, or what a recruiting expert is saying about a high school prospect. Alabama recruits from within its own walls. It can stay true to its system and operate independently of what everyone else thinks.

Take for instance, Huffman High School's Marcell Dareus, the Alabama All-American and first-round NFL pick. He was a three-star, but only because of concern over his academics. Dareus had few offers and was downgraded by the recruiting mavens.

Dareus was a late addition to the Alabama recruiting class in 2009, but everyone inside the building knew what he was. Dareus was 280 pounds when he arrived on campus and ran a freakish 4.68 40-yard dash. In practice, players usually run with their position group. Dareus was so fast, he ran with linebackers, not defensive linemen.

When I first saw Dareus during Bama's spring practice that year, I was shocked at the explosive power and quickness in his hips, hands, and feet. Dareus sure looked like one of those five-stars, but that is not how he was rated in high school. The fog had downgraded him, but Alabama coaches knew his skill level and waited for the fog to lift.

Certainly, recruiting in college is different from scouting in the NFL. In the NFL no fog is created by academics.

Here is another big difference between recruiting and scouting. While Belichick might be looking for a late-round player to fill a role on special teams, the Crimson Tide is recruiting twenty-five players to be four-down players, offense or defense, and become eventual starters. There are no roles, just starters.

When the Tide started looking at the class of 2017, probably 1,200 names were on the list, but over time the definitions helped cull the list to a manageable 350 to 400. Coach Saban personally gets a look at all of them in the various summer camps for high school underclassmen. Alabama tries its best not to get rushed into a decision on a player. That's why he does not like these so-called satellite camps that are far from campus.

The system is blunt. God's gifts of size and speed give you a better chance to play for Alabama. The Tide does not make many exceptions.

I still remember something Michael Lombardi told me after we played the Chicago Bears in Cleveland in 1993: "We want to be a size- and speed-based organization; we want big people that can run. We want to be a big, physical, hard-nosed team."

I remember vividly that game between the Bears and the Browns. We were starting to look like the vision Bill and Michael had for the organization. We were starting to get bigger, faster people, and in that game with the Bears the field looked as if it were tilted toward us.

We dominated that game and Lombardi told me, "That's what happens when you don't scout by using the measurables." The Browns were far superior physically that day. Chicago had taken some exceptions to build its roster and now had a team of undersized players.

A key thing to remember about the system is that it was modified as the game changed. Lombardi said the Browns had an idea what they wanted in linebackers, but when they saw the Cowboys in 1994, they felt Cleveland's linebackers were still not fast enough. The game was spreading out, and the Browns felt they needed to be a tick faster at linebacker.

The Book is written in pencil. The Browns erased and adjusted the critical factors of players, always chasing perfection. Saban has done the same thing at Alabama, evolving to deal with the prolifera- tion of the spread offense in college football. You will read about that evolution later in this book.

The Browns were starting to rise. In 1993, they finished 7-9. They went 11-5 in 1994.

In 1995, after moving from coaching to scouting and working the West Coast as an area scout, I was elevated to national scout by Belichick.

He came up to me at the Combine (1995) and said instead of my focusing on one area he would rather I went all over the place and see all of the players. Looking back, I now see it was a tremendous compliment and one that I probably took for granted. At the time, I had only scouted for a year and a half.

Ozzie Newsome was doing some on-field coaching, but was officially in pro scouting, as the Browns started to integrate the personnel department into both sides of the building in Berea.

Coming at it from completely different angles, Newsome and I worked closely as we both learned the numerical scouting system. Newsome, who did not miss a game in his entire thirteen-year NFL career and would later be inducted into the Pro Football Hall of Fame, became a perfect match for the Book. He was a former player committed to learning how to scout and run an NFL front office.

The incubation of Newsome and me from 1991 to 1995 was invaluable. We had to put it together as a player-personnel team quicker than we thought because the Browns were about to implode due to a major off-field issue.

In 1995, after Saban had taken the job as head coach at Michigan State, the trapdoor opened on Belichick and the city of Cleveland. The Browns started the '95 season 3-1, but then lost 9 of their next 10. In the midst of the downturn, owner Art Modell announced he was moving the team to Baltimore.

Modell's decree came within a month of the loss of the World Series by the Cleveland Indians, an offensive juggernaut in baseball, to the pitching-first Atlanta Braves. The city of Cleveland was reeling.

On Valentine's Day 1996, Belichick and Michael Lombardi were fired. It happened after the Senior Bowl and the Combine, which is unheard of in today's NFL.

A week later, I was sitting at my desk in Fairhope when Ozzie called: "Are you ready to get going on this draft?"

Newsome had been named vice president of player personnel for the new Baltimore Ravens. He wanted me to become his college-scouting director.

In the meantime, Saban was busy scouting and recruiting for Michigan State and getting the Spartans competitive with Ohio State and Michigan in the Big Ten. He compiled a 34-24-1 record in East Lansing.

In November 1999, Saban was named the head coach at LSU, in part because Brandt steered LSU chancellor Mark Emmert to Saban. In 2003, the Tigers won a national championship. Many of the players Saban recruited were part of the Tigers' 2007 national title team, which was coached by Les Miles.

Saban left LSU for the Miami Dolphins in December 2004, and some critics say the system did not do so well with the Dolphins, but Michael Lombardi, who is now an NFL analyst on Fox Sports 1, scoffs at that. He said the staff in Miami was not completely devoted to the system, and many were not familiar with what Nick wanted in a player.

Does Alabama miss on players with the system? Of course it does. But with four national championships in eight seasons, judge for yourself how much it misses. Analytics has become a force in sports, and the Crimson Tide has used data as well as any other organization, pro or college. The game is not simply about signing the best players and winning with force of will. Players have to be picked, then groomed.

One of Nick Saban's greatest attributes in recruiting is looking back through his vast mental library of players and saying to himself, "This guy reminds me of so-and-so that we had at LSU." Saban will look at that player and project him forward, just as Tom Landry did with the Cowboys. The human element served them both.

I wasn't born when the Cowboys became the first computer masterminds of the game. Nick Saban was pumping gas and washing windshields at his father's filling station at the intersection of Routes 19 and 218 on the outskirts of Worthington, West Virginia. The NFL was less than half the size (fourteen teams) it is today when the Cowboys started sorting players using computer-generated data.

Alabama's base system for assessing high school football players is not some random concoction that came out of a hat. This system, which is vital to the Process, came out from under the hat of Landry, the poised and stoic coach, who always seemed in control underneath that gray fedora that he wore on the sidelines fifty years ago.

The Process also came from Brandt, who is eighty-four years old and considered the godfather of NFL scouting. He is one of the creators of the NFL Combine, which is, not surprisingly, a data-driven enterprise.

The Process partly came from Schramm, who came up with the idea of instant replay, microphones for officials to inform the crowd about penalties on the field, and the wind socks used on the top of goalposts. It was also Schramm's idea for something not wholly related to data: the world-famous Dallas Cowboys Cheerleaders.

The Process can also be traced back to an immigrant, Qureishi. He came to the United States from India to teach at Case Institute of Technology, which is located in, of all places, Cleveland, where Belichick and Saban took the computer handoff from the Cowboys.

The Cowboys were labeled America's Team because they were on television so much that their faces were instantly recognized. They won and won and won, and TV always follows a winner. But the Cowboys could be known as America's Team because the organization was a melting pot of innovation. Schramm, Landry, Brandt, Qureishi, and veteran scouts such as Hickey and Dick Mansberger, among others, determined the direction of scouting for an entire league. The Cowboys created a two-hundred-page scouting manual out of their computer study, and scouts would joke the Book told them everything, including "How to Go Pee."

This system has been bedrock for Alabama football since 2007, the season Nick Saban became head coach. The Crimson Tide goes by the book. The Cowboys introduced a different kind of brainpower—a solid system using data—and Saban adopted it. Dallas did not just give the geeks of Silicon Valley a seat at the table; the geeks were handed the keys. Drive us into the future, the Cowboys said, and help us sort through players. Along the way, the data merchants gave a ride to Nick Saban and Alabama football.

The Process did not just materialize on a grease board in Tuscaloosa in 2007 when Nick arrived. It started on a chalkboard in 1963 in Dallas. It is important to understand the respect Coach Nick Saban has for the coaches that have come before him. He is an original thinker, but he also relies on some fundamentals of the game that were being taught a half century ago by Tom Landry.

The fundamentals are twofold: (1) players at each position need specific physical tools; (2) those tools need to be developed and the player needs to be trained at a deliberate pace. In eight years around Alabama football, that is what I have come to understand as the Process.

In Dallas, Gil Brandt and his personnel staff would get the players; Landry and his coaching staff would train them. In Alabama, Nick Saban runs the show on both ends, sorting through prospects and finding players who fit the system, and then coaching them up. He is the GM and the head coach. I have thirty years of experience in college and professional football, and I have not seen anyone do it better.

2
THE PRESCRIPTION

THE ALABAMA RECRUITING FORMULA

When you walk around the Alabama football practice field and look at the "big skills"—the defensive linemen, linebackers, the offensive linemen—you may not notice it, but these guys do not need a belt to hold up their pants.

Please don't laugh.

They have the "bubble."

Coach Nick Saban says the explosiveness of a player comes from that protruding rear end, the gluteus maximus, the bubble. The power to launch into an opposing player with a block or a tackle comes up from the ankles, to the knees, to the butt, and then through the hips. The arms, shoulders, and chest are making the impact, but football people know where the energy starts and how it transitions from the ground up.

The *bubble* is a fairly common term among scouts, and it is one of the reasons my friends in scouting refer to Alabama as the thirty-third NFL franchise. The Crimson Tide has a surplus of these bubbles.

In a manner of speaking, Alabama is the best-looking team in America.

The look of the Crimson Tide stems from that system of player evaluation the Cowboys created in the mid-1960s. The Cowboys of Tom Landry and Gil Brandt did not stray. They did not reinvent themselves season to season, the way you see in the NFL today. Their system was their system, and they had uniformity in drafting players.

Alabama, like the Cowboys, has definitions of players it sticks to. While Saban would tinker with height/weight/speed over the years, he stuck to what he believed in. Dallas was a perennial NFL playoff team because of its consistency, just as Alabama is a perennial national championship contender because of its consistency in choosing players.

You can see the consistency, the uniformity, of the players on the Alabama roster when they run out of the tunnel onto the field before a game. You can see the difference in "look" between Alabama and opposing teams on film and while watching them from the sidelines in pregame warm-ups. Alabama's power is unmistakable compared to that of some other programs, who might have seven or eight starters who look smart in a uniform, but not all twenty-two like Alabama.

I watched five tapes of Notre Dame in my home office a month before the 2013 BCS National Championship Game. I put the clicker down and walked into the other room and told my wife, Dorothy, "If Bama doesn't turn the ball over, they will beat these guys by three touchdowns. It won't be close."

Once we got to Sun Life Stadium in Miami Gardens and we were on the field during pregame warm-ups, I relayed to Rece Davis of ESPN, "Notre Dame looks like a MAC [Mid-American Conference] team compared to Alabama." I was not trying to disparage the Irish. It was just a scout's critical eye.

The Tide won, 42–14.

So the first point to make about the philosophy in the Alabama football complex when it comes to recruiting is:

"Big people beat up little people."

The Crimson Tide has some powerfully built—from the ground up—football players. I have had a number of scouts over the years tell me that Alabama is deeper across the defensive front than some NFL teams. Power is the propellant for five SEC titles, four national titles, and a 119-19 record since 2007.

The second point about the culture inside the Alabama program and how that culture influences recruiting on the eighty-five-man scholarship roster is this:

Coach Nick Saban is studious and disciplined in evaluating high school players. It trickles down to his coaches and his player-personnel staff. Once they have determined the player fits inside the height/weight/speed matrix, they look hard at a player head to toe.

Here's what I mean.

If you have ever been to one of Alabama's prospect or high school summer camps, you will see Nick Saban walk around with his head tilted slightly down under that straw hat. He is studying a player's flexibility from his ankles to his knees through his hips. Nick has developed a keen eye at surveying a prospect's joints.

Saban is measuring the player, and I'm not talking about height and weight. He is looking at the player's bend at the waist, his hip rotation, the flexibility in his knees and ankles; Saban is looking for any degree of stiffness that might indicate an athletic limitation in the future. The Alabama head coach is matching the player in front of him to what he has seen of that player on film. Coach Saban would make one heck of an NFL scout, to say the least.

The prospect could be a specimen, a six-foot-five, three-hundred-pound high school offensive lineman who could comfortably add twenty-five pounds. He could have "the look" and still get rejected by Alabama when it is awarding a precious scholarship.

Indeed, a member of Alabama's player-personnel staff told me, "If a player can't bend, Coach doesn't want him."

The high school players in summer camp go through all the drills Alabama goes through during the regular season. The head coach is looking for quickness (initial and lateral), agility, and balance, or what scouts call the QABs. The high school campers run through dummies and step over bags. If they get a scholarship, they will do these same drills their first practice in Tuscaloosa.

Former Alabama offensive line coach Joe Pendry, who was one of the best O-line coaches in college and pro football, would see a prospect in the hallway of the Alabama football complex and say, "Hey, do me a favor, stick your arms straight out and do a knee bend for me."

Pendry would also ask, "Bend over and touch your toes."

Thanks, kid.

Pendry was sly. He was looking at flexibility and balance. You could wreck your hopes for a scholarship in that hallway.

Pendry was an eyeball evaluator. It must be a West Virginia thing. Saban has the same vision as Pendry, who is a native of Welch, West Virginia. Saban is from Worthington, near Fairmont, West Virginia.

The third significant point to make about Alabama's prescription for building a team is this:

The Crimson Tide defines the characteristics needed for a position and rarely strays from the definition. A football player has to be a certain height and weight with the requisite speed for each position, and he needs to have the intangibles of character, competitiveness, and toughness. He also needs that "bend" and that "bubble." He must fit the definition.

Alabama builds from the inside out, not the outside in. The Tide sets the parameters for recruits; it is not the other way around. Brandt and Landry scouted for what they wanted to be as a football team and did not choose players here and there. Saban does the same thing as the Cowboys because he wants to accurately grade a prospect.

You think that is basic, a no-brainer? You would be surprised how many Division I programs detour in recruiting and pick outliers.

Based on Alabama's current and previous rosters since 2009, and talking to staff members in recruiting, here is my educated guess at their standards for height and weight at each position:

Quarterback: 6-2, 210
Running back: 5-11, 215

Wide receiver: 6-1, 190

Tight end: 6-5, 250

Left tackle: 6-5, 300

Right tackle: 6-4, 310

Guard: 6-3, 300

Center: 6-3, 290

Defensive end: 6-4, 285

Noseguard: 6-2½, 320

Jack outside linebacker: 6-3, 245

Mike/Will inside linebacker: 6-2, 250

Sam linebacker (over tight end): 6-4, 250

Cornerback: 5-11, 190

Safety: 6-1, 205

The size of the noseguard has changed the most at Alabama in the Saban Era. Remember Mount Cody, the giant of the 2009 national championship team? Terrence was six feet four, 365 pounds. The Tide has gone to a more mobile interior defensive lineman. Da'Ron Payne, the 2016 noseguard, is 315 pounds. Football has evolved from north-south to east-west, or sideline to sideline. You are now required to stack the run, but also move laterally down the line when the football goes away from you.

Alabama is looking for linemen who can run, but it also covets those old-school attributes of arm length and hand size.

The arm length should be thirty-three inches or longer because your lineman needs to be the first to get hand placement on the other guy and steer that blocker or defender. You can give a little bit for guards and center and allow thirty-one inches and thirty-two inches with arm length, but tackles have to be at least thirty-three inches to reach defensive ends in the run game and protect the edge in pass protection.

The arm length for linebackers is thirty-two inches for the inside backer and thirty-three inches for the outside backer in the Alabama 3-4 alignment.

The hand span should be at least nine inches for a high school prospect. Ten inches is ideal.

Every player that comes to the Alabama summer camp has his arms and hands measured. The player-personnel staff has started measuring the knee joints, as well, to judge growth potential.

With speed, the Alabama staff discards the 40-yard-dash times reported by the high school. The 40 time is too much home cooking. An official electronic time on a player from a state track meet is accepted. Otherwise it is done in Tuscaloosa, or it doesn't count.

The staff also wants to see a player run a 40 because not all 4.4-second times in the 40 are the same. There is straight-line timed speed and legitimate "play" speed, and a distinct difference in evaluating on a watch versus on videotape.

The Crimson Tide does not just recruit high school players, it evaluates them psychologically to determine if they can fit into the culture. Alabama is a demanding place to play, and the staff will dig in on a prospect and investigate how he handles criticism or being corrected. Mental makeup is important, critical, in recruiting a player. If you are a high school player with all the measurables and you did not get offered by Alabama, look in the mirror.

Something else to consider with the exact measurements of height and weight is that the staff tries to *eliminate* players. For twenty years in the NFL that's what I did every fall traveling from campus to campus; it was all about reducing the list of prospects and identifying the ones that fit our organization the best. That's what Alabama is doing now at the college level when it is recruiting.

Think about the sheer numbers. There might be fourteen hundred to sixteen hundred prospects in the class of 2018 when you consider the Alabama recruiting area and how many leads are chased. Natural selection—you must be this height, this weight—allows the coaches and player-personnel staff to eliminate some players immediately and save some wear and tear on their eyeballs with tape study.

Remember: height/weight/speed (verified) are the early critical factors in recruiting. That is exactly how the Cowboys started gauging players in the 1960s. It is how Belichick and the Browns started gauging players in the 1990s. It is how Saban does it at Alabama fifty years after Tom Landry and Gil Brandt.

In Alabama and the surrounding states, plenty of high school prospects fit the matrix guideposts. But other schools, Auburn, Georgia, Florida, Mississippi, and Tennessee, can find players, too. The Crimson Tide does not snap its fingers, as Steve Spurrier suggested, and the players sign up for Alabama.

The Alabama recruiters have some pet phrases. *Control the state* is heard a lot around the football building. It is similar to the *build a wall* phrase Saban used when he was the head coach at LSU (2000–2004) and he wanted to fence in all of Louisiana for himself. The thrust of recruiting—bayou first—yielded a national championship in 2003 and another in 2007 (under Les Miles). Michael Clayton, the All-American wide receiver, once said the whole LSU program turned around in 2000 because Saban built a wall around Louisiana.

Then there is the *five-hour golden radius*. Alabama wants the best players within a five-hour drive, so this covers the entire state of Alabama, Atlanta, Memphis, Nashville, New Orleans, the Florida Panhandle, and Mississippi. You think it is a simple concept, but you better understand how important it is for family and extended family to easily drive to watch their son/brother/nephew/grandson play major college football. It will not be NCAA rules limiting satellite camps that will prevent Jim Harbaugh from plucking players out of the South; it will be moms, dads, aunts, and uncles asking, "Why do you want to go way up there to Michigan? We will never get to see you."

The other reason the five-hour radius is key to recruiting is that high school players can be brought to summer camp in Tuscaloosa by coaches and parents. These summer camps are crucial because Nick Saban himself gets to put his discerning eye on most every player who is going to be offered a scholarship to Alabama. The man in the straw hat is the ultimate cross-checker. For any program, your batting average is higher with in-state recruits because you know them better.

The five-hour radius is ideal, but as Alabama has broadened its brand the last eight years, it has become a more national player in recruiting. Of the 116 players listed on the 2016 roster—which included invited walk-ons and scholarship players—71 were from out of state. Of those 71, 44 were from outside the five-hour-drive time.

There is one sure way to have a chance at getting in front of Saban as a prospect at an Alabama camp. The player-personnel staff gets the names of every high school player in Alabama who has an offer, from the FCS level all the way down to Division III and junior college. These players are worth a glance, at least. The staff eliminates some prospects because of the critical factors. Then they take a second look and eliminate players having studied them on tape.

By the third look, a prospect is not far from having Nick put eyes on him on film. Can you see how rigid the system is?

The player-personnel staff discards some prospects based on the early critical factors, but there are exceptions. Remember the fabulous high school running back Dee Hart? He was five feet nine, but was a good role player. Courtney Upshaw was an outlier, a linebacker with shorter arms, but he overcame the height/weight/speed formula and became a star.

The staff also collects tips on prospects from the recruiting travels around the region by assistant coaches. Perhaps the staff saw a freshman from McDonough, Georgia, while recruiting defensive lineman Dalvin Tomlinson and they added that younger player to the "follow" list.

Tips are left by voice mail for Alabama staff. You know how they go: "Hey, Bama needs to check out this guy."

Jeremy Pruitt, the Alabama defensive coordinator, got one of those phone calls. He was in the shower in the football facility the week before Signing Day 2016. A friend of Pruitt's sent a video using the recruiting tool Hudl. It showed a "wildcat" quarterback from McLain High School, north of Tulsa, Oklahoma.

I'm told Pruitt rushed upstairs to the football office and showed the video of Joshua Jacobs to Jody Wright, the director of player personnel. Wright watched it and popped out of his chair and took it down the hall to Coach Nick Saban. Wright did some research. Jacobs had one offer—from a midmajor, Tulsa. Wyoming and New Mexico had some interest, too. Saban was impressed with what he saw and he had Burton Burns, the running backs coach, get on a plane to go watch Jacobs in a basketball game.

Burns liked what he saw in person, but Missouri had also entered the recruiting picture, along with Oklahoma. Alabama hastily arranged a campus visit. Jacobs and his father visited Missouri, then drove ten hours to Tuscaloosa. Saban told them Alabama would not know until noon of Signing Day if a scholarship would be available.

When Alabama lost out on defensive end Jeffery Simmons, who signed with Mississippi State, a scholarship was suddenly available for Jacobs. Simmons, it turned out, was arrested in the spring of 2016 for assault on a woman. (He later pleaded no contest to the charge and apologized to the woman.) Jacobs, a five-foot-ten, 204-pound running back, received an offer. By the end of August 2016, his first summer camp with the Tide, he was among the top running backs for snaps for the 2016 season. He was a valuable contributor in the march to the national championship game.

Nick Saban has learned his lessons the hard way about chasing the leads you are given.

In 1999, while he was at LSU, Saban was contacted about another potential recruit who was under the radar. This recruit was a quarterback, a high school senior who had only one season of starting experience. Nick asked the contact, "Where are his offers?"

The friend said, "Duke and Miami of Ohio."

"Okay, we can't go all the way up to Findlay, Ohio, and beat Duke and Miami of Ohio on a quarterback, no way."

The quarterback, Ben Roethlisberger, signed with Miami of Ohio, and, well, you know the rest of the story. Saban is human, but he has learned to follow up with recruits and see for himself.

Alabama's staff will follow up on prospects suggested on social media outlets like Twitter and Facebook. Don't worry. No player is offered a scholarship based on a Twitter blast of "He's the next Derrick Henry!" It's just a lead.

The staff looks at Internet message boards and newspaper stories and jots down names. It is creating the database, the early catalog of names, just like National Football Scouting or BLESTO, the two scouting services that do the same thing for the vast majority of NFL teams.

Then the player-personnel staff—many of whom started as student assistants at Alabama—pour the names into a funnel. The databases for a particular class year may have as many as fourteen hundred names, but many are quickly eliminated using the height/weight/speed charts. The player-personnel staff collects tapes and watch prospects and makes notes for the coaching staff.

The player-personnel staff, the analysts, and the assistant coaches develop their own index, their own catalog, by walking the field during summer prospect camps, during spring practice, during August fall camp, and during the regular season.

That up-close exposure to the players starts from the moment you get a job at Alabama as a student assistant or as an assistant coach or "analyst." The whole staff create a catalog in their mind's eye of what a good player looks like. So when a summer camp rolls around, the staff can look at a prospect and compare him to a current Alabama player.

Alabama is renowned for collecting "analysts" such as Mike Groh, Steve Sarkisian, or Billy Napier, and guys let go by other programs because of a head-coaching change. They come to Tuscaloosa and get familiar with the system, then suddenly there is an opening and they become an assistant coach.

The new coach or analyst or staff member hired in the offseason gets his first look at Alabama talent during spring ball. The players are in pads and thumping against other players of a similar skill set.

If you want to see what a left tackle looks like on this level of college football, go down and watch the individual drills of Cam Robinson. Check out his body type and watch him move. Create a vision in your mind's eye of what a major-college left tackle should look like.

If you want to see what an edge pass rusher looks like at this level, go watch the one-on-ones of linebacker Tim Williams. Study the proportioned physique, the burst off the line, his countermove, and it's easy to see, okay, that's how an elite college rusher should look.

Once you have a vision of Julio Jones, you know what a big-time receiver looks like.

What is important is that everybody is looking through the same lens at Alabama.

There is a prototype, a vision, at every single position. This guy reminds me of tight end O. J. Howard. Hey, this guy is similar to cornerback Marlon Humphrey.

Do you understand? There is uniformity. *This* is our base. No other school adheres to the strict discipline of judging players like Alabama, and it starts at the top with the head coach.

When I was scouting director for the Baltimore Ravens, we created this same prototype system. Our 2000 Super Bowl XXXV winning team was loaded with these kinds of players. From Jonathan Ogden at left tackle to Ray Lewis at middle linebacker, Shannon Sharpe at tight end, Rod Woodson at free safety, Jamal Lewis at running back, and Chris McAlister at cornerback. Everyone in our personnel department had a vision at every position of what a big-time NFL prospect should look like.

In personnel and scouting, comparison shopping is important. In one year of spring ball, followed by fall camp, then a regular season, December practices, and a bowl game, these UA staffers can develop a library in their mind's eye of players. They can shop for something similar in a player during recruiting. Do not underestimate this part of the Alabama recruiting approach.

So when that kid from Wetumpka, Alabama, walks on the field for summer camp, you can say with reasonable assurance, "He fits." Some other recruit will walk out on the field, and he doesn't fit. He's duck footed, he has skinny legs, and he doesn't look the part.

Once again, the test is the Alabama team when it runs out of the tunnel at Arkansas. No duck feet, no skinny legs. The vast majority of the Tide players are well proportioned. They are not bulked up with a muscled torso on small legs, or vice versa.

Indeed, the youngest staff member at Alabama walking the hallway can say, "O. J. Howard looks the part of an impact tight end. Dont'a Hightower looks the part of a major league linebacker."

There is a staffwide cultivation of these mental pictures of the ideal prospect. You can take it further and expand the library of your mind's eye by looking at the opposing team. You look at Georgia and outside linebacker Leonard Floyd and you see a sleeker edge rusher. You look at Texas A&M offensive tackle Jake Matthews and see a starting left tackle in the NFL.

When these players move on to the next level, and if you are still at Alabama working in the recruiting office or working as an analyst or assistant coach, you can say, "So that's what an NFL defensive end looks like. I saw Jonathan Allen or Reuben Foster in two hundred and fifty practices and forty-plus games. We recruit according to *those* guys."

At the end of this chapter I will tell you what's cool about that and why it is proprietary to the Alabama franchise.

The student assistant is building his recruiting portfolio, but Saban is thirty years ahead of him. The Alabama head coach will often say in recruiting meetings, "He reminds me of Ryan Kelly," and he is referring to the former center. Saban will say a linebacker reminds him of Rolando McClain, or a high school running back reminds him of Mark Barron, who played offense in high school, but was switched to defense at Alabama.

The library-like card catalog of Saban is rows and rows of mental recall, and NFL scouts marvel at his recollection of players, not only his own, but players from other programs. The recall is important because in recruiting Saban tries to project how a player might play at Alabama after three or four years of detailed coaching and development.

The eye of Coach Saban is a recruiting ingredient few schools, if any, can match because he studies film of prospects like no other Division I coach.

You should understand that just because Alabama uses some "analytics" to look at players, they do not look at them on a computer. They look at them in flesh and blood.

Human science.

In April and May, Nick Saban's player-personnel staff will send him home at night with a tape of ten to twelve high school prospects. The Alabama head coach will watch the film and study players and tell the staff, "Let's get this guy to camp."

During the regular season, Saban will reserve an hour on Friday morning to watch tapes of these prospects.

The staff does *not* put together a highlight tape for the Alabama head coach. They put together a profile tape of the Good, the Bad, and the Ugly. That's what they call it. They have not cherry-picked a prospect's good games. They have watched all his high school games.

"We get the full picture," a staff member told me. "Player-personnel guys are cutting up a hundred guys a day and we want to see it all."

It is exhaustive work. Alabama has a player-personnel staff larger than most NFL teams. In 2012, each of the assistant coaches got his own player-personnel assistants to help with recruiting. Alabama, I believe, was the first to do it. Now others do it, too.

The nine assistant coaches would split up Alabama county by county in recruiting, and then each would get an area of the country. Former assistant coach Sal Sunseri would recruit Huntsville, but also get Pennsylvania and Ohio. Jim McElwain did Tuscaloosa, but also had to look at players west of the Mississippi.

I have had player-personnel people tell me the head coaches at other FBS schools do not watch as much tape of high school prospects as Nick Saban. Some big-school coaches do not watch tape of prospects at all. They simply close the deal on prospects they are told are worth the scholarship. These coaches—and you may find it hard to believe—check Rivals and 247Sports and find out who has offered a prospect and tell their staff, "Start recruiting him."

It is dangerous to rely on word of mouth and film only. You need to see a player eye to eye, face-to-face, and up close before you invest in him. Trust me on that one.

When I was with the Browns in 1995 as a scout—the year before we moved to Baltimore—I was asked to cross-check an Ohio State linebacker. I was sent three tapes, which I later found out were the three best games of his life.

The Browns' area scout, Ernie Plank, had given the prospect a fourth-round grade. I watched his film—a highlight show—and put a high grade on him based on those exposures. Others in the organization were given the same tapes, and all of our grades resulted in this player being lined up with our other potential first-rounders on the board.

We traded out of the No. 10 spot and down to no. 30 in the first round of the 1995 draft. We also picked up a future first-round choice in the 1996 draft. But, at No. 30, we were too far down to get any of our intended targets. When they all went off the board, one of our only options was to pick this particular linebacker at no. 30, and that's what we did.

Later that night, when our first-round selection walked into the Browns building, my first reaction looking at him was that this guy did not look like an NFL player. One school of thought in scouting very much believes in "face-grading" NFL prospects. Yes, he was tall and had long arms, but his shoulders were rounded, his legs were thin, and he had zero presence.

Terry McDonough, another Browns scout who is now the vice president of player personnel for the Arizona Cardinals, just looked at me as the player walked down the hallway, and we both thought something was missing with this guy. Almost simultaneously, we both said, "Uh-oh," let's go pull out some other tapes on him.

He was not good on any of the other tapes we watched. He was completely opposite of the three tapes we had been sent. He flashed straight-line speed, but showed little instinct and was a poor, low tackler. Needless to say, he never made it with us, then bounced around to three different teams in four years before ending his career in the ill-fated XFL. On paper, he was six feet four, 245 pounds, and ran a sub-4.7 seconds in the 40, but he had a bad face, bad motor, and no pass-rush skills.

From that moment on, I said to myself that I would never submit another grade without seeing the prospect in person. Once we moved to Baltimore and I became the scouting director, we never asked our scouts to evaluate a player on just film alone.

The good news? That 1996 first-round draft pick we acquired by dropping down from no. 10 to no. 30 turned into Ray Lewis, who became one of the dominant players of his era and one of our established prototypes for the Ravens.

There is no doubt, in my mind, that Alabama wants an in-person evaluation as well. You can be fooled by measurables on paper and manipulated tapes.

I think Nick Saban may have made the same mistake on another prospect back in 1991. The first time I ever met Nick was in the old Browns offices at Baldwin-Wallace College that March. He had a grainy black-and-white film on the screen, and I asked, "Who are you watching?"

"Some guy that can't play, Aeneas Williams from Southern University."

Williams was drafted in the third round by the Arizona Cardinals and was inducted into the Pro Football Hall of Fame in 2014. Film can be unreliable in grading a player, and when I asked Aeneas years later if he remembered working out for Nick, he said the Browns never came to see him in person. I believe that's why Nick is to this day obsessed in getting high school prospects to their summer camps on campus. He wants to see them up close and in the flesh.

Once the head coach has made his evaluation, the Crimson Tide grades high school prospects on a numerical scale with the top grade being an impact starter and future NFL player.

The player will grade himself if you watch enough film, but you want to always cross-check him with an in-person exposure.

Saban also brought to Tuscaloosa the Cowboys' methodology that made sure a player's blemishes or red flags are part of the record. On the recruiting board in the Alabama football complex, a yellow dot is put next to the prospect with academic issues. An orange dot is put next to the player with "character issues or concerns."

The recruiting board lists players who have been to high school camp at the Capstone, and those who have made it as far as a video conference call with Nick Saban.

Alabama's recruiting staff will make notes next to a player. This might come as a surprise, but one of the "critical factors" for a cornerback is the ability to tackle. The game has spread into space, and the Tide wants five-foot-eleven corners who can bring a receiver down by themselves.

The goal is always to find "clean" prospects. The clean prospects have the height, weight, speed numbers and no red flags.

What Alabama does better than most is take emotion out of the recruiting of a prospect. It evaluates in a coldhearted way. It pulls everyone on the staff together in the same direction so they are evaluating players for the same subset of skills. Rarely does Alabama take outliers in recruiting, because it is trying to play the percentages. Big people beat up little people in football; that's 100 percent true. Play that percentage.

The height/weight/speed charts rule, but "critical factors" and "position specifics," which were also at the heart of the Cowboys' system, are considered, too. For a defensive end, the critical factors are athletic ability, strength, explosion, speed, and competitiveness, while the position specifics include key/diagnose, point of attack versus the run, hands/controlling, and shedding blocks and pass rush. The body type—long arms, a streamlined upper body, and the power source, the bubble—are musts, too.

Alabama also asks, "What is the prospect's mental makeup and how much can he grow physically?" How much upside does the prospect have mentally and physically over the next four years?

It is vital to have an anchor system because you are less likely to get caught up in that fog of confusion I talked about in chapter 1. An old personnel adage is "You scout with your eyes, not your ears," and Alabama does that better than anyone else.

There is little "fog" for the Crimson Tide because, by taking a cue from the head coach and relying on their own system, the "chatter" is turned down regarding almost every prospect.

The exact definitions for players at each position must be followed. Assistant coaches cannot become general managers. They cannot have an emotional bias toward a player who does not fit the criteria laid out in the critical factors.

Just think about what happened at Tennessee ten years ago, after Phil Fulmer was fired. The Volunteers had four head coaches from 2008 to 2013, and the result was a disjointed roster with a random collection of players. The definitions of what made a good linebacker, for instance, were all over the place in Knoxville because there were four different coaching staffs. Tennessee was 14-34 in SEC games in those six seasons.

There needs to be continuity, and if there is one thing the recruiting staff at Alabama has told me, it is that the program is consistent. Coaches and player-personnel staffers tell me they have seen the inner workings of other FBS programs, and the leadership from the top down does not compare to Alabama.

"There is a feel here that you are always going in the right direction," a UA player-personnel staff member told me. "Coach has the ability to get everyone on the same page. There is an inherent leadership."

I've been told that Alabama, say for the class of 2017, made 100 to 125 offers over two to three years. Recruiting has stretched out to four years because talented high school players are being identified early and rival schools are forcing decisions.

The gatekeeper, Nick Saban, limits the mistakes in recruiting. Some SEC schools will sign twenty-five players, and ten will end up as major contributors. Alabama will sign twenty-five prospects, and twenty will become bona fide players because Saban stands at the gate. The depth of Alabama's roster, the competitive zeal up and down the depth chart, which makes players work hard in practice, is because Saban demands to see players in person at the summer camps and size them up with his well-trained eyes.

Sometimes other schools will offer a kid and try to get Alabama into the mix and make the Tide waste a scholarship. You will hear it in the rumor mill: "If this guy doesn't get an offer from Alabama, he's going to school X."

Alabama doesn't usually bite on it, but the Tide can make a mistake with the high-profile player who forces their hand early in recruiting. That's what some staffers say about why they have missed on certain prospects. A high school junior will insist he has to know and Alabama gets impatient.

Some high school recruits coming into their junior and senior years have multiple offers and feel they don't have to attend Alabama's summer camp. They feel they have nothing to prove. That's when the Alabama staff wonders about the player's competitive mentality. Why doesn't he want to come to the camp? A note might be slipped into the player's file about how he skipped camp, or he had to be persuaded into coming.

Some high school players such as Reggie Ragland come to summer camp ready-made physically. Reggie was the same weight his rookie year in the NFL that he was in high school. Ragland came to camp because his competitive juices stirred.

Coach Saban will watch others in summer camp and project them as starters four years out. Just look at Eddie Jackson, the safety. He came out of Lauderdale Lakes, Florida, and was just 149 pounds, according to a staff member.

Saban saw film of Jackson before the camp, then saw him up close and noticed Jackson's hands. They were as big as a catcher's mitt. Jackson had only decent straight-ahead speed, but he made up for it with lateral quickness, flexibility, long arms, and those hands. Eddie could press a receiver with his long arms and get those hands on a lot of footballs.

He sure was skinny, but Jackson was offered a scholarship, became a starting safety, and led the 2015 national championship team with six interceptions.

Alabama does not care so much "what" a high school player is doing on the field. It cares more about "how" a player is doing it. There is a big difference. What he is doing might look dominant against high school players, but how he is doing it—athleticism, instinct, explosiveness—might show his future potential.

Nick Saban would much rather take a guy with "tools" in his body that have not yet bloomed over a high school player who is "an effort guy" making twenty-five tackles through willpower. Saban thinks he can coach the player with tools so that his pure ability will allow him to far surpass the results of the overachiever with limited skills.

Some recruits are called value picks, such as former Alabama right tackle Austin Shepherd, from North Gwinnett (Georgia) High School. He did not get an offer from the University of Georgia and was rated a three-star. Kirby Smart recruited Shepherd, who was a starter for two seasons at Alabama.

What did Smart see? The left tackle on that North Gwinnett team was Ja'Wuan James, one of the best high school offensive tackles in the country. On that offensive line, James was the real target of the national recruiting analysts, and he ended up at Tennessee. Shepherd was overshadowed, but he had the attributes Alabama was looking for in a tackle. Sure, right tackle is historically the weakest position on a twenty-two-man roster, but a starting right tackle at Alabama is something to take notice of. Shepherd was drafted in the seventh round of the 2015 draft by the Minnesota Vikings.

Shepherd proved to be a great value.

Saban prefers flexible players and can also be a flexible recruiter. He has told his staff that the wide receiver corps needs to look like a basketball team. It needs centers, such as Julio Jones (six feet four), but it also needs point guards to play the slot. Alabama will recruit specifically to that role.

Mike Gundy, the Oklahoma State head coach, told me they save one scholarship a year for the slot receiver because that role is so important in their offense.

In 2015, Richard Mullaney was the Tide's point guard, that slot receiver. He was taller, six feet three, but he did the same things as the Patriots' slots: he read the interior of the opponent's pass defense. In 2016, the Tide recruited Gehrig Dieter, the fifth-year slot receiver out of Bowling Green.

You look at players such as Wes Welker and Julian Edelman with the Patriots, and some college coaches have wised up to how important the role can be. When you play two wide receivers, yes, you want two Julio Joneses on the field. But with three wide receivers, or four, on the field, there is a place for the slot-type athlete.

Mullaney and Dieter are bigger, which is different from the New England slot receiver, but they have a role. The slot guy gives you a three-way go, and with more defenders around him, he has to be aware of what the defense is trying to do so he can settle in a hole or run away from coverage.

Here was the other thing about Mullaney. He was a third wide receiver and could force teams to play an extra defensive back, but then he could motion in tight to the formation, creating a base offensive look and be an additional blocker in the run game against a Nickel defense.

The Crimson Tide seemed to have a perfect slot-receiver type in Blake Sims when he was recruited out of Gainesville, Georgia. He was six feet tall and a high school quarterback, but the Tide looked at him as a versatile offensive threat. A Bama staffer told me, "We didn't know what Sims was coming out: running back, wide receiver, defensive back. We had to have him, though."

The most important thing was that Alabama knew Sims was a football player. He was tried all over the field. In 2014, the Tide was desperate for a quarterback, and Sims stepped in and became the starter. The Tide won the SEC Championship and made the first-ever College Football Playoff.

I still think that 2014 team, with a six-foot, first-year starting quarterback, and a below-average secondary, was the best coaching job done by Nick and his staff during his time in Tuscaloosa.

Saban likes size and prefers the "centers" such as Julio because they can work above the five-foot-eleven defensive back. Nick is all about winning the matchups sideline to sideline. That's why when a prominent high school defensive back came to summer camp and was evaluated by the boss, Saban was not impressed.

"I could eat peanuts off the top of this guy's head," Saban said. The corner was five feet nine and a top-notch national recruit.

Saban prefers the five-foot-eleven, six-foot corners, the guys tall enough to duel Julio for a jump ball, but also flexible and fast enough to turn and run with Amari Cooper. This particular high school player could run, but he was under five-ten. The player went on to have a sensational college career, but not at Alabama.

Was it a mistake not to sign the player? Probably, but as Ozzie Newsome used to tell us every year before the scouts left training camp for the season, "Hey, there ain't no virgins in scouting, everyone has skeletons in their closet." Sometimes a prospect can beat the percentages, but Saban still had four national titles in a eight-year stretch during that time.

So you can't tell me his approach doesn't work.

The SEC is known for its speed, but Alabama understands it is going to have three games a year where muscle matters: LSU, Arkansas, and a likely Big Ten team, either early in the season (Wisconsin) or during the playoffs (Ohio State, Michigan State). Alabama stays prepared for the teams that are going to try to jam the ball down the throat of the Tide. Alabama recruits and signs one heavy lineman for the nose of the defense every year. They also recruit the 245-pound thumpers for the Mike and Will inside linebacker posts.

Alabama is built to play two different ways. It's why Saban said during the 2016 SEC Media Days about the 2015 national championship team, "We had the perfect mix of personnel: we had guys who could play specific roles against all the different kinds of offenses we see."

Alabama does not worry too much about the guys they take a pass on in recruiting; they worry more about missing out on the ones they really want. If a prospect that fits all the criteria goes to another school, that one hurts most. They don't worry about the ones that are not the ideal fit for their system and are signed by another SEC school.

Leonard Fournette was a big fish they could not get in the boat.

Was Jadeveon Clowney another? Yes, but . . .

Missing out on Clowney, who signed with his home state team, South Carolina, hurt because Alabama was in the hunt for an edge rusher with the 2011 recruiting class. They wanted to improve their outside pass rush, and he was the man to do it. It came down to South Carolina and Alabama.

When he got to Carolina, there were hints that Clowney would have had a hard time adjusting in Tuscaloosa had he signed with Alabama. He had poor practice habits under Steve Spurrier and basically was on his own program. Still, in three seasons, he racked up 24 sacks for the Gamecocks and emerged as the no. 1 overall draft pick by the Houston Texans because of his obvious natural ability. But you wonder how much more prepared Clowney would have been for the NFL if he had gone to Alabama. It was not until the 2016 season, his third in the league, that he reached his vast potential and became a Pro Bowler.

Coach Saban will tell players who enter the program, "Do you want the pain of discipline or the pain of disappointment?" Most first-year players immediately acknowledge that the man means business, and he has credibility to go with it. The recruits see the NFL carrot and they see the goal of the College Football Playoff, and most decide they would rather have the pain of discipline.

If you need another example of the system's foundation and how solid it is, just look at defensive end Da'Shawn Hand, who was a junior in 2016. Three years earlier, he was not just the top defensive end in the country as a high school senior, Hand was rated one of the top five recruits for any position in the country.

Hand (six feet four, 278 pounds) didn't start for three years at Alabama. He played in every game in 2016 and had twenty tackles and two sacks, but he was on the same development curve as Ryan Anderson and Tim Williams. Neither were full-time starters on the defense because of the veteran talent in front of them. Hand showed his explosiveness off the ball, his strength, and a feel for the system. NFL scouts take note of players such as Hand who show discipline and improve gradually and develop into a starter.

While he was in high school in northern Virginia, Hand was scouted for that resiliency and willingness to work and compete on the defensive line, which has, historically under Saban, been the strength of the team. Would Robert Nkemdiche of Grayson High School (Georgia) tolerate that stress of competition? Who knows, but he went to Ole Miss where he arrived as the most talented athlete on the team as a true freshman.

Like the Dallas Cowboys staff, Alabama's player-personnel staff could pick out the top 10 percent of players, the Nkemdiches—Gil Brandt used to say a housewife could do it—but it is that next 20 percent where you earn your money. To pick out those players just below the blue-chip line—the guys rated ten to twenty-five in your recruiting class—requires a devotion to tape study, a strict system, and an eyeball-to-eyeball test. That starts from the top at Bama with Nick Saban.

So this is the "cool" part I referred to earlier in the chapter when I was talking about identifying players.

You hear all the time in college football, "Coach X is off the Bobby Bowden coaching tree" or "Coach Y is off the Bear Bryant coaching tree."

Some coaches—such as Kirby Smart, Will Muschamp, and Jim McElwain—are off the Saban coaching tree. There is another Saban tree: a player-personnel tree. These limbs from the trunk of Saban spread wide.

How many coaches can claim a player-personnel tree? Not many.

That's what stands out about the Alabama system. It can train up young coaches, but it can also train scouts and front-office talent, too, to effectively evaluate players.

It is remarkable to me to hear some of the graduate assistant coaches or player-personnel assistants, maybe guys twenty-two years old, say, 'He's stiff in his ankles, he's really tight." That terminology comes from the very top of the organization, the Alabama head coach.

At least nine men who were on the Alabama player-personnel staff that constructed national title teams in 2009, 2011, 2012, and 2015 are playing prominent roles for scouting and player-personnel staffs in the NFL and in Division I football. That should tell you something about the impact of Alabama on our industry.

Nick has said the NFL gets one pick every thirty-two choices, but in college "if we are picking the right guys, we should be signing four or five first-rounders every year." In the six drafts from 2010 to 2015, Alabama has had sixteen first-round picks. It is not four or five first-rounders every recruiting cycle, as Saban insisted was possible, but it is more first-rounders than any other school. It shows you how high the bar is set.

Think about what these player-personnel "kids" helped accomplish in the run of four titles in eight seasons from 2009 to 2016, all because they were dutiful to the player evaluation system. In the six drafts from 2010 to 2015, Alabama not only had sixteen first-rounders, but they also had seven second-rounders.

The remarkable thing is those first- and second-rounders have been scattered on both sides of the ball. Remember when Tennessee was Wide Receiver U? Southern California was Tailback U? Penn State was Linebacker U?

Alabama is just U-Haul U. They haul in players at all the different positions who can become first-rounders.

In my opinion, Nick took the Browns' system of the early nineties and applied his own methodology and his own philosophies to it once he became the head coach at Michigan State (1995–99). He modified his system and improved it at LSU. He sharpened it at Alabama.

It is the ultimate combination of being able to recruit the top prospects and fitting those players into his specific roster makeup, exactly what talent he wants at every position.

When another Division I school insists it is going to recruit like Alabama, it better understand the underpinnings of recruiting at Alabama. The player-personnel system is disciplined; it has a barbed-wire fence. No coach or analyst is allowed to stray and declare a new definition of what a left tackle should look like.

It is true that Alabama can shop down the five-star aisle and find their definition of a left tackle. But it is also true that these prototypical players, once they are signed by Alabama, do not jump out of a box as SEC-worthy. Saban and the Tide have to develop these players mentally and physically. They have to bring them back from the disappointment of being sent to the scout team. Sometimes Nick uses the roughest sandpaper to smooth a player out, but this is football and it is not always pleasant. He does it with the best intentions: for the player to improve and his team to win.

Understand, Saban will do something so coarse—or so the player thinks—as to move a touchdown-making high school star to defensive back (Mark Barron at Alabama, Corey Webster at LSU). It can upset an entire family who believed their son was destined to be the next Jerry Rice.

Saban has gone so far as to visit a recruit's family in their home a year after signing to discuss a position change. He did that with Webster. He went and told Lorraine and MacArthur Webster their son could guard receivers like a great basketball one-on-one defender. Nick told Corey's parents their son had an instinct for defense and that he would break on footballs and make plays and he needed to be a defensive back. Webster said his parents wanted to throw Nick Saban out of their home in Vacherie, Louisiana, for disrupting the plan for Corey to be an NFL wide receiver.

Saban, who is a sensational defensive backs coach, converted Webster to cornerback for the 2002 season at LSU and developed him into a topflight NFL prospect. Corey Webster won two Super

Bowl rings with the New York Giants as a cornerback. In 2008, he signed a five-year contract extension with the Giants worth $43.5 million.

There is recruiting, and then there is the next step in the process, player development.

You think Alabama's head coach and his staff have a keen eye for recruiting, right? The development of players is even more impressive. Sure, the Alabama coaching staff is given amazing talent to work with, but look at what they do when a supremely gifted player gets injured or doesn't keep up on the practice field. I'm about to show you in the next chapter a good example of development for a dinged player.

The common complaint about development in college sports is that coaches are so busy trying to recruit the next great player that they sometimes cheat a kid already on the roster. The complaint is that they don't coach enough individual skills and fundamentals.

But few players walk away from Alabama feeling cheated when it comes to development. You are handpicked for the Crimson Tide and then you are handcrafted, even when your career appears doomed.

3
DEVELOPMENT

4TH AND GOAL ON THE PRACTICE FIELD

There might as well have been a flashing billboard hung over Alabama's left cornerback position in the 2014 Iron Bowl:

"Throw the ball here!"

Alabama was a desperate team in the defensive secondary that night in Bryant-Denny Stadium because left cornerback Eddie Jackson was on the field wearing a bulky knee brace. Healthy big-league corners don't wear knee braces in games.

Auburn attacked Jackson with gusto. In the middle of the third quarter, Bradley Sylve trotted on the field to replace the struggling Jackson, who could not cut off Auburn's wide receivers early in their routes as they ran past him for big plays.

Auburn led 33–21 when Jackson was benched. I remember watching him on the sideline. He was at rock bottom with a bum knee. The kid needed to get his health back; he had lost his downfield speed, and I felt bad for him.

I thought that was it for Eddie Jackson as a cornerback at Alabama. He was done.

Well, I was right. That was it for EJ's career as a cornerback at Alabama. He was demoted in spring ball to second-team corner.

But he was not done at Alabama as a football player the Crimson Tide could trust.

Jackson became All-SEC in 2015, a hero for the national championship team, and a sudden NFL prospect. He was moved twenty yards to his right to the middle of the field, where he thrived as a free safety in the high post.

This chapter is about the latent essence of the Alabama football program, those winding turns of player development that are an underpublicized part of Nick Saban's process. Development is the grinding and sharpening of the knife.

Recruiting is significant, but what they do best at Alabama is player development. Talk to any NFL scout and he will tell you that the Alabama practice field resembles a pro camp more than any other college program in the country. The drills and techniques being taught in Tuscaloosa are the same ones used during the week by NFL players who slip on pads for the Sunday games.

The Crimson Tide soaks its players in film work, fundamentals, repetition, and patience. This is mostly shielded from public view. It is a slow drip. It is a resolute focus on blocking and tackling and ball security/takeaway fundamentals.

Alabama also uses development to rescue careers, such as Eddie Jackson's.

We see the assemblage of top-five recruiting classes, but what happens when a player veers off course with an injury, such as Eddie, or has off-field personal missteps, or finds veterans stacked in front of him on the depth chart?

You should read carefully here about the examples of Eddie Jackson, Reggie Ragland, Tim Williams, and Derrick Henry and the influence of fundamentals and development. Careers are not readymade. Sometimes the ascendant high school superstar—such as Eddie—has his career hijacked by the various calamities none of us saw coming, such as injuries.

From the start of the 2014 regular season, Jackson looked less than 100 percent healthy and by the time of the Iron Bowl three months later, he was still wearing that bulky brace. Jackson became a target in a patchwork secondary during the 2014 season (Alabama was eleventh in the SEC in pass defense in 2014) and his pride was dinged.

EJ lost his job for good as a corner in spring practice 2015 when his burst had not returned. When he was moved to safety that first week of spring ball, he was made second team, and that caused him to simmer inside at Nick and the coaching staff. Jackson was angry at the Alabama coaches because he felt they had rushed him back too soon after a major knee injury in April 2014 and he was not given enough time to regain his speed.

Then the lifeline came. Saban and first-year defensive backs coach Mel Tucker met at the end of the first week of spring ball in 2015 and decided to move Jackson to safety.

Jackson not only had to be taught a new position, he had to be mentally reconstructed. He was at a disheartening moment in his career, and a little bitter. He had lost his job. Development at Alabama is mental as well as physical.

But before I tell you about Mel Tucker and Nick's work—and EJ's determination—digest these NFL facts. This is the undertow, the unseen data behind the EJ comeback.

A study was done on NFL safeties by a friend of mine in scouting. Forty-eight percent of safeties in the NFL in 2016 were former college cornerbacks. The NFL game had spread out with the more open formations, and pro teams were looking for taller, angular, 4.5 40-yard-dash guys to play the middle of the field. They were looking for players with the characteristics of a cornerback. The NFL found they could find these new "safeties" inside the bodies of these revamped college corners.

So the NFL started hiring these converted corners to play the middle of the field. The strong safety in the NFL, the six-foot, 225-pound missile and ferocious tackler, is a linebacker now. What the game is demanding are hybrids, the defensive back with corner skills—loose hips, coverage ability, ball hawk—to play a large patch of green in the middle of the field so an extra rusher can be devoted to pressuring the quarterback.

Alabama, among other schools, saw the trend. The Tide started searching for these hybrids, either in recruiting or in players already in the program, such as Eddie Jackson. The college offense was putting a faster and shiftier receiver on the field, and the defense's base scheme of two corners and two safeties on first and second down was becoming obsolete. The successful scheme now had defensive backs who could cover receivers put in a slot between the tackle and the split end, just eight to ten yards away from the core of the formation and lined up off the line of scrimmage.

In its Dime (six defensive backs) package in 2015, Alabama ended up with six defensive backs with a corner background. That was absolutely by design. They all had some experience in coverage and playing in space. Twelve of the fifteen Alabama opponents in 2015 dictated that Dime alignment. Arkansas, LSU, and Michigan State were the only rock-'em, sock-'em teams on the schedule, the only ones who lined up in base or regular personnel (meaning two backs with one tight end or one back with two tight ends).

So the evolving college game created an opportunity for Eddie Jackson. He brought a corner's instincts in seeing the football, which allowed him to play deeper at safety and use his range. Eddie's vision to judge the trajectory of the ball, to play it in the air aggressively, and his overall savvy saved his career.

This is how it unfolded:

When spring ball started in 2015, EJ still looked speed deficient and stiff. He struggled with the first team at left corner, and Saban and Mel Tucker saw it and took his job away.

When Saban and Tucker switched Jackson to safety in 2015 spring practice, they made him second on the depth chart, too. EJ didn't know the defensive calls or checks, and I'm told his resentment for Coach Saban deepened.

But instead of retreating into a shell, as some players will do, Jackson became more determined.

Mel, who is a longtime friend of mine and now the defensive coordinator at Georgia, managed the resurrection of EJ. Mel was the "translator," if you will, between the thick playbook and the defensive backs.

In 2015, Eddie was Mel's pet project. Mel had been a graduate assistant for Nick at Michigan State back in the mid-1990s, so Mel learned football the Saban way, Sabanese, I call it. These two coaches recognized Jackson's ball skills as exceptional and saw his football IQ as above average.

It turned out they were not demoting him, they were promoting him. You should also understand that Saban has and never will be a stand-around head coach. He is in the middle of everything, but in this case, more important, he is a superb defensive backs coach, and he helped with Jackson, too.

What Saban and Tucker saw simultaneously was Jackson's "command" of the defensive backs meeting room. EJ had credibility with the younger players; he was the alpha dog in the group. Leadership is an intangible that coaches see as a huge asset.

Ryan Anderson, the fifth-year senior linebacker in 2016, was a fatherly figure to players. He called Eddie Jackson "my son." When a reporter tried to ask Anderson about Jackson's losing his cornerback job, Anderson angrily snapped, "He didn't lose his job."

The change from corner to safety did not go smoothly, but Tucker buckled his own chin strap as a coach. In practice, Saban and Tucker would usually split up the defensive backs—corners for one coach, safeties for the other—but Tucker started spending more time with the safeties so he could coach Eddie Jackson. EJ started to learn the calls and to build back his confidence. He felt trusted again by the staff. He started to regrow as a significant player on the Alabama defense.

As Eddie got more comfortable at the position, he began getting his hands on the football in practices and in scrimmages. He was knocking the ball away, but not catching it, yet. He was getting in position to make plays, which was the important thing.

Tucker continued to coach Eddie. Mel told him he was faster than he thought and that his range was allowing him to get to the football in plenty of time. EJ just needed to catch it and then go score. Tucker had Eddie play several yards deeper than Saban preferred, so Eddie could have more room and time to see the field.

When I was the scouting director in Baltimore, we drafted a player named Ed Reed, who liked to play a touch deeper so he could "vision the quarterback" for an extra count before breaking on the football. Ed will be in the Pro Football Hall of Fame after intercepting sixty-four passes and making the Pro Bowl nine times.

Now go from Ed to Eddie. Jackson was beginning to show these similar traits in his deep coverage.

Tucker also convinced Jackson he did not have to go for the "big hit" as a safety. He was sturdy enough at two hundred pounds, but Mel told EJ to use his technique and lasso the ball carrier, giving the "posse" enough time to get there to finish the play. Mel wanted Eddie to utilize his angles and take the legs out from under the ball carrier with a low, cut tackle when necessary.

In the meantime, senior Geno Matias-Smith knew the defense better than anybody else, and that knowledge allowed Eddie to free up and play center field with fewer restrictions. Smith could play to the boundary where there was less ground to cover, and Eddie went to the field side.

Here is where Saban makes his money as a tactician and a coach who has his eyes open to change. Nick typically prefers left and right safeties, but he allowed Jackson and Smith to align by offensive formation and one a little deeper than the other.

The defensive coaches felt that if the front seven was good enough, Alabama could get by with these "cover people," Jackson and Matias-Smith, on the field together and not need the 225-pound strong safety against the run as an unblocked eighth defender. The Tide could lean on their dominant defensive line and efficient linebackers to control the run and allow these defensive backs to almost exclusively play the pass.

(Watch Alabama and Georgia in the next several years. Both will be recruiting more athletic cornerbacks and moving away from the one-dimensional, limited strong safety. Tucker at Georgia, and Saban at Alabama, will continue to build the front seven on defense, so that they can be more flexible in the secondary with their coverage people.)

What Mel wanted—and what Nick wanted—were interceptions and explosive plays from the back end of the defense. Eddie Jackson made it happen.

In Athens, Georgia, on October 3, 2015, Jackson intercepted a pass and returned it 50 yards for a touchdown in a 38–10 rout of the Bulldogs. Two weeks later, on the road again in front of another big crowd, Jackson had a 93-yard interception return for a touchdown in a 41–23 victory over Texas A&M. In 2016, Eddie turned a pick into a 55-yard touchdown against Western Kentucky.

Eddie started to add to the operation on special teams in 2016. Alabama coaches thought they'd missed some chances for good punt returns in the first two games of the season. The blocking was there, but it just didn't sync up. What did they do? They put EJ at punt returner, and his 85-yard return for a touchdown was the key play in the comeback win at Ole Miss.

With Eddie's successful move to safety in 2015, Alabama could now get highly regarded Marlon Humphrey on the field at left corner and have freshman sensation Minkah Fitzpatrick play as the slot corner, or inside-coverage defensive back, in the Nickel (which is five defensive backs). The transformation in the secondary from 2014 to 2015 was remarkable. Alabama led the SEC in passes defended (75), passes intercepted (19), and also returned four interceptions for touchdowns.

Losing Mel to the University of Georgia was a significant blow to Alabama because he was an ideal assistant coach for Nick Saban. He understood the system, could speak the lingo, and knew exactly what Nick wanted from his secondary coach. You couldn't blame Mel for

leaving, but I do think Nick was disappointed in Kirby Smart for taking one of Nick's trusted staff members. Mel has NFL experience, an
eye for talent, and is a terrific recruiter. He loves teaching players. He
was the key figure in resuscitating Eddie Jackson's Alabama career,
which helped the Crimson Tide to another title.

Understand this: It is not easy to play defensive back at Alabama.
Coach Saban uses a sophisticated system of defending the pass, and
Eddie had to learn a new position inside that NFL-level scheme.

For instance, a cornerback playing man-to-man is not looking at
the receiver's helmet and he is certainly not looking at the receiver's
feet. The corner is focusing on the wide receiver's navel. Watch where
his belly button goes, and the rest of his body will follow. The receiver's hips will tell you where he is going on a route. Most kids who are
defensive backs lack eye control and discipline with their hands and
feet. They just react to the first move and chase the receiver. Alabama
coaches say, "No. You do it this way. This is where your eyes have to go."

It is not just reading hips, especially in zone coverage. Alabama
cornerbacks are triangulating their eyes from the quarterback, through
the inside receiver, to the outside receiver, the one you are lined up
against on the perimeter of the field. You got that? You have two eyes
on three players, in focus all at once, the farthest away to the closest.

What Saban and his staff try to do is expand the vision of what the
player sees. They want you to understand where you fit in the whole
scheme. Player development is from the neck up, not just physical skills.

Temperament and instincts are significant. Awareness and coachability are key, too.

Here is an example of where a player did not fit in.

A sensational athlete named B. J. Scott came from Vigor High
School in Prichard, Alabama, a place that has produced college and
NFL players for decades. I conducted a "free" football camp for skill
players in the Mobile area for almost twenty years, and B.J. showed
up one summer as a left-handed quarterback. He looked like a "young"
Michael Vick.

B.J. wore green-and-white, Dr. Seuss–like striped socks, and he could run and throw the football with ease. He lined up in the shotgun, would get the snap, and take off as either a runner or passer. He was named all-state and rated in the same breath with Julio Jones, both five-star, can't-miss prospects.

Alabama signed Scott, but they told him, "We think you can be a great defensive back." B.J. balked. He spent a redshirt season at wide receiver, then agreed to move to corner after his first season.

It did not go well. He had no concept of what "pattern reading" meant inside the Alabama system. He did not understand how the receivers were "numbered" or how to vision the quarterback while covering his man.

In individual drills and the pure one-on-one coverage periods, B.J. had the skills to be an All-SEC corner. But he grew up as an offensive player. That's what he knew. His instincts were all wrong for defense. When coaching went to that next level, with all of the checks and calls, he didn't grasp it right away because of his offense-first background.

Scott's transition was going to take time, but there was frustration. He never got over that proverbial hump of getting into the playing rotation.

B.J transferred to South Alabama and played receiver. He went undrafted and spent some time in the Canadian Football League.

What happened?

Alabama, like every other major school that was recruiting B.J., allowed pure ability to trump everything else that is required to play in its system. In the NFL, we get endless opportunities to interview and determine what a possible draft pick actually knows about his position, scheme, and responsibilities, plus make a judgment on his character and personality. In college, there is not always time for that closer look, and sometimes you cannot "develop" that special talent such as B. J. Scott.

Minkah Fitzpatrick, on the other hand, can show up and grasp the concepts immediately. My first reaction on seeing him at an August 2015 practice was "Wow, he looks like an NFL corner right now."

Right away, Fitzpatrick was an integral part of Alabama's Nickel package as the Star or slot corner. He quickly became one of the secret sauces in 2015.

I am amazed when a freshman gets on the field for Bama's defense. If you walk into the defensive coach's room in the Alabama football facility and see the number of "calls" and "checks" on the grease board, it's mind-boggling. I mean, this Alabama playbook has continued to grow from its Belichickian roots in Berea, Ohio, to where it is now, some twenty-five years later.

Just as an offense calls a play, the defense calls "base" and then the "front" and then the "coverage." The fronts are usually words; the secondary coverage is usually a number. The check is a reaction to the offense's formation. For instance, what happens if a tight end moves from the left side to the right side of the line. What's the check? All eleven players have to know that because responsibilities change.

All this is written on grease boards in meeting rooms or has been put on iPads for the players. Numbers and lingo are the various calls and all the checks. You need to learn it all to play defense for the Crimson Tide.

Alabama does not go backward for any player as it teaches details of calls and checks. The freshman defensive prospect goes to his first meeting and might start with a few basics, but that train gets moving very fast, very soon. You better keep up, kid, or you're going to get left at the station.

When you are playing defense for Alabama and playing at Bryant-Denny, it is extremely loud. The defense has moving parts and many hand signals from the sidelines to get the calls to the field. If you don't have the system down and you are not dialed in, you won't play.

In the defensive backfield, you can't just yell out, "Hey, watch the Over route." It's too loud. Hand signals—hands crossed, palms up, hands moving in a circle, fingers giving number signs—replace audible commands. When the offense moves—a tight end shifts or a wide receiver goes in motion—hand signals run the communication and coordination on the field as the "check" is made.

If ten guys play one defense against a screen pass and the eleventh guy does something else, the defense will break down and can give up a big play. That's why visual language is so crucial to the success of the defense. There has to be immediate recognition. That's one of the reasons Alabama is so successful on defense. All eleven players comprehend the call from the sideline and know what to do to keep all the gaps filled for a runner and all the windows closed for a receiver. Watch a game this September and tell me how many times you see a receiver just flat out running all by himself. It happens to other teams a lot more than it happens to Alabama.

One of the sophistications of Saban's approach is that all the linebackers and defensive backs "read" patterns. They call it pattern matching. The linebacker, the safety, and the cornerback are reading the releases of the no. 1 receiver (outside wide receiver), the no. 2 receiver (slotted wide receiver), and the no. 3 receiver (usually a tight end or running back).

Once those routes declare themselves, the linebackers and defensive backs then "match" themselves to the receiver in their area. On the surface, it's zone coverage, but in reality, it's man-to-man within a zone concept.

For a high school player coming into major college football, this approach is more complex than he is accustomed to. People think that in "zone coverage" the linebackers and defensive backs drop to a spot and then react to the football being thrown. Most schools do it that way, but not Alabama.

If you want an example of the coordination it takes to play cornerback for Alabama, I want you to jog down the street patting your stomach and rubbing your head. It's not easy. It takes practice.

Here is something else about playing defensive back at Alabama: your position coach on most days is Nick Saban.

Nick is like a hawk when he is watching his guys in practice. If you are a defensive back in your stance, once you start backpedaling, you better have your shoulders over your knees and your knees over your toes. Nick can see if you are leaning back or you are too far forward. He wants your eyes up, too. Alabama is one of the few places where you see the coaches teaching a player how to backpedal.

Oh, some teams will work on the backpedal in practice, but you don't see much of it in games. At Alabama, NFL scouts get a chance to see the complete gamut of techniques needed to play professionally, from backpedaling to half turns to catching the football itself, in practices, during pregame warm-ups, and in the games. This is player development.

Saban did not put up with any "bullshit" from the Browns defensive backs years ago and he is the same way today with Alabama's defensive backs. No alibis are allowed. You come to work. When the Browns came out on the practice field, shirttails were tucked in, and uniforms had no extraneous parts. You came to practice, not to make a fashion statement.

"Development happens every day," cornerback Marlon Humphrey said. "Coach works with the corners, and every day there is some new tip he is giving you, something to work on."

If you think cornerbacks have a lot to learn inside the Alabama defensive scheme, consider the learning curve for middle linebackers, the guys who call the signals for the defense. It's why a spectacularly gifted athlete such as Reggie Ragland did not become a starter until 2014, his junior year.

Ragland, who is from Huntsville, Alabama, committed to UA his junior year in high school. Ragland was already 230 pounds, and he could dunk a basketball. He was what the staff term a "jumbo athlete," so gifted he could play inside linebacker and/or outside linebacker.

Ragland, who was part of the 2012 recruiting class, would make frequent trips to Tuscaloosa while in high school with his friend basketball recruit Levi Randolph. It looked as if Ragland, a dedicated student, would step right in and make an impact.

He didn't.

Reggie came on board as a Jack (weakside outside) linebacker to help ease the loss of All-American Dont'a Hightower. But Ragland was so big and fast, it was hard to know what to do with him. He learned

all four linebacker spots his freshman season, which was to his detriment. He was not just "Mike in the middle"; he was on the edge, he was
to the field, he was over the tight end. That slowed him from getting
in the lineup because he could not zero in on one position and take
the job.

You have to understand that Nick Saban and Kirby Smart had a
dialogue on the sidelines during a game that was in a language all its
own. Reggie had to learn that. An outsider would have no idea what
they were talking about if he was standing between the two:

"The next time they come out and motion the Z toward the tight
end, we're going to check that . . . let's go to [cover] 7 Nail rather than
trying to sky it [three deep]."

"They are hurting us on that counter-run, so let's reduce the front
so we can cover those two linemen and go to cover 6 and buzz the
safety down to the weakside."

Ragland had to translate it. It was a football code Nick and Kirby
had built over seven seasons, a dialect from outer space they could
decipher between themselves. I saw and heard the same lingo with
Belichick and Saban back in Cleveland, and now the same conversa-
tions were happening in Tuscaloosa between Kirby and Nick.

This Saban/Kirby lingo would be signaled to the middle linebacker, who has to communicate it forward and backward, to the line
in front and secondary behind. The Mike linebacker has to declare
strength of formation—strong left or strong right—then he has to set
the front and make sure everybody is in the appropriate position.

If an offensive player goes in motion, Alabama has what they call
double calls, which adds to the Mike's responsibilities. Say the offense
comes out two-by-two (two receivers to each side), and then a receiver
motions; the Mike has to check to the appropriate defense immediately. Now you know why Kirby was so animated on the sidelines trying to get all of the calls to his players, sometimes ninety times per
game.

What gets tricky, in my mind, is that all these teams are in shotgun formation with the running back next to the quarterback. If that

running back hops from one side of the quarterback to the other, that can often trigger a change by the defense, as well. The Mike has to be alert to that, too.

It's all part of development.

Veteran Trey DePriest was in the linebacker cycle ahead of Ragland. C. J. Mosley was the other inside backer, who was more experienced than Reggie. You better believe there is a hierarchy at Alabama. If you are a veteran player who has proven himself, the coaches are not going to straight out trade you in for another player with more ability. They are going to maximize what's best for the team.

Reggie finally stepped in as a starter at inside backer in 2014. He received a third-round grade from the NFL junior advisory board after the season. He opted to return to Alabama his senior year in 2015 to try to upgrade his draft position, which is what many players are encouraged to do by Coach Saban when they are not going to be a first-round pick.

Reggie had a terrific 2015 and improved his draft stock. He was selected in the second round, forty-first overall, by the Buffalo Bills, who traded up to get him. For a Mike linebacker in this era of spread football, forty-first is a very high pick. Anytime you evaluate a Mike linebacker in the draft, the concern is whether he can play all three downs and stay on the field in all defensive packages. Reggie did that at Alabama, where he was effective against the run and the pass.

When Reggie accepted his invitation to the Reese's Senior Bowl in January 2016, he wanted the opportunity to play outside linebacker during the week, so that he could show his pass-rushing ability. I told him and his agent, "Other than quarterback, we will let you play whatever position you want." By showing another dimension of his game, he added to his predraft résumé, and I'm sure his draft position was enhanced because of that versatility.

Reggie became a star because the Alabama coaches saw his devotion, and that is a significant thing at Bama. He stayed in shape and played hard as a freshman, even though he was not a starter. That kept him afloat with the coaching staff while they worked with him in learning the system. If you can check the box on two of those three demands from coaches—be in condition, know what to do, and play hard—the coaches will hang in there with you. If you can't do these three things that require "zero" ability, then the coaches will open the door for somebody else.

Alabama players are evaluated every day, but there are "marker" dates for getting, as Kirby Smart said, "the right seats filled on the bus." To me, those marker dates are the first six practices in spring ball, the first two scrimmages of August camp, and the early fundamental pre-bowl practices in December.

These critical moments, in a practice setting, establish a player's trajectory as a potential contributor or starter for the upcoming season. To determine who gets one of those coveted top forty-four spots on the depth chart, the coaches constantly ask, "What track is this guy on?"

At times the players feel hopelessly off track and left behind. Marlon Humphrey said some freshmen at Alabama complain about the lack of playing time and the rigor of practice.

"I know there are schools, programs, where other people aren't doing what we're doing, and there are people here who fall into the trap of saying, 'Other schools aren't doing this; why are we doing this?'" Humphrey said. "That's why everybody can't play here. We do things different. You just have to think about the team. Don't think about yourself.

"What you have to think about is 'plenty of seniors before me have done this, this is the formula.' Coach Saban talks about that process. Once you buy into the process, you'll always be able to play here. You see it with the younger guys when they come in; they have some doubts when we start. I remember being in their same shoes, and I see them complaining and I did the same thing. I tell them this is the formula. You have to think, 'The last guy before me did it; why can't I do it?'"

Think about Derrick Henry and his development. No matter how many yards he gained running the ball in high school, many of the na-tion's best recruiters saw him as a future college tight end or outside linebacker.

Henry was six feet three and a half, 235 pounds. His identity as a football player was put in a box. Recruiters said he would be an out-side linebacker.

Alabama told him, "If you come here, we'll give you a chance at running back."

Henry played sparingly as a freshman during the 2013 regular season, so no one seemed to know what track he was on. But in the early-December 2013 bowl practices, which are devoted to funda-mentals more than the upcoming opponent, Derrick started to show some understanding of the system. He was picking up the basics: aim-ing points, blocking scheme, the importance of pass protection and whom to pick up in the blitz, and running pass routes at the proper depth. He rushed for 100 yards on just 8 carries against Oklahoma in the Sugar Bowl.

In his sophomore season in 2014, Henry faced other challenges. NFL scouts saw him as a leggy, one-speed strider. They saw the size and the speed, but wondered if he could get through the smaller open-ings in pro ball. Could he get his pads down and change directions in a short area?

Some within the program still debated this, as well. Typically, Al-abama's running backs had been in the five-foot-ten to six-foot range.

Ultimately, Saban, running backs coach Burton Burns, and offen-sive coordinator Lane Kiffin decided height was just a number. Henry was different from other tall tailbacks. He could be elusive and squeeze through a crease. They saw something else, too. Burns, the only as-sistant coach who has been at Alabama as long as Saban, recognized that Henry's work ethic could make him special.

The Alabama coaches decided in 2014 that Henry was the next great back to follow Mark Ingram and Trent Richardson. So what hap-pened? Why didn't Henry emerge right away in 2014?

It was not the time for Henry to break out. He split time with

Kenyan Drake because Alabama used an east-west, sideline to sideline offense, to utilize the skill set of six-foot-tall quarterback Blake
Sims. The scheme had a lot of lateral movement.

But when Jake Coker became the quarterback in 2015, the Crimson Tide had one of the biggest backfield combinations in the nation.
Coker was six feet five, 245 pounds, and would hand or play-fake to
the six-foot-three-and-a-half, 244-pound Henry. The offense was now
north-south, more vertical in nature and straight at the defense.

This was Henry's style. He was a big back with bruising runs who
got better as the game progressed. Derrick would pound the middle,
with the defenses wary of his breakaway speed. They had a right to
respect his speed. When he broke through the line, he was gone. In
eight seasons calling Alabama games, I have seen every Crimson Tide
tailback angled off or tackled from behind, except Derrick.

Derrick Henry won the Heisman Trophy with 2,219 rushing yards
in 2015.

The NFL had its questions answered on Derrick Henry, too.

Alabama had another special talent in 2014 and 2015 who per-
plexed NFL scouts, Tim Williams, the outside linebacker/rush specialist. Who is this cat? Why is he not on the field more with that
first-step quickness and explosive pass-rush potential?

Williams could be an impact player on third down when rushing
the passer, but the Alabama coaches could not trust him on first and
second downs to read his run/pass keys. His rare pass-rush ability
warranted a role on the defense as one of those top twenty-two contributors on the two-deep depth chart, but he was not a starter. He
ended his junior season in 2015 with 10½ sacks but only 18 tackles.

Tim was a home-run hitter with limited at bats. He averaged
about a dozen snaps per game in 2015, which makes the 10½ sacks
remarkable.

The issue was simple: Tim was not a complete outside linebacker
in the 3-4 defense. When I would ask coaches why he didn't see more
playing time, the answer was the same: "He doesn't know the system,
he doesn't have it yet. He will play eight snaps and have four pressures

and four busts." One bust will get you scolded; four busts will keep you on the pine, at least until third down.

And that's what Alabama did. It kept Williams on the sideline before unleashing him in passing situations. In 2015 he was a force to be reckoned with and almost unblockable when racing off the edge.

Ragland had to prove he could play on third down; Tim Williams had to prove in 2016 he could play on first down. As an outside backer you have to prove you can play over the top of a tight end and get off a block. Ragland and Williams were two linebackers on the 2015 national title team with opposite challenges. Ultimately, Tim was a one-year full-time starter as a senior, and that's just how his development track unfolded.

I hope this much is clear: players at Alabama just don't jump out of a box.

Just look at what the defensive linemen have to master. They have to learn from day one that on the snap of the ball your hands are going to explode into the chest of your opponent, and with your thumbs up, you are going to shoot your palms and the butt of your hand into the breastplate of the blocker.

If your hands don't get in there first to the blocker's chest, you are taught how to hand-fight to get them inside, so that the blocker can be controlled.

Defensive linemen learn that Coach Saban demands a wall be built to defend the run. All seven guys in the 3-4 defense are building a wall and controlling the gaps the running back can run through. That is a fundamental of Alabama's defense. The Tide was textbook with the wall on November 7, 2015, when it held LSU running back Leonard Fournette to 31 yards and ruined his Heisman Trophy campaign.

Everybody in the Alabama defensive front seven understands how to shock with their hands, shed with their strength, and then go make a proper form tackle. What makes the Alabama defender special is that he can do all those things against a blocker while his eyes are reading his keys and he is also finding the football. As I said earlier, just try to jog down the street rubbing your head and patting your stomach.

This is development. This is why Alabama has won four titles in the last eight seasons.

You need to understand something else about Alabama and its development of players. When players go out for their first practice, they are treated as if they have never played football a day in their life.

Alabama coaches start with eyes, feet, hips, and hands. They emphasize eye control, footwork, contact explosion, and hands technique.

When Nick Saban talks defense, he always mentions eye control and discipline, and they work on that every single day. The players are trained to see one thing while doing another with their feet and hands. Saban frets every week about his players keeping their eyes focused on the right things. Read your keys, keep everything in front, don't take the bait of a trick play. Alabama spends tons of time on the coordination of getting everybody seeing and reading the proper keys at the same time. It's called team defense.

That's why Nick Saban is so bothered by the whole RPO movement (the run/pass option offenses that have become the rage in college football). The quarterback rides the ball in the belly of the back deciding to give or keep, then starts running laterally along the line of scrimmage. Offensive linemen are four, five, six, seven yards downfield, and all of a sudden the quarterback, when the defense reacts to tackle him, pulls up and throws the ball downfield.

This puts the defense in conflict between defending the run or the pass; it breaks all of the run/pass keys that players have been taught their entire careers. Technically, it's illegal with linemen downfield, but as my coaching mentor Homer Smith used to say, "The rules are what they call."

With that said, you can find examples of Alabama's offense doing the same thing with the RPO. It's become a major part of the college game, so if you can't beat 'em, join 'em.

The core elements of football are taught from day one: eyes, feet, hips, and hands. You see a five-star lineman on his knees in practice learning to strike a bag by exploding from the ground up through his "hips, hands, and hat." The training at Alabama starts from that basic technique of a six-inch punch; that core movement is at the foundation of the program.

Development has a psychological component as well. Years ago at Michigan State, Nick said he realized that not every player could be coached the same way. For over twenty years now he has demanded that his assistants know their players and understand how they respond to different coaching. While the coaching staff can be animated, they are all teachers first, and yellers second. They have a clear view of what each individual needs and how to maximize his potential.

The coaches are tuned in quickly in assessing their position groups. They must know who is making progress and who isn't and why. They must assess whether a redshirt year might be needed or if the prospect may simply never pan out as a starter. The position coaches and coordinators must evaluate their players just like NFL scouts, in effect, determining if a candidate is a starter, potential starter, backup, or will never play.

First impressions go a long way across the board. A true freshman gets there in June or July, and by the end of the camp in August the staff has a good idea about him. If you are not on that first bus of the two-deep by September, then you will have another chance to impress during the December bowl practices.

The coaches are honest behind the scenes with their players that last week of preseason camp in August. Sometimes it is hurtful to younger guys who have never been criticized. A player will be told, "Unless there is an injury, we need you to continue working in practice to get better. These are the three things you need to improve on between now and next spring."

The development of players at Alabama is the top priority of Scott Cochran, the energetic strength-and-conditioning coach. I think some of his best work is on the mentality of these players. Building strength and getting faster is physically hard, but the one-of-a-kind Cochran makes it fun. He is the opposite of what you would think Nick Saban wants in a coach—hype—but he is exactly what the program needs.

You hear Cochran before you see him. He bounces into the weight room at 6:00 a.m. with a loud "Awwwwwrightttt! It's going to be an awesome day!"

I haven't seen it, but urban legend has it that on some days Scott will drink half the Powerade out of the bottle, then refill the bottle with Red Bull, and off he goes.

Alabama's mental toughness and discipline under stress is born in the weight room. The coaches have complete faith that these guys are not going to have a false start or jump offside on defense because they are tired. Cochran gets a player to do more than he thinks he is capable of. If a guy insists he can only bench 300, Scott will gather other players around and push the player to do 315. They will cheer the player on, and the cheering will be led by Cochran.

Some NFL people I know sort of chuckle at Scott's antics. He is a sideline show, a one-man band almost, and the players love him. He's the only assistant ever allowed to do a commercial or to appear on the video board at Bryant-Denny Stadium. Among the fans, he has a cult-like following because they see him as the mechanic most responsible for their beloved team's physical engine.

He is a motivator every bit as much as he is a strength-and-conditioning coach. In those January workouts, Cochran is the one that has to keep everybody energized in that march to spring football.

I think Scott has a feel for each and every one of the 120 players in the program. He is their biggest cheerleader, and he comes at them with a positive approach. He can be sarcastic, but he is believable to the players and makes them stay on task and focused on their individual and team goals.

Scott also contributes to the evaluation of players by keeping the coaches updated throughout the year on each individual's progress in the weight room and during conditioning. Remember, in development, it's mental and physical, on and off the field.

Sometimes, Alabama's player development system misfires. Saban likes to have the pipeline filled at every position, but injuries happen or a player is unhappy with his playing time and transfers (rarely, other than at quarterback). It could also be that Alabama misjudged a player and the development system did not create the finished product.

So an unexpected hole may occur on the depth chart, and when that happens, the mechanism for finding junior college players kicks in. Terrence Cody (Mississippi Gulf Coast Community College) filled a major need in the middle of the defense in 2009. De'Quan Menzie (Copiah-Lincoln Community College) and Deion Belue (Northeast Mississippi Community College) filled vacancies in the secondary from 2011 to 2013. James Carpenter (Coffeyville) was a standout left tackle in 2009 and 2010.

Nick will fill a need for the team, but he will also fill a need for the player. For instance, Mark Barron was a terrific offensive player in high school, but he became a standout safety at Alabama and an NFL first-round pick.

While he was at LSU, Saban evaluated players early in their careers and moved them into position to be millionaires. Corey Webster was a receiver and became a wealthy defensive back in the NFL. Marcus Spears was a tight end and got paid in the NFL as a defensive end. Joseph Addai was a high school quarterback and became a rich running back in the NFL.

While he was at LSU, the defensive end Spears went in to see Saban and said he wanted to be a tight end. Saban opened his desk drawer and pulled out a sheet of paper with the salaries by position in the NFL. A defensive end would make more money.

Spears smiled and said to Nick, "I'm going to be the best defensive end I can be." He stayed on defense.

Michael Clayton, the former outstanding wide receiver for Nick at LSU, says that the players on offense thought Nick was out to get them when he moved them to defense. They scored touchdowns in high school, they wanted to be in the limelight. He switched them over to defense, taught them the fundamentals, and made them great football players. He coached them hard, instilled confidence, and helped them earn a living in professional football. Clayton said, "I saw it with my own two eyes."

One potential issue with Alabama players who make it through one of the most rigorous development programs in all of college football is, can an NFL team get more out of the player than Saban does in Tuscaloosa? Think about it. The Alabama player is inside an NFL-style system for three or four years and climbing toward a peak. He has been instructed by an all-time great coach, so how much upside potential is left?

As an NFL scout, one of the challenges in evaluating an Alabama player is trying to determine if a given prospect can function outside this controlled culture otherwise known as the Process. To a large extent, Trent Richardson, Rolando McClain, and Terrence Cody have proven they could not, while Julio Jones, Dont'a Hightower, and Amari Cooper, among others, have demonstrated the ability to handle their affairs off the field on their own.

The pros are persuaded to draft Alabama players—sometimes a full round or at least a half round higher than a Tide player is projected—because of the skill development and training in Tuscaloosa.

When NFL scouts go to Alabama, they see players performing tasks that are going to be required of them in pro ball. The scouts' dilemma is to project what a guy will be able to do when you give him a specific assignment. When they watch Alabama tapes, they are able to see it in living color. The Crimson Tide system, in many ways, takes some of the guesswork out.

The scout can say, "I have seen Reuben Foster do that. I have actually witnessed him doing this," rather than saying, "I think he can do it."

I think the people Nick has a relationship with in the NFL are always going to give him the benefit of the doubt when it comes to evaluating players. If Nick tells them, "Reggie did this, this, and this," it carries some sway. I know this much: if you are an NFL scout and go watch film at Alabama of their players, pack a lunch. The Tide will have twelve to fourteen NFL prospects for every draft, so plan to be there a while watching tape.

Scouts don't just watch film at Bama or evaluate practice. You can also get an honest appraisal of a player from an expert, Coach Nick Saban.

At times at Alabama practices, if Nick is not doing any hands-on coaching or the team is stretching, he will come over and shake hands with the pro scouts. Three or four will gather up around him, and he will give them a nugget. He might say, "Cyrus Jones hasn't done it in a game, but we've repped him as a nickel corner for two years, and I think he could be really good inside."

That is a gem for a scout. Saban has coached in the league and has put many of his players in the NFL. For a scout to get a solid tip like that from the head coach himself to put in a report is invaluable and will impress the scout's general manager to boot.

Some coaches in college do not have time to watch pro foot-ball on Sunday, so they will oversell a player thinking he can play in the NFL. It is important to Nick that he is honest and can fore-cast his players beyond the X's and O's. The college coach, Nick believes, has to help with the intangibles, such as what makes a guy tick.

Saban, more than any other coach in the country, understands the transition from college to pro and what it takes. Not all his guys have made it in the NFL, but a good many have, and his evaluation of that player means something to the GMs and scouts who venture to Tus-caloosa.

I hope you understood from reading this chapter that the Crim-son Tide takes nothing for granted in development. It does not assume anything. The motto is one technique, one play and one practice at a time. Nick is always figuring out ways to combat complacency in his program, and one of the best ways is the competition that comes from inside the player development system.

I went to twenty-five different schools in 2015 for practices. These were mostly FBS-level schools, the big schools. In just two programs did I see every player on defense take on a blocker, separate from that blocker, and go make a tackle in the open field, which is what college football is today, open-field tackling. Those two schools were Michigan State and Alabama, semifinal foes in the second-ever College Football Playoff.

Think back to the All-American Dont'a Hightower. He was six feet four, 255 pounds. Sure, he could run through most tight ends when he was playing at outside linebacker. But look at all these fundamentals he developed at Alabama:

- His punch and hand placement to the blocker.
- Maintaining leverage on a blocker and keeping his contain element.
- The eye control to see over the top of the tight end and into the backfield to read run/pass.
- The skill of reading the releases of the tight end and running back and then matching the proper receiver in his area.

It is a bottom-line existence at Alabama. Show a profit, stay in the black. At Alabama, you either devote yourself to the rigor of the fundamentals, or you get passed on the depth chart. Saban does not allow players' raw skills to dictate their place on the depth chart. He wants them to give some meaning to their careers, and that requires their acceptance of thorough training.

Some players, such as Reggie Ragland, have to wait in line. Some, such as Eddie Jackson, have to get back in line.

Jackson, after losing his job as a corner, was first-team All-SEC in 2015 and having an All-American season at safety in 2016 until he broke his leg against Texas A&M. Before the injury he had an interception return for a touchdown and two punt returns for scores. The fans didn't forget their hero. In the Georgia Dome, after Alabama beat Florida for the SEC Championship, they chanted, "Eddie, Eddie, Eddie!"

The message on the flashing billboard over his head in 2015 and 2016 was different from in 2014: "Quarterbacks beware: Don't throw it near EJ."

So you see, the Process develops and decides, and it can also mend. No one shows up as a "No Assembly Required" prospect, from Julio Jones to Dont'a Hightower to Derrick Henry to Reggie Ragland. No one is promised a smooth ride. What you get out of that collaboration between skill and the Process is a fulfilling career and maybe a championship ring or two or three.

The players that make it at Bama understand the mentality of development on the practice field. It is an uncomplicated deal between the staff and the players: we can develop you if you practice hard. We'll do our part, if you do yours. "It is fourth and goal every day, brother." We are going to pay attention to what you do Monday through Friday more keenly than what you do on Saturday. You better develop your skill in practice, that's all there is to it, if you want to get on that field on game day.

4
PRACTICE

"WE PLAYED THIS GAME . . . ALREADY"

"Can you throw today if we send a plane?" Lane Kiffin said in a text to quarterback Jake Coker.

It was a 911 text, no doubt about it. It sounded urgent. Where was Coker anyway? Why wasn't he on campus to begin with, and why did the offensive coordinator have to send a plane?

Well, the 911 was to get Coker to Alabama practice, but it was November 3, 2016, two days before the Crimson Tide had to play at LSU, and a full season after Jake had led Alabama to the national championship. The call from Kiffin was for Coker to show up to be the scout team quarterback. Thursday is the day Alabama practices inside and pumps crowd noise into the indoor facility.

Jake's college career had ended ten months earlier, but what kind of excuse was that? Mama was calling.

Okay, maybe it wasn't a totally serious idea to send a plane, but are you sure? It's Alabama. Practice matters. Practice is why, when the Crimson Tide huddles up in a "shitstorm," as Nick Saban calls it, like the one created at LSU by roaring fans, the Bama players say to each other, "We played this game four times already this week."

What they mean is they played the LSU game in four days of practice. The Crimson Tide rehearses in its own self-created "shitstorm" every day in practice.

"Our practice," said defensive back Hootie Jones, "can be tougher than the game."

A player's timeline has a string of events: recruiting followed by development, which is the daily test of practice. As crazy as this sounds, Monday through Thursday seems more sacred than Saturday within the walls of the football facility.

You should see one of these practices. Nick Saban quick-walks the practice field, and the pace is blistering from one eight-minute period to the next. Sometimes the period is started over if Saban is not pleased with the effort or focus that he is seeing.

In the Saban Era, Alabama pays him to be head coach, defensive coordinator, recruiting coordinator, defensive backs coach, and graduate assistant. The man keeps both hands firmly planted on the wheel of his football team. The school gets its money's worth with him walking, pacing, coaching, and teaching.

He may be with the defensive backs for a good part of the practice, but only a nosy neighbor keeps an eye on everything better than Coach Saban.

Alabama practice is the relentless pursuit of perfection. It is not rumor. It is real.

You know the old saying in the stock market: "Past performance is no guarantee of future returns." It is stamped into the mind-set of every Alabama football player every day at practice. The pressure is ratcheted up and maintained for one and a half to two and a half hours, depending on the day, and it's all filmed, so the players know that if they loaf, a record of their "loaf" will be shown to the squad the next day.

An even more serious message could be conveyed to the slacking player the next day: a bump down the depth chart in an ultracompetitive environment.

So with two backup quarterbacks hurt and freshman phenom Jalen Hurts working as the starter on the other end of the field, Kiffin might have been serious with his idea to send a plane for Coker. He at least wanted Coker to race up there in his pickup truck. John Parker Wilson, who played his last season at Alabama in 2008, had also filled in as scout team quarterback that week because the regular, Blake Sims, had other obligations and could not be there all week.

Coker said no to Kiffin, but Alabama didn't give up trying to get Coker back to help prepare for LSU.

Scott Cochran, the strength-and-conditioning coach, called Jake: "Hey, buddy, we'll get you a night at the Capstone," the on-campus hotel. "You can't beat that."

Seriously, this is how important practice is at Alabama.

I mean, look at the scout team that week before LSU. Blake Sims and John Parker Wilson were the quarterbacks. Trent Richardson was the Leonard Fournette stand-in, and Richard Mullaney was an LSU receiver. Alabama's compliance staff had found a little-used exemption for former players to participate in practice. Cal had invoked the rule when they opened the 2016 season in Australia and former running back Marshawn Lynch was utilized as a scout team runner.

Coker had to decline. Loyalty can go so far, then paying bills takes over.

"Man, I got to worry about grown-up stuff now," Coker said with a laugh. After tearing the meniscus in his right knee in camp with the Arizona Cardinals, he was considering jobs outside football.

"Jake sent me that text about a plane and coming back to play scout team quarterback," former linebacker Dillon Lee said. "Crazy. I'm not surprised."

Coker, Lee, and many other Alabama players saw practice as crucial, and a privilege. They never discounted the value of it. They saw tracks being laid for their careers in the sweltering workouts, which were preceded by meetings to install new schemes.

Coker found out about the intensity of Alabama practice during the 2014 summer workouts the first time he put on a jersey. He had transferred in from Florida State, and he joined his new teammates in a seven-on-seven workout. There was nothing casual about it.

Lee, playing outside backer, walked out to cover a slot receiver and knew Coker was going to throw a slant pass to the receiver Lee was covering. Sure enough, Coker stood tall and threw the ball to the receiver on a slant. Lee jumped the route and slapped the ball away.

"This ain't the fucking ACC, this ain't the fucking ACC," Lee yelled at Coker. The rest of the defense was delighted in the strut and the taunts and joined in with Lee to mock the ACC.

Coker laughs about it now. "I thought, 'Oh, well, I'm going to have to deal with this for a while.'"

So is that what newcomers, freshmen and transfers, should expect? To get smacked by a crimson-and-white welcome mat embroidered with a nasty face?

No, you have to turn the mat over. A smiley face is on the back side, the flip side to the intensity, which is the fun of competition. Alabama is not some unforgiving warden, Lee said.

You are expected to get used to the sniping at Alabama and come out the other end a better man and a better person. If you don't join in, it is hard to survive. Your attitude must be to be part of the ride, and the fun, or else. No one is allowed to sulk for long.

"I would run around talking shit every day to whoever, it didn't matter," Lee said. "It was not like I was angry; I was just running around having a good time. Some people get really offended by my comments, then they loosen up. They learn it's for their own good."

Coker was in Lee's wedding last February at the Ritz-Carlton in Atlanta, along with Ryan Anderson and T. J. Yeldon. The quarterback got over the ACC ridicule in a hurry. Most of the players who have come through the program put up with the shaming and earn one another's respect through their shared experience.

Lee said the players who sign with Alabama are ultracompetitive. They "get it" before they ever show up. One reason a player was offered a scholarship at Alabama is that he knows how to bounce back up and take some mental grinding.

"The majority of players at Alabama are not walking around like 'Man, if I miss a tackle, it's going to be on the board the next day, I'm in trouble,'" Lee said. "It's not like that. Everybody is too much of a competitor to let it bother them, which is huge when you start talking about what happened with the Ole Miss games and falling behind.

"See, when you get down in a game and everything is going wrong, it is built into the program that you do not shut down. If I miss a tackle in practice, I just can't shut down the rest of practice. That carries over to the games."

Last fall, Coker sat back in his chair in my office at the Reese's Senior Bowl in Mobile and marveled over the Alabama Way, which is obedience to practicing hard: "You just can't match it. Other programs try to copy it, but they can't. I don't know if it is how Coach Saban drives his team through practice that they can't copy, or what. People try to copy what he does, but you can't do it without a leader like him. It's impossible to copy because of the uniqueness of his personality."

For a moment, in his mind's eye, Coker traveled back to his playing days. "Coach is running back and forth from field to field making sure he is letting everybody have it equally, and then he gives it to everybody again that is standing between the fields and in his path.

"Spectators just watching, if they are not watching with intensity, he's pissed off at them. It is something to see."

I usually go to a handful of practices each season. Never do I look away from the field or down at my cell phone. This time is for practice, putting my depth charts together, assessing the seniors, looking at the young players, forecasting what these prospects may become as NFL candidates. You also don't want Nick Saban to see you looking at a phone.

Lee said that when he got to the NFL, it was a practice paradise compared to Alabama. He played four preseason games with the New Orleans Saints in 2016, which means about five weeks of camp.

"In fall camp at Alabama, you get a water break, one, for every practice. It's two minutes long, that's it," Lee remembered. "After that, you have to get water on your own and practice is two and a half hours.

If you are on the field for five or six plays with the ones, then the twos come on and you go off, you better get a sip of water on the sidelines.

"When I was in New Orleans, almost every period we had five-minute water breaks. It was water and Gatorade. It was crazy, it blew me away. I was like, 'No freaking way.' I was like in heaven. It doesn't matter how hard practice is, we're going to have a water break next period. A real water break, more than one hundred and twenty seconds."

Lee says an Alabama equipment manager walks around Alabama practices with an air horn and a timer and is never far away from Saban. You get moving on the sound of that horn and make sure you find some water.

There are some rules. Players get dressed for practice and then go to team meetings. It is usually the other way around in the NFL, Lee said. At Alabama no hats or hoodies are allowed in position-group meetings. You can't be sleeveless in the meeting room.

Here is another rule: no music in practice.

As I travel the country looking for future NFL prospects to invite to the Reese's Senior Bowl, virtually every college program has music in practices. Alabama does not because the coaches are teaching fundamentals and technique and you don't need to be yelling over the music.

The energy other programs have in practice comes from the music, I guess. Alabama has strength coach Scott Cochran and the players themselves providing the juice. Plus, the man in the straw hat absolutely loves practice and keeps it upbeat.

As far as I know, Nick has never had a formal fitness workout routine, yet has kept himself in excellent shape, which is how he gets around so well from field to field at practice at sixty-five years of age. He plays basketball between the end of recruiting and spring football. In the old Browns days, he would play racquetball, but as far as I know, he has never been a runner, walked on a treadmill, or done an elliptical.

You should see him at practice. He can show these kids every backpedal, plant and drive, and form tackle. You can see him physically living through the players. His whole body will tense up in every individual drill, almost like an isometric exercise.

I talked earlier in the book about the primary role of fundamentals in the success of Alabama. Your progress in learning those fundamentals and acquiring technique to play a position is measured in practice. It is not measured every week, or every day. It is measured every hour, Monday through Thursday.

This is important because this is what makes Alabama upset-proof. The fundamentals and practice regimen require players to play to a standard. They do not play to the level of their opponent. They play to a standard set by Nick Saban and established by the team leaders.

So what does that look like?

It's film work. A lot of it. Film doesn't lie. Practice tape is evaluated almost as strictly as game tape. In other words, every practice is valued and treated almost like a game by the Alabama staff. That is another difference between the Crimson Tide and other programs.

"Strip attempts and forced fumbles and missed tackles and made tackles, they keep track of all that," Lee said. "They do a little production sheet for what we did at practice, and you get it the next day. If we're doing something at practice, it is getting filmed, watched, and coached. It's not graded, but it matters. It will have everyone's name up there on the board and how many strip attempts and how many loafs and who had zero loafs. They know who had forced fumbles and fumble recoveries. That's for every practice."

Lee said the production sheets go both ways. It is not just to criticize a player for his mistakes. The sheets are there to reward, as well.

"How many times you can be on the sheet for good things, you always want to maximize that," Lee said. "Then there is how many times do you want to be on the sheet for bad things. Say you walk in and your sheet is shown on the board and you had three interceptions and a forced fumble and five strip attempts. Every coach, all of them, know you were on fire at practice. Everyone knows you had a great day. There are two sides to it."

Do you get a sense of the essence of Alabama, the practice sessions? This is what has led to four national championships in the Saban Era. The four-star and five-star high school superstars are assembled on one field and they practice as if it were Saturday, all of them, freshmen to fifth-year seniors. They do not stop a play on the sound of the whistle. You play through the echo of the whistle, that's when the play is over.

"You have an entire team where everyone on scholarship is the best from somewhere in the country," Lee said. "You've got to come every day with everything. It's always going to be competitive, and that scares some people off; they don't want to sign with Alabama for that reason."

We have talked about it before in this book. Nothing is tailored to a specific player so that the player enjoys a break now and then. The superstars—Julio Jones, Mark Ingram, Amari Cooper, Ryan Kelly, Reggie Ragland—they all went down the same chute.

Lee said his friend Ryan Anderson saw the bottleneck at linebacker coming out of high school, and Anderson still signed with Alabama. Lee had at least thirty-five offers coming out of Buford (Georgia) High School. He wouldn't be scared off, either.

Anderson was a highly recruited player out of Daphne, Alabama, but he got no promises of playing time from the head coach. The only thing he was promised was stern competition. Anderson was redshirted his freshman year; he saw the possibility of waiting until his senior year to be a starter. He stayed.

In 2016, Anderson was a candidate for SEC Defensive Player of the Year. NFL scouts commented to me throughout the season that he might have been the most consistent player on what was a ferocious defense.

It is players such as Anderson—and Lee—who fuel the practice mentality. It is a competitive rage, with some fun mixed in, and the goal is to get everyone to play to the Alabama standard.

Lee said, "If you are thinking one day, 'Oh, I don't have to do this' or 'I might not have to be that physical today,' or maybe think, 'I'll just make it through practice today,' you can't do that, not at Alabama. There is a guy on the scout team who was a four- or five-star coming out of high school, and he is waiting for you to do that so he can take your job. He is trying to beat you and bring his best, and you better do the same thing."

Scuffles break out in practice. It is intense, period.

The defense always thinks the offense is holding on every play. Coker shook his head slowly from side to side thinking back at the scrums on the field: "The defensive line would get mad because the O-line would punch them in the mouth. Everybody is working to kick the other guy's ass and make them better. 'Walk-throughs,' those practice sessions while you are wearing only helmets, don't accomplish the same thing as being in pads. It was important for us to be in pads."

Lee said it was easier to get teammates locked in during the 2015 national championship season because you had defensive linemen A'Shawn Robinson and Jarran Reed stirring it up on the practice field. Lee was a fire starter, too, and it revved up the workouts daily.

"You can't argue with them or talk back to them and say you don't want to do something because they are so huge and physical and they are bringing it," Lee said. "They are not kind of bringing it. They will get mad if somebody blocks them in practice. They wanted to dominate every snap, everything we did at practice. If you say you want to do it, that's one thing. Doing it is a whole other thing. They did it."

Tuesdays and Wednesdays, when the ones go against the ones, those days are the most intense. No school has more NFL prospects on the same field, and with the first-team offense versus the first-team defense, that is as legitimate a practice as you can get anywhere in America.

Lee has had a chance over the last five years to compare notes with players who came out of other FBS college football programs.

"You hear about how they do things at other places, and it's like, 'No way, really?' That's not how it is at Alabama," Lee said. "We are not going to practice in just helmets. We're not going to do just a shadow tempo. I have talked to some people whose teams did helmets-and-shorts practice on Sunday and have Monday off, then shells (helmets and shoulder pads) on Wednesday, and back in helmets and shorts on Thursday and go play the game.

"We will do shells on Wednesday, but it is full-speed thud (no tackling low or to the ground). If we are in pads, it is full-speed thud. On Thursday before the game, everything is full-speed thud except for two-minute drill at the end of practice."

Here's another snapshot of practice Bama-style.

During the 2016 preseason camp, Jamey Mosley, the brother of former Crimson Tide star C. J. Mosley, was finally awarded a scholarship. He had been a hardworking walk-on, a six-foot-five, 228-pound outside linebacker. But in his first practice with scholarship money, the younger Mosley lined up playing the wrong leverage on a tight end. Nick Saban erupted with almost no memory that a few hours earlier it had been all smiles and hugs for what Jamey had done to earn that scholarship.

I thought, welcome to the program, no time to rest on your laurels; that was then, this is now.

Dillon Lee smiled when he heard that story. He's seen the fangs of practice before, mostly with the younger players as the coaches try to establish a foundation of accountability.

"They don't do that with older guys, they don't scream at them like that," Lee said, "but that's how it happens if you are young. You can't do that with older guys. When that happens with a young guy, you usually get sent down to the scout team.

"It's crazy how much it means to go to practice with the ones and twos, to fill in even for a couple of plays when you are a freshman. It just feels like a huge accomplishment. Then, you get sent back to the scout team and you have to earn your way back."

Courtney Upshaw, an All-American outside linebacker, was practicing with the ones and twos when the wrath of Saban descended on him: "I remember my freshmen year getting chewed out by Saban and having to go over to the scout team squad on *that* practice field. I was over there for two plays maybe and I said, 'I can't stand this, I can't be over here like this.' I made up my mind not to mess up and really worked to stay with the ones and the twos. It was a punishment thing. I was demoted, but I took off from there."

It's funny. The Alabama players see the risk/reward of stern practices, and most of them always talk about the reward before the risk.

"We all said the same thing when we got to the league: Alabama was NFL-type everything from the off-season to the practices to the training, and we liked that," Upshaw said. "One of the reasons I wanted to go play there was the NFL-style practices. Saban coming from Miami, I felt like it was a great chance to learn something and get into the league.

"The practices were fun, and we battled. If we messed up, he would start the periods over. He wanted the best out of us, even on the practice field. He has always been hands-on."

Offensive lineman Bradley Bozeman said everybody on the roster has that "Oh, shit, moment" when you realize at a practice that you are at Alabama playing for a national championship contender: "We got in full pads freshman year, fall camp, and I'm hitting with guys and I'm saying, 'I can compete here, I can do this,'" Bozeman said. "We ran a play with a pulling guard where I kick out the end man on the line of scrimmage.

"Well, that end man on the line of scrimmage happened to be Ryan Anderson. I hit him with everything I had, and he moved about that far [hands spread several inches apart]. I went, 'Oh, shit,' because in high school that guy would have been in the stands the way I hit him. That's when I knew where I really was."

The challenging Alabama practices had a reward, besides the preparation for the games and building toughness. Geno Matias-Smith, a starting safety for the 2015 national championship team, said when practice was over, it was over.

"We did a lot on the big screen in the meeting room before practice, and Coach Smart or Coach Saban would explain a lot of things,"

Matias-Smith said. "Then we got a lot done in practice. So, we didn't have to dive in at night after practice. You could work on your own back at your room, but our practices and meetings were so thorough that we didn't always have to do that.

"If you wanted to review practice on the iPad, you could do it. If you wanted to look at extra tape on the iPad, you could do that, too. I did that on my own, but you didn't have to go home and watch practice all over again."

That is important because some Alabama players needed to leave the anxiety of practice on the practice field. It can be mentally exhausting trying to keep up with schemes or to hold off the player trying to take your position . . . daily.

"Damion Square told me my freshman season, 'Don't take this shit home,'" said Ryan Anderson. "Don't be frustrated at home, don't be mad walking down the street. Leave the football stuff at the football field and you will be better off."

The football field "stuff" was tough enough for two and a half hours. It only made sense to leave it at home. While they are at practice, Nick Saban never stops telling his players to be dutiful to the drills. It truly is 4th and goal every day. The head coach does not take a practice off, and neither do his players.

"The thing Coach Saban harped on the most—always he said this—was that you play the game the way you practice," Matias-Smith said. "I know everyone says it. All teams say it. But he never let us forget it. I still remember we had those bad practices the week of the Ole Miss game [2015] and we lost. We played as we practiced. Bad."

Alabama players insist that practices were the reason they dealt with adversity so well against Mississippi State in 2014, Clemson in 2015, and Ole Miss in 2016, all come-from-behind, pressure-filled wins.

"We already played this game four different times, that's what we say," Lee said. "We would go in the game and everyone just feels like we played this game. It's not going to be more physical than practice, it's not going to be harder than practice. Everything will be slower, based off how we practiced."

One of the interesting parts of Alabama practice is the rehearsal of practice itself. Players don't just walk out on the practice field and the fire drill starts with shouting and commands. Nick starts with a walk-through, maybe on pattern matching for the defensive backs, or some seven-on-seven drill that has to do with the opponent's scheme. The players are warmed up mentally for fifteen minutes to a half hour on what the day's chore is going to be.

Then the whistle blows and Scott Cochran, the strength-and-conditioning coach, goes to work warming them up physically, and stretching them. That's when the organized chaos starts.

Creating that organized chaos and a cauldron in practice started the first spring of the Saban Era at Alabama. The coaches were teachers, but they started fires in practice to get the vibe they wanted in the program. They wanted the players to know just how important practice was to the operation.

I'll give you an example from 2007 and 2008 when the foundation was being put down.

Offensive line coach Joe Pendry would routinely yell at quarterback Greg McElroy in practice because he was holding on to the ball too long. And McElroy was the backup!

McElroy said the coaches were in his face constantly some days, along with the actual pass rushers. They were testing him over and over.

Several times McElroy took the bait and snapped back in anger. It was all part of Saban and Pendry's approach, another piece of the Process, if you will. Saban wanted a quarterback who could survive and thrive in an SEC fourth quarter.

"They had half-field drills where you would have four defensive backs, or maybe three DBs and one linebacker, covering a receiver and a running back, which is two guys trying to get open against four," McElroy said. "It was totally scripted to put pressure on the offense. The defense was practicing its half-field coverages and trying to teach the quarterback not to be greedy and take what's there. It was a drill where they said, 'It's okay to take a check down.'"

The natural inclination of a quarterback, though, is to make the big play. All young quarterbacks want to make a play, especially if one of the receivers is Julio Jones. But if McElroy tried to wait for Jones to get open, instead of finding the running back, all hell was coming at McElroy . . . pass rushers and Pendry.

"I remember one practice it was raining a little bit and I was frustrated because we were doing a nine-on-nine," McElroy said. "It was a seven-on-seven drill, except there were two offensive linemen going against two defensive linemen.

"Seven-on-seven is supposed to be a passing drill. It is supposed to feature the passing game and coverage. But our coaches would put two defensive linemen in there to simulate a live rush, and it was more spread out and the defensive linemen would practice stunts and twists and their games. More often than not, the defensive linemen are back in my lap. I remember Joe Pendry screaming at me, 'Get rid of the ball!'

"I remember yelling back at him, 'What the f—do you want me to do?' They were on me and he was chewing me out. I was getting hit in seven-on-seven and the ball was wet, too. It was all part of their deal in getting the quarterback ready to play in tight situations."

If the feisty McElroy wasn't getting into it with Pendry, McElroy was getting into it with Rolando McClain, a player who seemed to enjoy the idea of teammates not liking him. McClain, a menacing inside linebacker with ideal size and temperament, thought it was his job to keep things stirred up in practice.

McClain's style was also part of the development of the program. It is not just up to coaches to keep the players on edge. They have to do it to each other, and McClain was a champ at it.

"Rolando McClain hated me," McElroy said. "We were two leaders on the team, and we did not like each other at times. I love him now and wish him the best, but there were some days . . . oh, man.

"I remember in scrimmages I would make an adjustment, and Rolando would make an adjustment that would blow up the play I adjusted to and I'm yelling, 'He's knows our plays.' Coach would create competition whenever he could. Brothers fight all the time. You are challenging each other.

"I was pretty fiery. I would occasionally get chippy myself. I think when they yelled at me, I would actually play better in a lot of ways. They like putting you in spots and testing you mentally. Physically, they can see what you got. You are not going to be on the team if you can't make all the throws, but Coach wanted to try you and see if you would fold or thrive in pressure-filled situations. That is harder to figure out for a coach sometimes."

McElroy, now a nationally known college football analyst, was thinking back to the games in 2016 when Alabama trailed, but the pressure never became too much for the Crimson Tide. Instead, the Tide played better when behind against USC, Ole Miss, and Texas A&M. Saban has baked his players in pressure situations over and over and over in practice.

"The tough coaching in practice is one of the reasons why his teams have responded so well in championship settings and big games," McElroy said. "They always seem to play pretty well and seldom wilt at the moment. He started that in the spring of 2007, making things hard on everybody so they would get ready for those big games.

"You come to expect that Alabama will play well on the biggest of stages. Now, they are just so dang talented and mentally tough."

Between the loss to Florida in the 2008 SEC Championship and the last-second defeat to Clemson in the 2016 national title contest, Alabama won nine "championship" games in a row, which included five conference and four national crowns. I have no doubt that those results come directly from Alabama's devotion on the practice field.

The rigor of practice prepares Alabama players for the NFL, but does it overprepare them? Are they maxed out when they leave Tuscaloosa?

NFL scouts must understand and be able to decipher which Alabama prospects still have "upside" for development at the next level, and which players have almost reached their full potential under Nick Saban and his staff. An NFL personnel evaluator has to determine if what he is seeing at an Alabama practice or game is what his team will get at the next level, or does the Crimson Tide prospect still have more room to grow physically or in technique?

Nick has expressed frustration when some in the media who cover the NFL draft have been critical of certain Alabama players who have "washed out" in the pros and have made blanket statements about his program and his approach to practice. Running back Trent Richardson did not thrive in the NFL, and some conjectured that once he was out of the regimen at Alabama, he could not cope on his own. Rolando McClain seemed to have All-Pro potential, but he has had to deal with drug-related suspensions. Barrett Jones was an Outland Trophy winner and Rimington Trophy winner and had one of the greatest college careers in the history of the sport, but his NFL career never took off.

This is not Nick's fault.

Alabama gives more access and is more wide-open to pro scouts than any other program in the nation. The NFL scouts are treated in a first-class way and always welcomed to Tuscaloosa. They get the opportunity literally every day to see the Alabama players do NFL-like things in practices and games.

It's their job, not Nick Saban's, to determine if a prospect has the mental makeup, physical attributes, and overall ability to make the transition to professional football. Most of Alabama's players in the Saban Era will tell you that their practices prepared them not only to win college games, but to succeed at the NFL level, too. Some Alabama players do not thrive in the NFL for all kinds of reasons, but to blame it all on Nick's practices is not accurate at all.

The Alabama practices reveal the grit in their players, one by one. Players learn determination and how to deal with adversity.

"My freshman year [2014] Trey DePriest sprained his MCL in camp and they said he was going to be out a while," defensive back Marlon Humphrey said. "He came out the next day and was practicing and limping. I mean, he was just limping all over and couldn't really practice, but he wouldn't go in. That's when I realized that at this place you just had to do it. He couldn't practice one hundred percent, but he said he was going to practice anyway."

What parents want to happen after four years is to see that their son came out the other side of the Process with resolve and a will to succeed in life. The parents covet the diploma, but they covet most the work ethic players are taught in practice, the forty-year bargain with Nick Saban, not the four-year deal.

Dillon Lee can check all those boxes about life skills. He didn't catch on in the NFL, but he has caught on in life. Lee is working for a construction company in the Atlanta area and thriving.

"I wake up every morning and I go to work," Lee said. "When I'm at work, I work. This is what you learn playing football at Alabama. You do honest work. People at Alabama are not emotional, they handle their business no matter what's said, or what's done. No one gets too worked up.

"At my job, people get emotional. Working hard day in and day out is not common. I work as hard as I can and get it done as fast as I can. Then I go home. I see a lot of people that are not doing that. They are just hanging out, punching the clock.

"You are accustomed to every day being a workday at Alabama, not just physically, but the mental part, too."

Three years ago, I was on a training-camp tour with SiriusXM and visited a number of college and pro teams in August. My final stop before the season would be Tuscaloosa to check in on the Tide before the first game of the year.

It must have been one hundred degrees that day, but Alabama worked on everything: first- and second-down plays, third-down or sub situations, red-zone offense and defense, short yardage and goal-line and two-minute. It was a long, hot, physical practice.

I saw Nick in his office an hour or so later and said, "One of the reasons you will always win here is that your practices are tougher and more comprehensive than any other program. No one does it the way you do anymore. I go to these other places and they play music and have walk-throughs, maybe spend a few minutes on techniques and tackling, but nothing remotely close to how you do it. You make it so hard on these guys in practice, the games are almost easy. When the pressure arrives in the fourth quarter, they have been there before and know they are going to win."

He shrugged his shoulders. "So these other teams aren't doing this?"

"No. you're one of the only teams in the country that has a practice like what I just saw. I haven't seen one close to that this year, pro or college."

The players wrap up an intense practice by walking to tables that are laid out with cut-up fresh fruit and personalized smoothies. Orders are taken before practice from each player, so that they can get exactly what they want after a demanding two hours on the field. They've earned the right to have their names on those cups, too.

Practice is the fuel for Alabama's football program. It is fuel because Alabama has enough kids eighteen to twenty-two years old who believe in the meritocracy of practice. There is no debate about that, and everyone in the building understands it. You compete or go home. That practice field represents the true test for every Alabama football player. There are no shortcuts to game day at Bryant-Denny. You earn your way there, and on that practice field is where the Crimson Tide develops the "brotherhood" that has been mentioned so often by players like Jonathan Allen and Eddie Jackson.

"This place isn't for everybody," 2016 right guard Korren Kirven said. "The dog. You have to have the dog in you for what we do at practice."

It's not just talent that drives Alabama football, it's the fundamentals and the practices, the absolutes of the Process. A player has to be resolute and driven. A player has to like the regimen of practice and the details that go into being a good football player. I've looked into the eyes of players—in college and the NFL—who are obsessed with the game.

I was raised by a man, a son of Alabama, who could have played for Nick Saban. The toughness he showed on the football field and passed on to me is the epitome of the modern Alabama football player. The football "dog," as Korren Kirven put it, has been bred in Alabama kids since the 1950s and before. It is important to know where it comes from because it does not just materialize on the practice field when the players turn eighteen years of age.

5

OPTIC YELLOW GOALPOSTS

FOOTBALL PLAYS BIG IN ALABAMA

My state, Alabama, is the wellspring for Nick Saban's football program. I'm not just talking about my state's sending forth big and fast football players to Tuscaloosa. I'm talking about sending him football players who have had the parentage necessary to play for Alabama. Think of peewee, middle school, and high school football as the main aquifer for Nick and how some of these kids are raised in the game. The very core of what these kids bring to the university is this:

Football is a big deal here, you cannot play small.

You need ambition and confidence to play at Alabama, and Nick is given ambitious and confident boys, most of the time. They play big. It is not necessarily a feeling of superiority. It is a feeling of "I can do this. I'm made to do this. I was born to do this." Linebacker Reuben Foster, from Auburn, described the hyper-driven Alabama players, somewhat inelegantly, as "savages, goons, monsters, beasts."

So you need to hear a few stories—several of them personal from me—to understand better what Nick has borrowed from us in

Alabama. A fierceness is in our souls that translates to the competition on the field.

You want to get to the bottom of the Process, don't you? My experience can help you understand the attitude around the Alabama program, the poetic power behind the Tide.

I can relate right away to the father of the Alabama football coach, Nick Saban Sr. He would drive a school bus through the coal-bearing hills of northern West Virginia in the 1960s to pick up his players for football practice. My grandfather Hastings Savage drove a bus through the iron-ore hills east of Birmingham in Overton, Alabama, and carried children to ball games and special events, too.

Hastings Savage parked his bus behind the Alabama Fuel & Iron Company commissary late in the afternoon of January 27, 1941. He was walking toward the back door of the commissary when another miner lunged at Hastings with a knife and stabbed him to death. The man was angry that Hastings had been promoted ahead of him.

Hastings was thirty years old when he died and left behind a widow and three children, one of them my father, Phil Savage. I call him Big Sav. He was a football player, and football was a big part of his growing-up life.

Big Sav was a classic hard-nosed pulling guard for the Murphy High Panthers in Mobile from 1953 to 1956. He was a muscled-up five feet ten, 180 pounds, with a barrel chest and thick neck. Years later, after I had become an NFL scout, I watched some tape of my father, and Big Sav could play. He was a tough ass, could run, and played with relentless, and I mean *relentless*, effort. For such a sweet person, he was a mean football player.

As a side note, his head coach was Joe Sharpe, an upperclassmen teammate at Alabama to a more soon-to-be-famous coach, Paul Bryant, back in the 1930s. Sharpe was legendary with his old-school tactics and, ironically enough, sent Big Sav's quarterback, Bobby Jackson, to the Capstone where he ended up as Coach Bryant's first quarterback in 1958.

You have probably heard about some of the discourtesies that went on in Big Sav's era of high school football. There were no such things as automatic ejections and one-game suspensions for unruly behavior and "targeting" fouls. For instance, they threw elbows on just about every play. These vicious elbows would draw blood because there were no face guards or mouthpieces. A kid would get popped in the nose or the mouth, and nobody on his team would have to say, "Hey, you're bleeding." The kid could taste the blood himself. Smears of blood on the jersey were as common as today's jersey patch commemorating some special occasion.

Elbows did not deter my father. He threw them back where they came from. But the flying elbows were the least of his problems. My father suffered full-body cramps, usually late in the fourth quarter. He would fall to the ground and fight to get back up.

That was "the dog" in him that current Alabama players refer to, the willpower they see in practices in Tuscaloosa. So flash forward from 1954 to 2012.

From linebacker Ryan Anderson:

"My freshman year we are out there in camp in the heat and Jarrick Williams [defensive back] tore his ACL. He still finished his rack of plays. No lie. He had two plays left and stayed out there and finished his rack. You don't expect that from nobody, but if you want a practice story that's insane, that's one. It was unreal what he did."

Football was important to my grandfather J. T. Savage, who stepped in and married my grandmother, Mildred, after Hastings's death. My grandparents allowed my father to play even with this obvious medical issue, which would have outraged today's football-nervous citizenry. Back then, coaches didn't believe in giving players water during games or practices, which would have been an obvious remedy to cramps. Coaches said if players gulped water, it would make them sick.

When the Murphy linemen would push the blocking sled around the field following a typical afternoon thunderstorm, the center would purposely drop his towel into a puddle. It would soak up the rainwater, and then the players would steer that sled back around to the towel lying on the ground. They would slyly pick it up and pass it around so that everyone could squeeze some water from the cloth.

My father's first cramping episode came early in the 1954 season, Big Sav's sophomore year at Murphy. He was running down the field for a kickoff and a cramp hit him in the stomach. Then the cramps moved to his legs, then his upper chest. His entire body cramped from neck to toe.

Big Sav lay on the football field unable to move. The coaches had to cut off his uniform with a razor blade so they could try to massage his muscles with a wintergreen balm. They finally carried him off the field and put him in a car and raced him to a hospital. A doctor and nurses were waiting for him with a gurney and wheeled him into the hospital. He was wearing just his jockstrap.

Today, a school board member, or a lawyer, would have stepped in and put Big Sav on the sideline for good, or until an independent medical evaluation cleared him to play. But sixty years ago, the parents ruled. Big Sav would be back out there the next Friday night, and the Friday night after that. There were more cramps and the meat wagon was on standby. Big Sav, a key member of the powerhouse Murphy team, was a regular at the hospital for fluids along about 9:50 p.m. every Friday night.

Big Sav was cut up, "ripped," as the scouts say. He was imposing with a crew cut and a square jaw and the kind of face you take seriously. Bryant Coker, the father of Jake Coker, the Alabama national championship team quarterback in 2015, said Big Sav was a hero to kids in Mobile. He was among the best football players in the entire state.

"He reminded me of Mickey Mantle with that crew cut," Bryant Coker said.

Big Sav's story is raw Alabama football. High school football programs in the 1950s did not have these glistening steel weight rooms or detailed strength-and-conditioning programs. Big Sav would run five miles a day up and down the sand dunes during the summer on Dauphin Island for his conditioning. Some days he did sit-ups with blocks of cement, which had been dried to rebar, hanging around his shoulders. He wanted to make his neck bigger so his head could withstand the whiplash from those flying elbows.

Big Sav's neck size was seventeen inches. They had to custom-order his shirts because he didn't really have a neck.

My grandmother Mildred started saving the juice from the pickle jar for him to drink because they said it would help with cramps. My aunts would eat the pickles and Big Sav would drink the juice.

Once, Big Sav ate "fifty to seventy-five" salt tablets the day of a game against rival Vigor so he wouldn't fall out with cramps in the fourth quarter. He finished few, if any, games his senior season because of this debilitating condition.

My father said all the other parents were looking at my grandmother and grandfather going, "Why are you letting him play?" My father said it would have torn him up not to play football. He told me, "I wouldn't have been worth two cents if I didn't play football."

He meant it. He didn't want to quit. He strived to be the best he could be.

My father played his last game on the University of Alabama campus in what was Denny Stadium (capacity thirty-one thousand). He was an all-state player and had been selected for the Alabama high school all-star game in the summer of 1957.

Tennessee and Auburn had been recruiting Big Sav, but his cramping condition scared off recruiters and he was not offered a scholarship. He was good enough to play Division I football, no question about it. I saw the tape.

It nearly broke his spirit not to play college football, but Big Sav became a successful businessman, full of the same stubbornness he had on the football field.

Now do you understand where some of this allegiance to the game comes from in Alabama? It comes from the family, the taproot.

Flash forward to 2016 and a lesson center Bradley Bozeman of Roanoke, Alabama, learned from his father:

My dad [Barry] said he messed up his chance for a scholarship and slacked off in high school as a football player. He thought he could have gone somewhere to play football in college and he didn't. It's the last thing he wanted to happen to me. My dad has been a huge factor in my life. My brother was seven years older than me, and he pushed me, too. I wanted to be bigger, badder, in everything. They gave me a competitive edge.

I've always been the guy that has had to bust my butt getting to where I wanted to go. I have always done extra, stayed extra. I am the first one there, last to leave. It has helped with my dad as peewee coach. If I wasn't doing right, he would let me know.

He had this distinct look he would always give me. It would be the first quarter and I would come to the sideline and he would just look at me, and I would say, "I better pick it up or I am going to hear it." I'm so grateful for that. By my junior year I stopped getting that look. I finally figured it out a little bit.

The football field in Alabama is a proving ground. It's where boys go to test their toughness. It's where the townspeople go to support their local high school team. It's symbolic of the culture that exists within the state. Football is important, and for many in Alabama it has become our identity.

"A lot of these guys from the West Coast and the North don't really know the deep roots," Bozeman said. "We know Bear and Gene Stallings and everything that comes behind the name *Alabama football*. It means a little more to us having that pride behind us.

"You can't quit the team here and go home and blame it on somebody."

The scene sixty years ago of a fiercely competitive seventeen-year-old being carried off the field in only his jockstrap is all relevant to the scene in the fourth quarter on September 3, 2016, in Dallas where Nick Saban is barking at the officials and the Alabama fans are cheering him for complaining about a call. Bama led Southern California, 45–6, but the ultracompetitive Nick Saban behaved as if it were 0–0. The fervent attitude around football grips the state today just as it did sixty years ago when Big Sav was knocking teeth loose. Enough is never enough.

This reverence toward football is passed from generation to generation. It was passed on to me.

The 2017 season will be my forty-sixth year in football, and I couldn't imagine one September without being a part of the game in some fashion. I started playing tackle football when I was six years old.

My first in-person "big-time" game was December 3, 1976, when I was eleven. Murphy High School of Mobile was playing Mountain Brook at Legion Field in Birmingham for the state championship.

Only the south entrance was open to fans, so everyone walked into Legion Field on the ground level. When we emerged from that entrance and into the lights, all I saw were these optic yellow goalposts right in front of us. I was mesmerized. I thought, this is where Alabama plays its most important games, the Football Capital of the South. I couldn't take my eyes off those optic yellow goalposts, and I was hooked.

Major Ogilvie rushed for 339 yards for Mountain Brook in the 52–26 win over Murphy. Bear Bryant offered Major a scholarship after the game, which he accepted the next day. My heroes were Murphy quarterback John Holman and receiver Mardye McDole, who went on to play for Mississippi State and the Minnesota Vikings. Holman had a fine career at Northeast Louisiana (now Louisiana-Monroe), passing for 4,863 yards, which was a lot of yardage in those days.

I wanted to be Holman, or maybe Richard Todd, the last Alabama quarterback picked in the first round of the NFL draft, and the pride of our neighborhood in west Mobile. I had to play football.

Can you see the desire in this story from 2016 linebacker Ryan Anderson, who is from Daphne, Alabama?

"I was the youngest of five, and you had to fight for everything, you know what I mean? I had a big brother who was six years older, and if I had a game, he wanted it. I had to fight him. I had that mentality my whole life, pretty much since I stepped on the football field. If you are the toughest player out there, I am going to try and hit you as hard as I can. I feel like I was born to play here."

Me, I thought I was born to play at Murphy, a Mobile institution. I begged my parents to allow me to transfer from a private high school to Murphy. They let me transfer, and I waited my sophomore (1980) and junior (1981) years as the backup quarterback behind Pat Washington, who would go on to play at Auburn with Bo Jackson.

In 1982, two weeks before preseason practice was scheduled to open—which was going to be my chance, finally—the longtime Murphy coach, Robert Shaw, retired. Larry Henderson was named head coach and he went into a rebuilding mode. I was benched at halftime of the first game.

Henderson called me into his office Labor Day morning and said, "I don't think you're good enough, we're going to make a change."

Coaches have an influence on how a kid's life can go. They can give hope or strip hope. If I had accepted "Okay, I'm not very good, I need to figure out something else to do," my life would have completely changed.

I didn't accept Henderson's declaration. Football was too important. There are kids like me all over the state; kids like me who make football the national pastime of our state. I kept practicing. I didn't quit. Every coach I ever played for before or afterward absolutely loved my work ethic, passion for the game, and will to win. I wanted to prove Henderson wrong in the worst way.

Can you see *me* in Eddie Jackson, the Alabama safety? He lost his job as a cornerback in spring 2015 because the coaches didn't think he was good enough. Eddie did not retreat. Instead he fought back.

"It was a tough adjustment," Eddie said after Alabama won the SEC Championship Game over Florida in 2016. "But you don't quit."

So while I was dejected about being benched my senior season, I didn't give up. I got to play some that season and threw a few touchdown passes. Murphy was 3-7, probably its worst season in one hundred years, but I persevered through a long fall. Never take anything for granted in sports, I learned. Nick Saban has learned the same thing, which is why Alabama is the most consistently winning team in all of college football.

In this state there is a culture of refusing to play small, no matter what level of football you're playing. It's a big deal around here.

Look at my brother, Joe, in the fall of 1983. How close did he come to tragedy because of football? I was a freshman in college and Joe was a freshman in high school when he went through an old-fashioned one-on-one drill where two players butt helmets with each other. They collided eight or nine times, like rams on the side of a bluff.

Joe woke up the next morning with his vision seriously impaired. Doctors found a blood clot, likely a result of that head-knocking in practice. He was scheduled for surgery the following day.

My father prayed overnight for Joe. "Lord, you can do whatever you want with me if you spare his life."

The next morning they did another scan of Joe's brain. The clot was gone. My mother insists it was divine intervention, so Joe could find his calling in the ministry and go on to serve people across the country and around the world. I'm not arguing. Fourth and goal, indeed.

Here in Alabama you do what you're told in football. It can work out just when you think it can't.

Look at me. A benched senior quarterback, and I still got a chance to play college football.

The University of the South in Sewanee, Tennessee, is a Division III school, and its head coach, Horace Moore, came to Mobile looking for a quarterback. Horace walked in the front doors of Murphy High School on a tip from Jim Seidule (soo-juh-lee), the headmaster at my brother's school, and saw athletes filling the main hallway. My teammates were big kids, kids who looked like athletes. Horace's eyes lit up.

When I came down to the office to meet Coach Moore, he said, "Hell, son, if you can play here, you can play for me."

Then he said, "Hell, I'm told you play baseball, too. Hell, you can play both and get a quality education." Horace, as I quickly learned, started every sentence with *hell*.

When I got to Sewanee in early August, Coach Moore didn't tell me that he had recruited five other quarterbacks in my class, but I didn't tell him I was a benched senior quarterback, either. I played college football because I refused to quit and I put the work in. Today, I am a member of three Halls of Fame, became an NFL general manager, and now direct the most prestigious college all-star game in the country. I didn't fold easily because football meant so much to me and our family.

The labor around football prepared me for life beyond football.

Coach Homer Smith, my mentor at Alabama and UCLA, said when you are doing the laborious work involved with football—strength and conditioning, film study, meeting with coaches, drills in practice, the summer workouts—it is preparing you for something else in life.

That connects to what Nick Saban has preached to his Alabama teams since 2007.

You hear other coaches say these things about preparation, but after being around the Alabama program the last eight years, I can see that Nick is unwavering in always having his staff and team totally prepared.

Think about a player such as Alabama outside linebacker Ryan Anderson. He was a fifth-year senior in 2016. He had not started *one* game at Alabama. By the week-seven, 49–10 Alabama win over Tennessee, NFL scouts were telling me that no. 22 was the most productive player on the Crimson Tide defense. He had one season to make his résumé shine, and he did it.

He put in the work. He kept striving. Ryan Anderson learned that. I learned that. It kept my football dream alive several times.

In January 1987, just four months before I was set to graduate from Sewanee, I sent seventy letters out to college football coaches looking for a graduate assistant position on their staff. The first rejection letter was from Joe Paterno. This wasn't so bad, I thought, I had a letter from Paterno himself. Then a rejection letter came from Danny Ford at Clemson. Then there was a rejection letter from Don James at Washington. I finally realized they were form letters. I received sixty-five of those rejection letters with three no responses and two maybes.

Tulane and Alabama were the two maybes. Jack Fligg, who was Bill Curry's football operations director, called and said they had an "administrative" GA position available. If I could get to Tuscaloosa, meet the staff, and pass the Miller Analogies Test, I might be their choice. My big toe was in the door. I started at Bama on July 6, 1987.

I sat in meetings, filmed practices, made copies, and generally did the typical work of a first-year grad assistant. After that first season, Coach Curry changed offensive coordinators and hired Homer Smith. I had never heard of him. Little did I know, he was about to become the most important man in my football life.

In his first meeting with the offensive staff, he walked to the whiteboard and drew the foundation play of his passing offense. I was sitting there thinking to myself, "Wait a minute, he just drew up our base pattern at Sewanee." It was the BYU offense I had learned in college from our offensive coordinator, Dewey "Swamp Rat" Warren.

That BYU scheme was built on rhythm and timing. I knew it like the back of my hand. The very first play Homer Smith drew on that board was the very first play Dewey Warren showed me as a college freshman at Sewanee.

I could run that play right now as a fifty-two-year-old.

A few weeks later, that proverbial door opened again. Ken Walker, the graduate assistant who was the on-field tight ends coach, decided to go back and coach high school football. We were in a staff meeting when Coach Curry asked Homer whom he wanted to coach the Alabama tight ends.

I'll never forget Homer wheeling around in his chair and saying, "Bill, I got my man right here." And Homer pointed at me. By early March, I was coaching Crimson Tide tight ends Howard Cross and Lamonde Russell, two outstanding players.

But the grind of football can humble you, too. A year later, before our summer camp for high school players, Coach Curry told the graduate assistants, me included, the tight ends coach, he wanted the parking lot of the dorm spotless. We GAs ended up on our hands and knees picking up cigarette butts.

Coach Curry would often say to us, "Sometimes you have to do things you really don't want to do. You think Jesus really wanted to go to the cross?"

Alabama was 7-5 in 1987, then 9-3 in 1988, and Coach Curry had his own cross to bear. Fans were unhappy. A brick was thrown through his office window following a 22–12 home loss to Ole Miss. Then we lost to Auburn, and I don't have to tell anybody familiar with the Iron Bowl rivalry about the teeth gnashing that went along with a shutout defeat in Birmingham.

It started to turn for the better in 1989. We were 10-0. Alabama was going to Auburn for the first time in history. In the modern era, the Iron Bowl had always been played at Legion Field. This time it was on the Plains, and the Bama Nation, the whole state, was uneasy.

Before we left Tuscaloosa for the ride to Auburn, a bomb threat was called in, so we had a police helicopter escort. The chopper stayed over the team buses from Tuscaloosa to Montgomery, and then Montgomery into Auburn. I have never seen that done before or since.

We lost the game, 30–20. We were 10-1.

Noise of unrest swirled around the program. People were talking at restaurants and the barbershops about how Bill Curry had to go. The way I understand it, Coach Curry was approached quietly by Kentucky to become its head coach. Maybe Alabama was going to fire him, but he got out before they could "officially" get him.

There was no formal word of his leaving until January 1, 1990, when we were in New Orleans for the Sugar Bowl to play Miami. Coach Curry gathered his staff at 8:00 a.m. in the Hilton Riverside.

"Hey, guys, I want everyone to know I'll be leaving for the University of Kentucky after this game. My plan is to take as many of you as possible."

After Coach Curry told us he was leaving, Homer and I were walking down the hall from the meeting rooms to the elevator.

Homer said to me, "I didn't come to Alabama to coach at Kentucky. I'll be going back to UCLA. Would you want to go?"

"Coach, I would like to see if I have any options before I take another graduate assistant job."

Homer looked at me with a little disdain and said, "You are like all these other coaches; always looking for options."

Then he told me the story about how at the annual college coaches' convention one year, an assistant coach fell out of an eighteen-story window and a group of bystanders ran over to see what had happened. While the medics worked on the man, a coach leaned through the crowd and asked, "Anybody know what school he was at?"

I'm not sure if that story is true, but Homer made his point. Coaching is as competitive an arena as you are going to find, and everyone is looking for that perfect opportunity. Nick Saban was an assistant coach at seven different schools and for two NFL clubs during his first seventeen years of his career.

My football dream almost flickered out before I got the biggest break of my career, a chance to coach with Bill Belichick and Nick Saban.

First, though, I went to UCLA with Homer as a GA. When I left UCLA after the 1990 season, I took a job with the San Antonio Riders in the World League of American Football. The head coach was Mike Riley, an Alabama graduate, and now the head coach at Nebraska. I was slated to make $1,000 a month for four months with the Riders, and then the team said it would get me a job at a car dealership owned by Larry Benson, the owner of the Riders.

I was in San Antonio just six weeks when I got a call from Ernie Adams, the longtime confidant of Bill Belichick, who had just become the head coach of the Cleveland Browns. The next thing I know, I'm in the NFL because the Alabama man, Riley, pushed me out the door of the WLAF when I really wanted to be loyal and continue with him and the Riders.

"I'm not going to advise you as to what to do, I'm going to tell you what to do," Riley said when I debated whether to stay in San Antonio or go to Cleveland. "Those other coaches on this staff would give their left arm for a chance to go to the NFL. That's what this league [WLAF] was designed for, to get training and promoted into the National Football League. It just so happens you are the first one to get that chance. Call them back and take that job."

On March 18, 1991, I started my professional football career with the Cleveland Browns. You don't need one hundred opportunities. You need one.

So I arrived in Cleveland with Bill Belichick and Nick Saban, and they had this take-nothing-for-granted approach to winning games. I knew what to do on 4th and goal every day with these two men. I kept my head down, did my job, and paid attention. Bill and Nick showed all of us how to survive and thrive in a bloodthirsty, competitive industry. The rest was up to me, and I had the ambition because, well, I grew up in Alabama and football is important here.

By the time I was thirty-nine years old, I was the general manager of the Cleveland Browns.

This much I learned. Whether I was a GA or GM, my passion for the game, my work ethic and devotion to details has never changed. I was always overprepared. That's the Process, isn't it? Results matter, but the daily consistency of effort and focus, 4th and goal every day, is what separates Alabama (and the New England Patriots, for that matter) from other programs. I learned that much.

You have to play big. In this case, I am not talking about the catchphrase you often hear in football: "Big people beat up small people."

I'm talking about playing with a big heart. Nick Saban demands it, and it is essential to the success of his program.

Nick's schemes are complicated, but the mentality necessary to play for him is not. You have to be tough, work hard, and understand your assignments. You not only have to play big on Saturday, you have to play smart and have Plan A, Plan B, and Plan C. I like the details of the game, but I had a lot to learn from Belichick and Saban about how to break it down and then prepare a team to win. A player needs an entirely different level of training to be part of the Process. I found that out when my career path made a life-altering stop in Cleveland.

6
TRAINING THE EYES

FROM THE RAT, TO HOMER, TO BILL AND NICK

March 18, 1991, was my first day on the job in the NFL. I was twenty-five years old and the new "offensive quality-control coach" for the Cleveland Browns. I was going to be the "breakdown" scout with a vampirelike existence. I would be spending most of my time in the dark watching the Browns' opponents on tape, then writing the reports that would be the foundation for our weekly game preparation.

When I arrived at the Browns offices in Berea, Ohio, at 8:00 a.m., I was introduced to a few staff members in the lobby. I was taken to my "office," an open room in the center of the building.

Then, from around the corner, came the new head coach, thirty-eight-year-old Bill Belichick.

"Listen," he said after a quick introduction, "we hired you for the offensive job, but instead of having to hire another quality-control coach for the defense, I want you to do both sides of the ball for now, so you can learn and then teach the other asshole we hire later in the season what to do.

"We said we'd pay you twenty thousand dollars a year; we'll give you an extra five thousand dollars. That okay?"

I stood up, shook Bill's hand. "Yes, sir, that's great, Coach. I just want to thank you for this opportunity."

I had just gone from $1,000 a month for a four-month season in the World League of American Football to $25,000 a year, and I'm saying to myself, "I can't believe it. This is the NFL, a five-thousand-dollar raise in the first five minutes in the league!"

Six months later I was like, "Is there any way I can give these guys a refund?" I had never watched more tape and made more notes in one season in my life.

I didn't know it at the time, but that first meeting with Bill was my early indoctrination into the bullring of Alabama football. It started with Belichick's being direct and succinct, which is how it is at Bama many days.

Here is the position, take it or leave it.

The operation was moving way too fast for me to debate and negotiate my first day there. That's what you need to take from this chapter and my early exposure to the Belichick/Saban freight train. Get on, we're not waiting for you, not even to stow your gear.

It was my early training in the ways of Saban, fast and furious. Something clicks in your brain . . . or doesn't. You either mesh with it, or you don't.

I worked directly for Nick during the 1991 through 1993 seasons, then moved to scouting and saw him literally every year from that point forward as I evaluated his prospects at Michigan State, LSU, and Alabama. I jumped at the chance to reconnect, albeit indirectly, with him in 2009 as a broadcaster for the Crimson Tide Sports Network. You love the training and the rigor of working around Saban, not to mention the devotion to detail. That's what this chapter is about: training the eyes to see all sides of the game, big and small . . . and getting hooked on the pace of the job and the thrill of the ride.

In that respect, the lightning-fast pace of my first interaction with Belichick/Saban clued me in to the culture of these two and what was in store for my future training.

"Let's walk down to the defensive coordinator's office. They're short one coach on that side of the ball, so you'll be spending more time with them," Bill said. "I'll introduce you to Nick Saban."

I didn't know Nick Saban from Lou Saban, the old Buffalo Bills head coach. I just knew he was the Browns' new defensive coordinator and had come from college football, the University of Toledo.

On that fateful first morning in professional football, I met two Hall of Fame coaches within ten minutes of each other. Belichick, then Saban. I was not only going to have a desk in the same building with, arguably, the greatest pro and college football coaches of this generation, maybe of all time, but I would be a part of the ultimate football "think tank," one of the most impressive staffs ever assembled.

Bill introduced me to Nick as being from UCLA. I'm sure Nick looked at me and his immediate reaction when he heard "UCLA" was "Oh, great, a surfer boy coming in here from LA." It probably took a year for him to realize I was actually from Alabama.

Nick was sitting at his desk, rocking in his chair, looking up at the screen with a cowboy remote (clicker) in one hand and a spit cup in the other. I asked, "Who you watching?"

"Some corner from Southern University that can't play; you can hardly find him on this tape," Saban muttered.

When Nick said he could "hardly find him," he meant the player was not easy to identify and was not showing up in the middle of the frame making plays. Video technology was not the best, so it was difficult to get quality film from smaller schools. Nick was not impressed with this player he was watching, Aeneas Williams, a cornerback from the proud HBCU program located in Baton Rouge.

Williams, an ordained minister and one classy individual, was a future third-round pick of the Arizona Cardinals. Nick was discounting a guy who ended up playing fourteen years in the NFL and was inducted into the Pro Football Hall of Fame in 2014.

I tell that story of Aeneas, and the day I met Nick, to the young recruiting assistants at Alabama so they understand no one bats 1.000 when evaluating players. Remember the quote I gave you from Ozzie Newsome about everyone having "skeletons" in their scouting closet?

Nick Saban has limited his skeletons more than others because of his eyes. Nick sees things most of us don't see. He sees clearly, without the prejudice of a four- or five-star rating, and that is one of the hallmarks of his Process. He will decide if a player is worthy and will not let a "star" system tell him what to think. He has his own system, one he didn't have in place in 1991 at the Browns when he was grading Williams.

Nick can almost immediately determine a player's flexibility, explosiveness, and football speed from film. He has constructed a catalog of players to reference and compare because Saban studies more film than any other head coach I know, college or pro, this side of Belichick.

Film study also allows Nick and his staff to find gems of intelligence on other teams in preparation for games.

Alabama won one SEC game a couple of years ago because the staff saw an offensive player from the other team tip off run plays with his stance. I won't tell you which team or which position, but Alabama saw it on tape preparing for the game. It was right there for the taking and it helped Alabama win the game.

That's what I mean about training the eyes. You *learn to see* those things.

When I started with the Browns, I had to run to catch up with Nick. It wasn't easy, but at least I had a foundation that was different from that of most new assistant coaches in the NFL. I had Dewey Warren, also known as the Swamp Rat, and Homer Smith, an offensive mastermind, in my back pocket.

The Rat and Homer stretched my mind and sharpened my eyes in college football. I could "see and think" the game. I never felt left behind in Cleveland working with Bill and Nick, because of the education I had received before working with the Browns.

Here is some background on the Rat. You don't know this. Few people would, and it will surprise you and give you an appreciation of a quarterback who beat Bear Bryant once and almost did it a second time.

Some of you may remember when BYU, under head coach LaVell Edwards, burst on the scene in college football in the mid-1970s. The Cougars built themselves into a powerhouse—they won the national title in 1984—with a cutting-edge passing offense.

Edwards hired Warren to coach the offense at BYU in 1972. The Swamp Rat created a scheme that utilized all five eligible receivers and changed the college game. Gary Sheide became the quarterback in 1973, and the Cougars dazzled their opponents with formations and motions, all while hunting the mismatch of a good receiver on a lesser defensive back.

Warren, known in his hometown of Savannah, Georgia, and in his playing days at Tennessee, as the Swamp Rat, was my quarterback coach at the University of the South in Sewanee. He installed that offense at BYU in 1972 and was the creator of the Cougars' version of the so-called West Coast Offense. There were three run plays: draw, trap, sweep. There was little talking in the huddle; it was all a numbered system.

"It was one hundred percent Dewey Warren," LaVell Edwards told me years later after a BYU practice when I was an NFL scout. Edwards won 257 games at BYU from 1972 to 2000, and he said the Rat drew up that offense in year one. Bill Walsh had his version of the West Coast Offense, but the Rat swears Walsh came out to Provo to watch Warren's scheme first.

Dewey's offense was based on rhythm and timing. BYU turned out some terrific quarterbacks, such as Gifford Nielsen, Jim McMahon, Steve Young, Marc Wilson, Robbie Bosco, Steve Sarkisian, and Ty Detmer, who won the Heisman Trophy. BYU expanded the offense after the Rat left, but the basis of it was what the Rat put in for Sheide.

We had the same offense when I was the quarterback at Sewanee. It was a full-field read, a progression system, from left to right, or right to left. We had straight drop backs and sprint-outs and would also move the pocket for the quarterback to set up behind the left or right tackle in order to change our launching point.

We threw to X, Y, and Z, and the running backs. We threw screens and delay routes, where the tight end or running back would release late after a count or two. We had bootlegs and waggles and counter-runs. You would typically not get this foundation in football at the D-III level.

Sometimes we would even get some Yogi Berra–isms from the Rat. "It's like taking baby from a candy," the Rat would say as he drew up the game plan.

Here is some background on the Rat, with a Coach Bryant twist.

Coach Bryant went to Savannah in the fall of 1962 and tried to recruit Dewey as a linebacker. Warren wanted to play quarterback, but the Bear told Warren he already had two out-of-state quarterbacks in mind, Joe Namath of Beaver Falls, Pennsylvania, and Steve Sloan of Cleveland, Tennessee. Bryant could not take a third.

The Rat's home-state school, the University of Georgia, would not recruit him so he went to Tennessee. He was the starting quarterback for most of three seasons and led the Volunteers to a 19-6 record as a starter (1965–67).

The Swamp Rat was 1-1-1 against Bama in 1965, 1966, and 1967. Warren still insists Tennessee's 19-yard field goal with twenty seconds left in the 1966 game was good. The Tide won, 11–10, and finished the season unbeaten; that was the "Missing Ring" team for those who re-member.

"I was the holder," the Rat said. "The kick was close, but it was good. We should have been undefeated against Alabama while I was at Tennessee."

The Swamp Rat was the Tennessee quarterback in 1967 when the Vols beat Bama and Bear Bryant, 24–13, in Birmingham.

I went from the charismatic, cunning of the Rat to the cerebral, understated Homer Smith.

He was the offensive coordinator at Alabama (1988–89) under Bill Curry and became my football mentor when I was a graduate assis-tant there. Homer was the first coach I ever heard declare that the future of offense in college football was going to be the dual-threat quarterback. This was almost thirty years ago.

Just look around now at the college landscape. Alabama's Jalen Hurts, Ohio State's J. T. Barrett, Louisville's Lamar Jackson, Oklahoma's Baker Mayfield, Clemson's Deshaun Watson.

Homer saw the run/pass option (RPO) coming before it became a thing.

Coach Smith was not only a football coach, but the most brilliant man I've known. He earned an undergraduate degree at Princeton and an MBA at Stanford. Homer studied divinity at Harvard with the same devotion that he studied football.

He coached at the Air Force Academy, Davidson College, the University of the Pacific, UCLA, and the US Military Academy (Army), as well as Alabama. He knew the history and background of offensive football from the single wing and the Notre Dame box in the early 1900s all the way up through the wishbone and to the modern-day sophisticated passing attacks utilized in the NFL.

He was the master teacher of the game of football.

Homer would sometimes speed up the tape on us and make us see quickly and call out the play and the defense. Homer is widely recognized as one of the best tacticians in college football history, but he would also ask players what they thought about schemes. He asked Hall of Fame receiver Lynn Swann one time, "How do you read coverages?"

"Homer," the former USC and Pittsburgh Steelers great said, "I look at the corner all the way on the opposite side of the field. That will tip me off to what the corner lined up against me is going to do, man or zone."

Coach Smith was fascinated by the eyes of his quarterbacks and wanted to know what they saw. He would say that a QB's eyes were not like a movie camera, but would jump from one fix to the other. He would do a drill where his quarterback would close his eyes, blink them open and closed, and then describe what he'd seen in front of him. Try it, it's absolutely amazing the picture you can put together in the blink of an eye.

Before he passed away in 2011, Coach Smith dedicated himself to developing a system for managing the clock. He believed the sole responsibility belonged to the coach, so he wrote *The Complete Handbook of Clock Management*, which, to this day, is the most trusted reference book on the subject in virtually every football office across the country.

I got my undergrad from the Rat, my master's from Homer Smith, and my PhD from Belichick & Saban University.

It quickly became apparent to me at the Browns that the guy Belichick leaned on the most was Saban. Of all those people in the building, all those fantastic football minds, Belichick and Saban were the closest. These guys could talk man-match zones, rush-game keys, and sub packages without even going to the board to diagram. They had a clear vision of what the other one was explaining without the need to draw. Everyone else needed a board to explain himself. Kirby Smart and Nick developed that same rapport at Alabama and did it with headsets and one hundred thousand people screaming in the background. Now, Jeremy Pruitt and Coach Saban continue to do the same thing.

When Belichick and Saban talked, it sounded incredibly complicated. But when we got on the field with the players—I was Nick's assistant—their ideas appeared to crystallize right there on the green grass. It seemed easy to comprehend when they talked to the players during practice. That's why they are great coaches. They distilled some complicated schemes into words the players could comprehend and put it into place during our walk-throughs and two-hour practices.

Belichick and Saban always specifically emphasized fundamentals. Always. You see one wearing a cutoff sweatshirt (Belichick), the other in a neat polo shirt (Saban), and they look different, but not when it comes to coaching fundamentals and scouting the other team.

I spent the spring and summer of 1991 scouting the Browns' upcoming opponents. This is where I got the first inkling of the devotion to film study and the insight of men such as Belichick and Saban.

Three weeks into the 1991 preseason, Belichick called me into his office to tell me that the tape breakdowns I had been working on were not up to speed. I had taken notes in a spiral notebook for several months.

"Hey, this ain't really what we're looking for," Bill said. "Sit down, and let's watch some tape together."

Belichick went over receiver and linemen splits, the linemen stances, and the initial movements of every player. Then, I got a real tutorial.

Belichick started charting the quarterback's head movement. The Browns coach, who would go on to win five Super Bowls with the Patriots, was looking for any edge, and a quarterback's doing the same thing over and over with his head was a chance for a defensive lineman or blitzing linebacker to jump the snap count and get a sack.

You are taking it to another level when you are charting a quarterback's head movement. Professional players love when coaches find these tips for them. As you can imagine, Alabama's players routinely get these kinds of tips.

Belichick kept my attention with all these details of a single play. Nothing was overlooked. It was mesmerizing.

The clock in his office said we were on one play for twenty minutes. An NFL game has sixty plays, so that's three plays an hour. I thought to myself, "If I break down a game like this, I'll never sleep again; that's twenty hours per game and I am supposed to do three games on each side of the ball!"

Take a simple play such as I-Right, Lead 44, against a 4-3 Under defense. Bill wanted every player drawn, and he wanted it neat. Each sheet would have two plays on it, so there were usually about thirty pages of diagrams.

I would make multiple copies of the "pad" of thirty sheets. I would divide the plays by down and distance, third and short/medium/long, red zone, short yardage and goal-line, gadget plays, etc.

It was a lot of manual work, but those sheets are the core of your opponent scouting information. All of this stuff is done by computer today, but even now, I still hear the word *pad* used inside the Alabama football building. They still do it the old-fashioned way.

The tricky part when I got to Cleveland was that I had been a quarterback in college, then an offensive coach at Alabama. I had been on offense since I was seven years old. You move over to defense and all the diagrams are upside down because the offense is on top with the defense on the bottom of the page.

That was a real adjustment. I remember thinking, "I'm trying to help Nick Saban with defense, and I haven't tackled anybody in twenty years, except after I threw an interception."

Video can be viewed in two different ways. The coaching view is primarily of schemes, tendencies, and tips—you know, those bird/rabbit indicators where a guy's stance tips off whether it's to be a pass or a run.

Then you have the individual player evaluations for assessing a prospect's lateral and initial quickness, his flexibility, his strength and explosion, his competitive spirit.

I learned to watch tape from a coaching perspective with Homer, Bill, and Nick, but when I went into NFL scouting, I learned of the player-evaluation way to watch tape.

Terry McDonough is a friend of mine in player personnel. He is with the Cardinals and very good at what he does. We worked together back at the Browns and Ravens, and I would use a coaching term and he would say, "I have no idea what quarters coverage is; all I need to do is assess a player's ability to make it in the NFL."

I liked having that coaching background and knowing where a player is supposed to be and what he is supposed to do. Nick Saban, of course, is a master at both views.

The good NFL scout will see things like this: Are the heels of the defensive lineman way off the ground or closer to the ground? If they are closer to the ground, it means he has decent ankle flexion. Just look at a player in a three-point stance. If his heels are three or four inches off the ground, that's almost a ninety-degree angle. He is likely going to be stiff in the ankles and not have the explosion needed to get off the mark.

Saban can see all that, and he can see it in an instant.

Here is a key thing about Nick's approach to scouting teams in college:

In the NFL, you are trying to get the football to your best playmaker, while the defense is trying to take away that first option. What I found in college is that coaches are more concerned about their schemes and systems. If their scheme has a successful pass to the left, it doesn't matter if a great corner such as Darrelle Revis is over there to the left, they are going to throw it at him anyway.

Saban might say, "Our best pass may be to the left, but that's where Darrelle Revis is, so let's stay away from him. Let's go after the guy on the other side, who is a street free agent."

Saban's goal is to make teams beat him left-handed. I don't see that across the board in college. Schools are scheme oriented. The pros play more of a personnel-driven game. They target certain aspects of an opponent, and that's how Saban thinks every week.

I saw this approach back in 1992 when Nick was defensive coordinator of the Browns. We were on *Monday Night Football* against the 49ers, and we played a hard Cover 2, jammed up their wide receivers Jerry Rice and John Taylor at the line with our cornerbacks, and won that game.

The game plan was to take away what the 49ers did best, which was the timing routes to Rice and Taylor. Now, the players still had to execute it, but Nick worked our guys all week at disrupting routes and breaking quarterback Steve Young's rhythm. Nick coached a "physical" Cover 2 that week. We wanted to push Young off his first read and make him look for his second or third option. The goal was to break down their timing, and it worked to perfection.

That game was a validation of Nick as a defensive coordinator in the NFL.

I remember being at my first Browns practice in 1991 with veteran linebackers Clay Mathews and Mike Johnson, two great, great guys. It was like trying to learn a new language when those two started discussing schemes with Saban.

In practice they were chirping out, "Bird, bird, bird, rabbit, rabbit,

rabbit." They were reading stances and formations and calling out the run or the pass. That was the first time I had been exposed to that kind of intel.

Saban had coached for Jerry Glanville for two years at the Oilers, and the Browns were his first chance in the NFL as a defensive coordinator. This was his defense now, but veteran players will always challenge a new, young coach and find out what he's made of. The veterans can be skeptical about a new coach and first-time coordinator. Early on in Nick's tenure, Clay Mathews would ask how Nick wanted a certain route to be played, almost in a way that said, "Hey, we know football, too." Mike Johnson would do the same thing.

At times the veterans had philosophical disagreements with Nick, and he was open to suggestions from Clay and Mike because he had great respect for them. Clay and Mike could tell Nick, "I don't think this is going to work" or "Let's do it this way when they motion to go to slot." The approach was more collaborative than it is now at Alabama, no question about that.

The Cleveland veterans figured out quickly that Nick was further advanced than your typical college coach coming into the pro game. He was much more intense and much more savvy on the X's and O's.

You look at Nick Saban back in 1991 through 1994 and he was trying to prove himself. He was a demanding coach, but he was also breaking into the league at that next level as a coordinator. At times he would put his foot down and say, "This is how we are doing it," but in the meeting room with the Browns back in the early 1990s, he was principled but open to players' suggestions.

So fast-forward to where he is now when he walks into that defensive team room at Alabama. There may be some debate about a particular scheme or how to play against a certain route combination when he is talking upstairs with the coaches, but once they are in front of the players, Nick Saban sets the table for the game plan to be installed his way. And that is not to say that defensive coordinator Jeremy Pruitt doesn't have his own ideas and thoughts, he absolutely does, and that's why he and Coach Saban work so well together, because Nick has a true appreciation for someone who understands the game at his level.

Nick might have been respectful of the veterans in Cleveland, but he was tough on rookies. He sat on Eric Turner in 1991, I'll tell you that. I was tight ends coach at UCLA when Eric was an All-American free safety there in 1990, and who knew four months later we would both be in Cleveland working for Nick Saban.

Nick felt that he had to get Eric reined in and teach him the subtleties of the game and discipline with his eyes and being more vocal on the field. Nick applied an intentional pressure.

I picked up Eric the day he arrived in Cleveland after the draft. We were thirty minutes later than the schedule said we should arrive back at the Browns complex. This was Eric's first day in the facility, mind you, as the no. 2 overall choice in the 1990 draft. Still, Nick let him know it better not happen again. It wasn't Eric's fault, but Nick acted as if it were. He didn't let him off easy on anything.

Eric was one of the top prospects in the country and about to become an instant millionaire, but Nick coached him as if it were his first day of ever playing football.

It's just like the five-star showing up in Tuscaloosa. It doesn't matter what your background is, when you fall under Nick's coaching, his tutoring, it is going to be his way or get out. There can be some butting of heads, but if that player will commit to the techniques and fundamentals that are required, he will become a good player at the college and, maybe even, pro level.

By 1994, Eric had nine interceptions and the team made the playoffs. Rick Venturi had been hired as the secondary coach for the 1994 season to take some of the load off Nick, who had been defensive coordinator and secondary coach. One of Rick's jobs was to bring along Eric Turner. He and Nick turned him into one of the best players in the NFL in 1994, not only with interceptions and pass breakups, but with sacks.

Nick and Rick came up with a delayed blitz for Turner to utilize his explosiveness. The Mike linebacker would come up the middle on a blitz and the fullback would pick him up. Well, the Mike would grab the fullback and Eric would be coming full speed from behind as the "trailer" blitzer. Not everyone had that concept back then.

Players and coaches have to understand that Nick is going to test them, and at some point you are probably going to say to yourself, "This guy is impossible. I can't do this anymore." That's what happened in Cleveland. When it came to rookies and young defensive backs, Nick was the bad cop, and I was the good cop.

We had Stevon Moore, a Plan B free agent, a super human being. He was from Wiggins, Mississippi, and had played at Ole Miss and then the New York Jets. The whole Saban methodology was different to him upon his arrival. Nick's system and lingo were hard for Stevon to understand, and Nick would rip him on the practice field. I would pull Stevon off to the side and tell him, "Forget the bad part. Here is what he is trying to tell you, and all you have to do is look at it this way."

How did the relationship work out between Nick and Stevon? Moore was the junior college coach who called Nick in 2007 and said, "Hey, we got this noseguard down here that fits your 3-4 defense perfectly." It was Terrence Cody.

I was younger than some of the players and the same age as some others. When you are in the NFL, you must be able to talk to the players, and they don't care if you are fifty years old or twenty-two, if you can give them something that will help them become a better player and make more money, then they will respond to a coach of any age.

Alabama trains its analysts, who are behind the scenes, to break down the opponent and look for all the opponent's tips on "birds and rabbits," the passes and runs. Those tips are there. You just have to dissect film and find them. It takes hours of watching tape, and the players love you for it.

Maybe the left guard barely has his fingertips touching the ground in a left-handed opponent's stance. An Alabama analyst has noticed it and has tipped off the defensive line that means a pass is coming.

Perhaps the left guard has got more weight on his left hand, and an analyst—maybe another veteran coach such as Joe Pendry—has found it. The Mike linebacker is coached during the week to look for that tip and yell, "Rabbit, rabbit, rabbit," it's a run. That's all part of eye control and coaching.

So when you take the five-star athlete, the five-star development, the five-star coaching, and you add intelligence-gathering on a scale that is unmatched elsewhere in college football, you are going to be in the hunt every season and win four national championships in eight years.

You know all those analysts Alabama has hired the last five years? Believe me, they are there for a reason, and they are given specific tasks to help win games.

All of us who were in Cleveland in the 1990s gained an appreciation for the work ethic required to meet every eventuality on game day. We didn't leave a lot of stones unturned, no detail was too small, and that came from Belichick. It resonated through the whole staff. Bill was such a detail-oriented person it put pressure on everybody else to be the same thing.

This demanding style said, "Look, this is the NFL and it's hard to win. Everybody has talent, let's find an edge."

The edge might come from watching an extra tape of a game. There might be additional study on an opponent's third-down reel. Going beyond the minimum started with Bill, and Nick applied it to the defense. I promise you, we led the league in "projects" both during and after the season.

Rick Venturi had been in the NFL twelve years when Belichick hired him. He had not coached the secondary, but Bill wanted him there for his overall defensive expertise and experience. Saban and Rick met every Saturday from March until training camp in 1994, and Saban taught Rick every scheme and detail about coaching defensive backs.

Rick made a notebook, which he still has, and he thinks that notebook should be in the Hall of Fame.

Rick has told me, "There is not a better defensive backs coach who has walked the planet than Nick Saban, NFL or college. No one knows more. He is the gold standard."

Rick said he could use that notebook, created twenty-three years ago, to coach defensive backs today. It was technique, footwork, body control, and a series of "absolutes" for secondary play. When Rick coached the New Orleans Saints' defense and Nick was at LSU, Rick had Saban come talk to his staff about defensive backs. Imagine that. A college coach teaching NFL coaches.

The drills we used in 1991 when I was Nick's assistant are essentially the same fundamentals taught today at Alabama.

We had to play in the same division in 1994 with Houston and quarterback Warren Moon and the run-and-shoot offense. Belichick lined up a preseason minicamp of three days against the Atlanta Falcons, which ran the same offense as Houston. Nick put in a defense where the entire "back seven," linebackers and secondary, turned instantaneously on the movement of the offset running back. If the running back went one direction, our defense turned that way and became zone on the front side and man-to-man on the back side. In other words, fourteen eyeballs had to see the same thing for the plan to work.

The Falcons smoked us on the first day as we tried to sync up that scheme. By the third day we were winning the scrimmages. We beat Houston in the regular season and won eleven games and a wild-card game against the New England Patriots. That was pure Nick Saban.

Venturi did a lot of game planning with Nick in 1994 when the Browns turned themselves around. Rick always marveled over how Nick could take the big picture of a defense and simplify it for a player.

Nick never ever wanted his man-to-man defense in the secondary to play "off." The idea was always to "choke off" the offense, applying constant pressure, rushing the quarterback and challenging every throw downfield. Sound familiar? The 2016 Alabama defense was suffocating in pressuring the QB and confronting routes down-field.

Rick says it was not wise to use the term *keep it simple* around Nick Saban. Saban heard Rick say it once, by mistake—"Hey, keep it simple"—and Saban bellowed, "Dammit, Rick, simple is not always better. Sometimes complex is better."

Rick says Saban always coached toughness in the secondary. Nick wanted the players to be hitters and to never concede anything. They had to learn how to play bump-and-run man-to-man, but to always know there is help somewhere.

If I've heard Nick Saban say it once, I've heard it hundreds of times: "Cornerbacks need to be able to do three things: cover man-to-man, tackle, and play the ball in the air."

When I was at the Ravens as the scouting director, we developed the Triangles of Success for each position with Saban's trifecta of what a cornerback needs being the model. We used that Saban approach to drill down into what it takes to be a successful center, tight end, or defensive tackle and created a Triangle of Success for those positions, as well.

On game day, Nick was always on the field; he wanted to coordinate the defense from the sideline. I was his set of his eyes in the coaching box above the field. One coach would look at the front; I watched the pass routes and our defensive backs. During those years, we had Polaroids, black-and-white pictures that were printed on the sidelines to show the opponent's formations and plays. These pics were taken both pre-snap and when the QB would hand the football off or reach the apex of his drop.

(In 2016, Microsoft paid $400 million to have their Surface tablet on the NFL sidelines, only to have Bill Belichick destroy his in disgust because of its inconsistent execution. He referenced going back to the days of the Polaroids in his postgame news conference.)

Twenty-five years ago, Nick Saban was more impatient and wound even tighter than he appears today. It was tough to see how much everyone was learning and growing as individual coaches and scouts, because the demanding atmosphere did not allow for a moment of self-satisfaction. It was not much fun during the week back then, but Sunday, game day, was a completely different experience. It was exhilarating, the culmination of all the preparation coming to life and paying off with a win on third down or a short yardage stop.

It was pure strategy and adjustments and thinking on the fly. It was Saban and Belichick reviewing a drive, going through the pictures, and coming up with a plan for the next series. It was me describing to Nick how the left corner did not sink in Cover 2 or how the outside linebacker widened too far in Quarters with no threat to the flat and opened up a throwing lane to the inside. It was football strategy at the highest level with two of the best coaches in history on the same headsets.

I learned a ton from Nick Saban, which helped my career first as a coach, then as a scout, and ultimately as an NFL general manager. I also had a chance to share some of that experience of working with Nick with a number of others over the years.

When Nick was the head coach at Michigan State, I went to East Lansing to scout some players for the Browns. A young assistant coach walked in while I was watching tape and said, "I'm Mel Tucker, I'm a graduate assistant here. Are you Phil Savage?"

"Yes."

"Man, I don't know what you did on those tape breakdowns and how Nick wanted you to watch the tape, but you have to show me what to do because he is on my ass all day every day about it. He says you're the best one he ever had to do it."

"That's funny. He never told me that. I was getting my ass chewed out just like you guys."

That's when Mel and I became good friends. Saban wanted those pads, two plays per sheet, sorted out and ready to go when he was the head coach at Michigan State. That's the underpinnings of the preparation needed to get ready for an opponent. "We don't want to be talking about this on Sunday," as Belichick has so famously said.

Here is a snapshot of that Saban/Belichick culture. In 1993, the

Browns staff coached one of the Senior Bowl teams. I was going to be working in my hometown, Mobile, for a week in late January.

I think I spent a grand total of fifteen minutes visiting my parents at our house during the entire six days we were there.

Belichick wasn't satisfied for us to work with just our team of college prospects. He wanted us to maximize our experience in Mobile, so while he and the other coaches met with our team, Ernie Adams, his longtime aide, and I would go watch and study the other squad's practices and players.

We were doing two jobs in one day, evaluating both the North and the South teams.

While most NFL coaches and scouting staffs were attending practices and meeting for a few hours, then going to eat Gulf seafood on the causeway, the Browns staff worked 6:00 a.m. to 2:00 a.m. We were not only preparing for the game, we were getting a jump start on the 1993 NFL draft.

I started jogging every day in July 1987 with Tommy Bowden, who was on the staff with me at Alabama. Tommy would later go on to be the head coach at Tulane and Clemson. Since then, in only one three-day stretch in the last thirty years have I not found time to work out. That one time was the 1993 Senior Bowl with Belichick and Saban. I might miss a day here and there, but never three in a row as in that week. There was no time to even walk around the block in downtown Mobile.

That Senior Bowl week I learned an early scouting lesson.

Ernie and I were watching Blaine Bishop, a short, bowlegged corner from Ball State. He was just five feet nine and a half, but was an aggressive defender who might not have an ideal position. According to most scouts, he was not fast enough for NFL corner and was too small for safety. But he was all-out in those Senior Bowl practices. Blaine hit people, covered people, and was a general nuisance to the offense. He wanted a professional football career and was putting himself out there in a big way.

So this is the lesson in scouting: Every once in a while outliers, players who do not fit the mold—too short, too slow, too light—can still play. A scout might be impressed with a player's skill, but backs off because the critical factors of height/weight/speed do not measure up. You Alabama fans remember defensive back Javier Arenas, right?

The NFL shrugged at Blaine Bishop's performance that week at the Senior Bowl. He wasn't drafted high, an eighth-round pick of the Houston Oilers in 1993, which means he wouldn't even have been drafted in 2017 in a seven-round draft.

Bishop had a terrific career with the Oilers/Tennessee Titans as a safety in Jeff Fisher's hybrid 46 defense. His career was worthy of a second- or third-round pick. One team I know backed off him because they thought he was so aggressive that as a rookie he might get a veteran hurt in training camp. That was our team, the Browns. Flash to Arenas. He had a terrific career at Alabama after receiving just one Division I scholarship offer out of high school.

We all have misses. Blaine, despite his height, was a perfect fit for the Titans. Bishop made his way in the NFL with that competitiveness he showed at the Senior Bowl, and we looked right past it. There's one of Ozzie Newsome's skeletons for you.

Skeletons never weigh Nick Saban down. He might make a mistake calling a coverage—just like a lot of coaches—but he was confident in his ability to scheme and coach NFL players through the week.

Throughout his time with the Browns, I always thought Nick wanted to prove to Bill he was just as knowledgeable on the defensive side of the ball as Belichick. We had game-plan sessions with volumes and volumes of information. We had every piece of information you could imagine to defend for base downs, sub downs, pressures, and special situations. Nick thought of everything. We were never underprepared. We might not execute, but we had answers.

We would get in our staff meeting, though, and Bill would try to simplify all of it. Nick would put everything in the game plan, and Bill would say, "We're going to do this and this, and we're not going to do this." Nick knew what he was doing twenty-three years ago, but the head coach is the head coach and Bill ruled.

I think that is one of the contrasts between the two. Nick wants a full toolbox, every remedy for every situation. Bill wants a hammer and a screwdriver.

Few people have worked for Homer Smith and Nick Saban and Bill Belichick, three brilliant minds in football. I might be the only one. I learned to be determined, resourceful, and complete. I learned that mistakes are part of the business, and that overpreparation and having quick answers on game day were requirements of the job.

What Saban has done at Alabama is limit mistakes because of the training of the eyes across the organization. You need to see things that are right in front of you and make immediate decisions. Sometimes it is easy to make decisions, such as in 2007 with Saban's first Alabama team. He saw a Crimson Tide team with little NFL-caliber talent in its junior and senior classes. He didn't need to look at tape, he saw it with his own two eyes on the practice field and then recognized it again in a landmark Alabama game in 2007 against LSU.

That 2007 Alabama-LSU game in Tuscaloosa, which I attended as an NFL general manager, was a reckoning for Alabama. The Crimson Tide was far behind LSU in talent and schemes. Saban saw just how far behind, and he went out and did something about it.

7

A TILT TOWARD
THE TIGERS

...AND THEN A TURNAROUND

An hour before Alabama's kickoff against no. 3 LSU on November 3, 2007, I was standing on the sidelines of Bryant-Denny Stadium next to Rich McKay, the president of the Atlanta Falcons. I was the general manager of the Cleveland Browns, and Rich and I were among a group of ten to twelve NFL scouts watching the pregame warm-ups of the Tigers and the Crimson Tide.

None of us were on the Alabama side of the 50-yard line evaluating Bama's players. We were all on the LSU end of the field evaluating the Tigers, which included players Nick Saban had signed for LSU before he left for the Miami Dolphins in 2005.

I turned to McKay and said, "We're all standing down here on the LSU side, but in three or four years, we'll be at the other end of the field looking at Alabama's players."

"You're exactly right," Rich said. "Nick is going to get players in here."

It didn't take three or four years for us to move thirty yards. It didn't even take a year for a population shift of scouts to the Bama side of the 50.

It took just three months.

On February 6, 2008, Alabama signed a recruiting class that included Julio Jones, Courtney Upshaw, Barrett Jones, Mark Barron, Mark Ingram, Dont'a Hightower, Terrence Cody, Brad Smelley, and Michael Williams. The class would later add Marcell Dareus. It has been called one of the greatest recruiting classes in the history of college football because that group became part of three teams that won national titles.

That February the page turned at Alabama under Nick Saban. Talent started coming in the door to supplement good players left over from the Mike Shula era. Then that talent started being developed. Then a practice culture took root. All around the program was a new mind-set, something akin to twenty-eight-hour days and eight-day weeks. You get the point, right?

Greg McElroy, the quarterback of the 2009 national championship team, and a recruit of Saban predecessor Mike Shula, said he saw an overnight transformation in the look of the roster. Big, fast people started filling up the meeting rooms in August 2008, just as McKay and I predicted.

"It was a different feel in regards to the recruits," McElroy said. "They brought in guys that were program-changing guys. There was a foundation of good players in 2006, but the depth wasn't there and we weren't as skilled as we needed to be to compete for a national championship. Then the bodies began to change and we got depth and skill.

"Julio was obviously one of those program changers because at seventeen years old he looked like an NFL receiver. But the guy that stuck out the most and made me go 'Wow' was Michael Williams, who was a defensive end who transitioned to tight end. We had a lot of good-looking players, guys who looked the part of elite college players, but when Michael Williams walked through the door, he was six-foot-seven, 280 pounds, and a freshman in college. It was pretty amazing."

That Alabama-LSU game in 2007 was a benchmark for the Bama program because it was the last time in the rivalry that the Tigers could physically lord over the Tide. I'm positive Saban looked across the field at the LSU team he helped recruit—a team that won the 2007 national championship—and thought one thing:

"WE'RE CHANGING THIS PICTURE."

One man predicted that Nick was going to circle back to the college game after the NFL and sign a class like Julio and Ingram et al. Jack Marucci is the head athletic trainer at LSU, and he knew in 2005, when Nick left for the Miami Dolphins, that Nick was going to be back in the college game. Jack is one of my closest friends in football. We were graduate assistants together at Alabama under Bill Curry in the late 1980s. Jack ended up at Florida State for a number of seasons working for Coach Bobby Bowden before landing at LSU as the athletic trainer.

Jack was at LSU when Nick arrived as the Tigers' coach in 2000. Jack called me when it was rumored that Nick was going to become the LSU coach, and I gave him some advice on how he might keep his job with the new boss and become a trusted confidant of his.

Their relationship was strong over five seasons, and Jack became a core member of Nick's staff.

I was on the verge of accepting the position of general manager with the Cleveland Browns on New Year's Day 2005 when Iowa defeated LSU on a last-minute drive. That night, Jack called to tell me that Nick was leaving for the Dolphins. Jack said, "Nick's got to take it. Five years, twenty-five million dollars, but mark my words, he will be back in college football within three years."

We thought Nick might come back and be the coach of Notre Dame, or West Virginia, his home-state school or Georgia, which he talked about. Nick owns a house on a lake in Georgia. Alabama never crossed our minds.

Two seasons later, it happened. Nick went back to the college game as the coach at Alabama.

I called Jack, and we laughed about how his prognostication had come true. We both agreed that the Crimson Tide makeover was about to begin. Alabama was about to become bigger and faster and much more competitive. The rough ride of the past ten years was about to end.

Alabama's program had been ransacked by coaching changes and NCAA sanctions from 2001 to 2007. All you had to do was look at the 2008 NFL draft to see how depleted the roster had become in NFL talent. Alabama had zero players picked, while Vanderbilt had three selected. Think about that for a moment.

Indeed, from 1997 to 2006, Alabama was a modest 67-55. It had fallen behind LSU, Florida, and Georgia in talent and had lost five straight to Auburn when Saban was hired in January 2007.

Alabama's reclaiming of its place as a national powerhouse happened faster than anyone imagined, including Nick Saban. In May 2007, he told me in so many words, "This program is thirty years behind where it needs to be in recruiting, video technology, and facilities. We have some catching up to do."

Remember, Alabama had four coaches in five years. That's one of the reasons it fell behind the rest of the SEC. Dennis Franchione abruptly left in 2002 for Texas A&M. Mike Price was hired in December 2002, then fired in May 2003 after his foray into a Pensacola strip club. Mike Shula was immediately named head coach and then terminated after the 2006 season. Saban arrived in January 2007.

The coaches all had their own philosophies and offensive and defensive schemes. So imagine the scene around the program from 2001 to 2007. Four different head coaches had proclaimed how things were going to be inside the program. A cast of assistant coaches also came and went, so high school recruits were confused. Prospects had no time to build critical relationships with staff. Even a proud program such as Alabama's cannot withstand that kind of upheaval and expect to win.

I think back to the circumstances of Price's departure in 2003. Before his ill-fated trip to Pensacola—the Arety's Angels strip club episode—he had been warned by Mal Moore to stop buying drinks for students on campus. Then, the morning of a scheduled golf trip to

Pensacola, an Alabama track athlete suddenly died, and Mal stayed behind in T-Town instead of traveling with Price to the Gulf Coast.

I've always believed when Price landed in Pensacola, he may well have thought that he was in South Florida and not the Panhandle, the northwest part of the state that is almost like south Alabama in its passion for the Crimson Tide. When you're the Washington State coach, you can stay relatively anonymous in your travels across the Palouse, but that's not the case when you are the head coach at Alabama.

Price ended up at an adult-entertainment establishment, an activity he would never have considered had Coach Moore been with him, and one thing led to another. The strippers wound up at his hotel and tried to charge $1,000 to his room. It did not take long for this news to go public.

The Alabama coach did not know the strippers, but they recognized him. The fifty-seven-year-old coach, who was going to make $10 million and modernize the Crimson Tide offense with his passing game, was quickly fired.

Alabama fell off the map with a 4-9 season in 2003 and 6-6 in 2004 for another reason. The Crimson Tide had to endure scholarship limitations—twenty-one lost scholarships over three years—because of NCAA sanctions for major violations. Bama had just nineteen scholarship players in the class of 2004 because of sanctions, which was Shula's first recruiting class. He recruited some NFL draft picks in his tenure—running back Glenn Coffee, offensive tackle Andre Smith, offensive guard Mike Johnson, quarterback Greg McElroy, defensive back/return man Javier Arenas, defensive lineman Brandon Deaderick—but it was not enough talent to win an SEC championship, much less a national championship.

(You have to give Mike credit, though. some of his recruits were on the 2008 team that was undefeated in the regular season and on the 2009 team that won the national title.)

Not only were the sanctions wearing Bama down, but the NCAA in 2002 threatened Alabama with the Death Penalty, a shuttering of the program. Imagine the chill that can put into a high school coach, player, or booster: your favorite school is in a police lineup. The threat of the Death Penalty was real; former NCAA Division I Committee on Infractions chair Tom Yeager confirmed that to Dennis Dodd of CBS Sports in 2015.

Nick Saban, I'm sure, would never have set foot in Tuscaloosa if the NCAA had shut down the program. The Death Penalty would really have put Alabama thirty years behind. Just look at what happened at SMU.

The first thing Nick had to do when he was hired was get off the celebrity tour bus. The Alabama football coach is a figurehead in the state, and the fans wanted to see their new coach. While he recruited in the spring of 2007, Nick also made speaking stops to get acquainted with his win-starved constituents. But he grew weary of it because it took too much time. Saban didn't object to meeting the people, but everyone affiliated with the program needed to get their priorities in order.

"Do they want me to make speeches or coach the football team?" Nick asked. "I can't do both."

Saban understood that Alabama was not preordained as a permanent winner, and he had to dig in as a coach and a recruiter. Eventually, Saban cut a deal. He would give Mal Moore and the university a reasonable number of speeches per year, and they would be scheduled well in advance. Nick was able to reduce some of his road time, and I'm sure the fans are not unhappy with the trade-off in national titles.

Nick was not starting from scratch in 2007. The tradition and passion around the program were tangible elements that could trigger a turnaround. You can work with that in recruiting. A month after he was hired, Signing Day 2007, he was able to hang on to some key Shula recruits, which included the immensely talented linebacker Rolando McClain.

Still, significant restocking had to be done, and Nick went to work in the winter and spring of 2007 with his recruiting pitch that had worked successfully at LSU.

"MAKE A FORTY-YEAR DECISION, NOT A FOUR-YEAR DECISION."

Saban told Alabama's prospects that choosing a school would impact their lives for forty years, not just four years of college. Corey Webster, the All-SEC cornerback, said Saban had the same message for LSU recruits seven years earlier. Saban built a fence around Louisiana to keep other college programs out and the top prospects in, and it led to two national championships in five seasons.

Meanwhile, the recruiting fence around Alabama was getting lower and easier to climb over to leave the state, or to walk across to rival Auburn. Brad Smelley, who was part of the epic 2008 recruiting class, committed to Alabama in the spring of 2007, but he and other in-state prospects had been uneasy about the Alabama program prior to Saban's arrival.

Ole Miss and Tennessee had also offered a scholarship to Smelley, who was a multitalented player at American Christian Academy in Tuscaloosa: linebacker, receiver, quarterback. He was practically a lock for Bama when offensive line coach Joe Pendry started recruiting him. But the door was cracked open just a little for Smelley to look elsewhere for a degree and a college football career.

"Other schools had been coming into the state, and Alabama was letting some of the prospects go, not getting all of them," Smelley said. "Alabama was my place; I had been sitting on the fifty-yard line for games since I was a kid, but I don't know, the program just wasn't going in the right direction. I guess I was pretty certain I was going there, but . . ."

Then Saban was hired in January 2007, and there were no more ifs, ands, or buts. The top in-state prospects suddenly had a different perspective. People were excited about the program again, Smelley said, and in-state prospects had a less difficult decision to make.

"All the in-state prospects were ready for someone to take the bull by the horns," Smelley said. "When Coach got the job, there was a buzz again when I went to games. Everyone knew the program was about to change, and it was about to change fast.

"We all saw his pedigree and how he coached. So the best players in the state jumped on board and started recruiting each other. Alabama was turning in another direction."

While Smelley was almost a lock for Bama, Saban did not take anything for granted to make sure he signed. Nick got involved in Smelley's recruitment and met with him in the press box of the ACA stadium one afternoon. Saban and Pendry laid out the plan for him to become the H-back in their offense. Nick Saban does not do courtesy calls, and he wasn't just showing up because Smelley was a Tuscaloosa-area high school star and it looked good for the Alabama head coach to be at his high school.

Saban recruits as earnestly as he coaches and does not leave a lot to chance. He saw Smelley's potential as a receiver and did not want to lose him, so Nick stayed active in closing the deal. Smelley was light, 195–200 pounds, but Saban saw the potential of Smelley's playing different positions. Saban liked his makeup, his football savvy, his ability to get open, and his hands. Saban kept recruiting him even after Smelley committed to Alabama. That's recruiting at its best.

In the fall of 2008, after Smelley had passed for over 300 yards in a high school playoff game, Pendry told Smelley that Alabama would even give him a chance to play quarterback. It was a done deal, Saban-style. The head coach was not leaving any room for Smelley to go somewhere else. He was going to give the kid a chance to be whom he wanted to be. Smelley became a key contributor at tight end, where he had 7 catches against LSU in the 2011-season national championship game that Bama won, 21–0.

"He came to the house, talked to my parents, and he visited me at school a few times," Smelley said. "The one thing I remember he said that impressed us was 'We're going to help you be a better man by the time you leave the program.' It sounds like a cliché until you hear it from one of the best coaches in the history of the game."

Alabama's 2008 recruiting class, which was Saban's first full recruiting effort, was a mirror of the 2001 LSU class. It was full of big men; big bodies, big frames, just big guys. That class gave rise to a slogan you first heard at LSU when Saban was there: big people beat up little people.

Saban stayed fixed on his height/weight/speed matrix in recruiting and did not detour those first two seasons. He identified his players and closed deals. Tom Lemming, the national recruiting analyst, routinely talks to high school football players as they are being recruited, and over the years they have told Lemming that Saban talking to parents in a living room is unmatched in persuasiveness. Only Urban Meyer is close.

Linebacker Courtney Upshaw, who was in the Alabama class of 2008, said Auburn and Georgia were his front-runners until Saban came to Eufaula, Alabama, Upshaw's hometown. The new head coach told Upshaw, "You will get a degree and we will win."

"He didn't have to work very hard for me," Upshaw said. "I knew I was going to Alabama pretty quickly after I met him."

By 2011, Nick had another recruiting pitch that was resonating more deeply with high school players:

"IF YOU WANT TO PLAY IN THE NFL, COME PLAY FOR ME."

Nick didn't have to say NFL directly all of the time because Alabama was loading its media guide with color pictures of its players on draft day. Every major program makes the NFL wonderland seem accessible, but only if you use their school as a launching point. Alabama really sold it. The Tide sold it so well the NCAA started to restrict the number of pages allowed in the media guide because of all the costs associated with the promotion. One SEC official said, "Alabama has taken it to a new level with the media guide."

(Oregon had also taken its marketing campaign a little too far starting in 2005. The Ducks designed comic books for each of its recruits, portraying them as superheroes, and sent those out to recruits a page at a time.)

The media guide restrictions became Saban Rule I.

Then there was Saban Rule II.

The NCAA cracked down in the summer of 2007 and banned coaches from making off-campus visits from mid-April to the end of May because of complaints that college head coaches were illegally "bumping" into players during a noncontact period. It was called the Saban Rule, but it also affected Florida's Urban Meyer and Southern California's Pete Carroll, who were also tireless recruiters.

The rule was put into effect after the 2007 spring recruiting period, but by that time Saban had teed up his 2008 class. The players in that class—Julio, Dont'a, Upshaw, and others—were finishing their junior years of high school, and Saban was putting them on the bus thanks to his nonstop visits to high schools.

Saban's hard push in the 2007 spring recruiting period ties back into his recruiting mandate, which is to get his own visual of a player, a "live" look at either a baseball game or a track meet, or maybe a spring football practice, or even of a walk down a hallway. He might not always have been able to shake the player's hand, but Saban could see him up close one way or another and start to form an opinion of whether the player fit his plan.

Just remember that familiar picture of Saban on the practice field, his head cocked down underneath that straw hat, judging flexibility and explosiveness. He could make judgments of players even if they were in street clothes at schools.

Saban wasn't the only coach the NCAA took aim at for recruiting. Ron Zook, when he was the head coach at Florida from 2002 to 2004, was up and down in a private plane day after day during one spring recruiting period. Zook said if a Florida town had a great player, the local booster club would set up an event in said town so Zook could fly in and be visible in the high school during the day and speak to the boosters that night. Zook was so successful with his all-in approach that his three recruiting classes made up twenty-two of twenty-four starters for Florida's 2006 national champions. Zook said that in one recruiting period he once visited 101 high schools.

That's when the NCAA started to get phone calls from rival coaches complaining about Saban, Zook, Meyer, and Carroll. "Those coaches just wanted to go play golf," Zook said of the coaches calling the NCAA and complaining. "They did not get out there and recruit like Nick and me."

In the summer of 2007, the NCAA banned coaches from off-campus visits in the spring, starting in 2008. Zook, who was coaching at Illinois by 2007, said he called Saban the day after the rule was put in and told the Alabama coach that the rule was directed at both of them. "Nick, they put us on the sidelines," Zook said he told Saban.

It is the Zook-Saban Rule, the Zooker has reminded people, not the Saban Rule. It figures that Ron Zook's father was a traveling salesman.

Saban's 2007 spring recruiting march could do nothing to save the 2007 Alabama season (7-6) a few months later. The Tide was 6-2 when it met LSU that November, and it just didn't have enough skill for the upset against the Tigers. Alabama lost four of its last five games, including another bitter defeat to Auburn.

That 2007 team was in the tank by the end of November, which brings me to another aspect of the Saban Era that started with that LSU game ten years ago.

I call it the carrot. When the Crimson Tide lost to LSU and dropped out of the SEC Western Division race, the squad lost some motivation. The seniors had bought the Saban message until they were eliminated, then the attitude changed and they were done. I have no doubt some of the passion was stripped from the team by its disheartening loss to LSU, and it spiraled into defeats to Louisiana-Monroe and Mississippi State. Saban has, since then, always had that carrot dangling out in front of his teams: *we're playing for a championship*.

Since the start of the 2008 season, all but three of Alabama's regular-season games have had national championship implications, which is an amazing run. For nine straight years, the Tide has entered the month of November in the hunt for a national championship. The Alabama program is not for the faint of heart, but when you take away the shot at championships and rings, it's tough to keep going.

The big carrot might have been gone for the 2007 team by the time it lost to LSU in 2007, but Alabama had something else to grab on to with that LSU game—the proverbial silver lining. LSU needed a late turnover to pull out a 41–34 win, and even though it was a loss, you thought, "Wait a minute. If Bama can play LSU off its feet like this with one-sixth of the talent LSU has, what's it going to be like when Nick Saban gets his own players and systems put in place?"

Here are two key things to remember about "systems," said McElroy, who was the backup quarterback in 2007. These are often overlooked as to why Alabama built a winner so fast.

- When he got the job in 2007, Saban treated the players left behind from the Shula era as his own players. He did not immediately put them down by telling people, "I have to get my own guys in here." McElroy never heard that declaration.
- Saban pushed and developed Shula's recruits as if they were his own recruits. There were no alibis that this player was "too small" or this player was "too slow."

Shula had just three recruiting classes before he was fired and replaced by Saban. Those Shula players would be core contributors to the 2008 team under Saban that went 12-0 in the regular season, and the team that was unbeaten and won the 2009 national title.

"There were a lot of role players in those 2005, 2006 classes that were significant contributors for the 2008 and 2009 teams," McElroy said. "Maybe those '05 and '06 classes didn't have the star power of 2008 class, but they were foundational players. The development of those guys in 2005 and 2006 was accelerated when Coach was brought in.

"That's what is most impressive to me. He recruits extremely well and finds guys that do what he wants to do, but he took guys that were there when he got to Alabama and put them on the field and maximized their ability. He filled in with the 2008 freshmen and put together a championship team with players he did not recruit."

When they got off the bus, the 2006 recruits were not imposing. One of those players was Arenas, who was five feet eight. With the Saban height/weight/speed recruiting matrix, Arenas, a defensive back, would likely not even be recruited by the current Tide program.

Arenas was hardly recruited by Division I schools as it was. He had one other offer, and that was to Florida International University. Alabama recruited Arenas because the Tide was desperate for a return man after the horrific leg injury to Tyrone Prothro against Florida on October 1, 2005.

Arenas came in, and by the time he left in 2009 he was a standout defensive back on the slot receiver. Known as the Star in Saban's lexicon, Arenas became a good kick returner, too.

McElroy said half the team in 2008 and 2009 were made up of players from the recruiting classes before Saban arrived.

"When the 2006 guys got on campus, if you would have told me we would win a national championship in three years, I would have gone, 'I don't know about that,'" McElroy said. "It took Coach to get us there. He doesn't get enough credit for that."

McElroy said people should go back and really study the 2008 and 2009 teams, which were 24-0 in the regular season, and see just how many NFL guys were starters on those teams.

"It's not as many as you think," the quarterback said.

The offensive line of the national championship team had two steady NFL players, guard Mike Johnson and tackle James Carpenter. Julio Jones was the only one of the wide receivers who had an NFL career. Mark Ingram, who won the Heisman Trophy, has played his first contract through with the New Orleans Saints. McElroy was part of the New York Jets from 2011 to 2013. Smelley played four years in the league, but he was not a three-down tight end for the 2009 team.

That's five starters from the 2009 offense that were drafted. Five, not eight, nine, or ten as most people would assume.

"Our 2009 team was close, we had chemistry," McElroy said. "We had some Pro Bowlers like Ingram and Julio. But remember, Hightower was out most of that season with an injury. We weren't as top-to-bottom talented as the Alabama teams you see now.

"That 2009 team survived off adversity because of how bad things were at the early part of our careers. We went six-seven, seven-six my first two years. We had been calloused a little bit and put through it and we were hungry."

The coaches really put McElroy through it. Some days in practice Saban and offensive line coach Joe Pendry were merciless with McElroy. They had a starting quarterback in 2007 and 2008 with veteran John Parker Wilson, but Saban and Pendry didn't think at first that McElroy was capable of replacing Wilson. They went after McElroy to test him to see if he could be handed the team once Wilson left.

"Coach's friend, Lonny Rosen, told me later that Coach didn't think I was the guy who could replace John Parker," McElroy said. Rosen is the sports psychologist from Michigan State who talks routinely with Saban on the mental training of athletes.

"That's the cool thing about Coach," McElroy said. "He doesn't come to conclusions about a player until he gives that player every opportunity to prove what he can do. Rosen told me that when Coach got to campus, he had to recruit a replacement for John Parker. He didn't know anything about me and he had no tape. He went into it believing he had to find a backup.

"But he gave me a chance to prove him wrong."

In 2009, Star Jackson, a prized recruit from Florida, was brought in to compete with McElroy. Jackson transferred to Georgia State. Thomas Darrah, a six-foot-six walk-on, got a look. McElroy said Darrah threw the ball as well as any quarterback McElroy ever saw in college or the NFL. Still, McElroy kept the job. AJ McCarron, a true freshman, was ruled out and redshirted.

"Coach changed his mind about me," McElroy said. "He was skeptical because I'm not the biggest guy in the world, and not the most physically intimidating quarterback you will see, but I had my fair share of strengths. There are coaches who come to conclusions and are unwilling to change. Coach changed his mind about me, and I don't think there are a lot of coaches like that."

The talent started flowing into the program using the 2008 class as a blueprint. Saban had a vision of what he wanted on the team, and when you actually get those players on the practice field, everybody in the program can see what the ideal wide receiver and outside linebacker looks like in person. The 2008 team was full of living, breathing examples of the Alabama prototype I wrote about in chapter 2. There was no theory.

That class was the powder keg, so to speak, the fuse for the program. That group won three out of four national titles.

"It's amazing to see Alabama's personnel now that I get to go everywhere in the country and compare what other teams have," said McElroy, who is an ESPN/SEC Network football analyst. "Ohio State and Alabama are in a league of their own, as far as how they look coming off the bus."

The Saban approach included much more than recruiting and development and forging a capable player through practice. The Alabama head coach got under the hood of the entire program and started fastening in new procedures, new strategies off the field, and used his vast experience to set his team up for victories. The head coach's full playbook came to bear on the SEC.

The Saban playbook even had a chapter on scheduling. Where could Alabama play to increase exposure to recruits? Where is the best stage and who is a fitting opponent? Could the fans get there?

Saban signed up for a 2008 game against Clemson in the Georgia Dome in Atlanta to start the season. Saban saw the high school talent in the state of Georgia and wanted to expand into the state and not leave it all for Auburn and Georgia. He told Gary Stokan, who runs the Chick-fil-A Kickoff Game, that Alabama's playing Clemson to start his second season in Tuscaloosa helped ignite the Crimson Tide program because it was on national television and the game was in the middle of the Georgia recruiting hotbed.

Saban has made it a habit to play these high profile season openers in football hotbeds such as Dallas and Atlanta. The Crimson Tide has played three season-opening games in Arlington at the Dallas Cowboy's magnificent AT&T Stadium, to get itself in front of recruits and spread its reach.

The other Saban scheduling move that sticks out was Alabama's arranging an off week after Tennessee and before the LSU game. By 2009 it was almost a matter of course that the Tide would have the week off before the Tigers, thanks to Saban. It was important because by week eight teams are feeling some of the grind of the season with injuries. Also, the physical nature of the LSU game demands a rested team (in 2012, Alabama beat Mississippi State in a rare game the Saturday before LSU).

Another part of the Saban playbook from 2007 is not a scheme, but a guy. Running backs coach Burton Burns. He is Saban's surrogate, a player's coach, father, and mentor. Burns is the last original member of the first Saban staff in Tuscaloosa.

Burns taught the position to Mark Ingram, Trent Richardson, Eddie Lacy, T. J. Yeldon, Derrick Henry, Damien Harris, and the emerging Bo Scarbrough. Burns coached the first Heisman Trophy winner, ever, at Alabama (Ingram). He coached one of the most dominant college backs of this era (Henry). If Alabama didn't have so many All-Americans at other positions, it would be known as Running Back U.

Burns went to Oklahoma in late January 2016 to watch an add-on recruit at running back named Josh Jacobs in a high school basketball game. Burns came back to Saban and said, "We need to offer him." Jacobs was a revelation his freshman season in 2016.

Burns is a legend in New Orleans. He was a successful high school coach there for years before he was hired at Tulane in 1994. Tommy Bowden said that when he took over as head coach at Tulane in 1997, his father, Florida State coach Bobby Bowden, told Tommy that whatever he did, he had to keep Burns on the Tulane staff.

For Tulane, Burns outrecruited Tennessee and Auburn for several sensational New Orleans high school players, Bowden said. Burns brought in the Offensive Player of the Year from New Orleans to play for the Tulane Green Wave, not LSU. Burns was no ordinary college football assistant coach, it seemed.

While at Clemson, Burns and Dabo Swinney won a colossal recruiting battle against the SEC for running back and future NFL player C. J. Spiller, who played high school ball in Florida.

When Bowden left for Clemson after an 11-0 season at Tulane in 1998, Burns went with him, but Nick Saban was stalking Burns. Saban tried to bring Burns to LSU when Saban was building his first staff in Baton Rouge, but Burton stuck with Bowden. When Nick got to Alabama in January 2007, however, the Crimson Tide had too much money for the Tigers. Burns walked into Bowden's office one day and said, "Nick made me an offer I can't refuse." Bowden hated to lose one of his most valuable and trusted coaches, but the allure of Alabama was too much.

Incidentally, Burton was first named wide receivers coach in January 2007, but moved to running backs a few weeks later when Steve Marshall, the new offensive line coach, left for Romeo Crennel's staff in Cleveland (where I was the GM) and Joe Pendry was moved from running backs to the offensive line, which opened up the spot.

Burton has recruited some sensational players out of Louisiana and away from LSU to Alabama. Safety Landon Collins, linebacker Tim Williams, and Lacy are just several. The Alabama players and staff have found Burns trustworthy, and that is the foundation of his success. He is a father figure and extremely respectful of other people.

Burton's running backs corps, if you noticed, is as consistent and dependable as he is. In 2016, they were working on a ratio of 145 touches for every fumble, which is remarkable. They are secure with the football because Burns emphasizes it every day and has taught them a physical, downhill approach to the run game. That's not surprising. When he played in college himself, Burns was a full-back in an I-formation offense at Nebraska. Burns and Saban are like-minded thinkers in believing that running backs should be 220-pound thumpers.

One more thing: an Alabama running back has a trademark look. A thickly muscled arm holds the football high and tight against the front of the shoulder pad with the hand above the elbow. Other schools teach it, but Burton Burns requires it.

Since 2007, running backs and defensive linemen, the positions with the greatest depth at Alabama, are the trademarks of Saban's teams. He gets those players because I think he truly enjoys recruiting. It is a break from the X's and O's. It is a whole different challenge. The recruiting wears out most mortals, but he keeps going and going and going. Once you have the taste of getting a commitment from a no. 1 recruit, you want the next one and the one after that, too.

Saban's skill at recruiting showed in 2008 with his first full recruiting class. Now you can really see his expertise with the stockpile of talent on the eighty-five-man scholarship roster. Players such as Ryan Anderson and Tim Williams, current NFL players, could not get on the field as full-time starters until their senior seasons in 2016 partly because of the waiting list of players in front of them.

Saban's recruiting made the rivalry with LSU extraordinary. By 2011, you could see the magnitude of the game just by looking at the two-deep rosters. When the Tide and Tigers played the Game of the Century on November 5, 2011, over sixty players in the game ended up getting a chance in the NFL.

That November 2011 game, which LSU won 9–6, was an NFL game wrapped in a college football setting.

So when you spin forward ten years—2007 to 2017—Alabama is the team on the sidelines with the cookie-cutter, dominant player at every position. It was exactly what McKay and I talked about in November 2007. Nick would get his players.

Nick lost that first game against LSU and Les Miles in 2007, but Saban went 6-2 against Miles and LSU before Les was fired in September 2016. Things have been turned upside down, and LSU is now the program trying to get traction under new coach Ed Orgeron.

Meanwhile, Alabama has become a routine stop for NFL scouts. To imagine not a single player from Alabama being picked in the 2008 NFL draft to where it stands now is a testament to Nick Saban's vision, work ethic, and ability to evaluate and then develop high school athletes into potential professional players.

From 2009 to 2016, Saban's Crimson Tide program has produced eighteen first-round draft picks and fifty-five overall selections. The scouting real estate on the Alabama side of the 50-yard line is back to being as valuable as beachfront property. The scouts' reason for getting back to the beachfront is Nick Saban, because they know his track record as an evaluator and developer of talent.

In 2005, after Nick Saban left the LSU facility for the last time, head trainer Jack Marucci called me and made his prediction that Nick would return to college football within three years. Sure enough, it was actually less than three seasons, but to our surprise, it wasn't Notre Dame, Georgia, or Texas, programs that always seemed to interest Nick. Nope, to the delight of the Crimson Tide faithful, it was Alabama, and the rest, as they say, is history.

Nick started reeling in players and developing them with fundamentals, then he started adding the polish with game plans and schemes and X's and O's. Nick was not going to just out-talent teams toe-to-toe, he was going to add creativity and wrinkles, modernize his offense, and install a variety of defensive looks. Like an accomplished construction contractor, Saban has filled his toolbox with all of the equipment needed to build a complete program and one that can win, again and again and again.

8

THE FULL TOOLBOX

SABAN HAS ALL THE DEVICES AND GADGETS TO WIN

Nick Saban has big, fast, skilled players. But that's not all he has. Nick has an ace up his sleeve, a rabbit in his hat, and can pull a quarter from behind your ear. Saban's teams have talent, but they also have the capacity to adjust and surprise.

It's not as easy as you think to hack into Nick Saban's mind.

He has the ability to call any scheme, or any play, on offense, defense, and special teams at any time. In ten years, Saban has built volume into the Alabama roster, that is, players of every style. He has all the tools needed to win.

But it's one thing to have tools, it is another to have the resolution to use them.

So rewind to Alabama versus Clemson for the 2015 national championship and the wholly unexpected onside kick in the fourth quarter. In my estimation, it is the signature play of the Saban Era because skill and daring were summoned from the Toolbox and combined to take a national championship, the fourth in eight years.

Here is the backstory. Ohio State was the inspiration, in case you didn't know.

The Clemson offense with quarterback Deshaun Watson had plundered the Alabama defense for three quarters. It was 24–24 and Nick had to steal a possession from Watson.

Saban gave the okay for an onside kick, a "pop" kick, as in pop fly.

Linebacker and special teams ace Dillon Lee said the kick was set up because, for the 2015 season, Alabama had changed its traditional spacing on kickoffs. In the 2014 College Football Playoff, the Crimson Tide had watched Ohio State bring its far-right kickoff coverage player all the way to the hash mark, squeezing eleven players into 33 yards of a 53-yard-wide field. The Buckeyes' idea was to cut off a quarter of the field from the kick return team and pin the returner to one side.

Alabama started doing the same thing in 2015, using its exceptional athletic ability to its advantage by pinning the opponent into 75 percent of the gridiron, left or right.

"The way we were lining up, everyone's kick return teams started cheating in because they were saying, 'Why would we stand way out there when the last person on the Alabama kickoff team is so far inside,'" Lee said. "They are thinking, 'Okay, Marlon Humphrey is really fast, so I have to move in from the sidelines and get as close to him as I can to block him.'"

Alabama's formation—squeezed in 20 yards from the sideline—opened a 20-yard window on the right side of the field because Clemson's kick return team mirrored the alignment to match the Tide, head up. The Tigers' outside guy on the front line of the kick return, Jayron Kearse, could retreat and then turn and cut off a speedster such as Humphrey (4.40-second 40) and not let him jet right down the field to cover a kick.

Kearse was a six-foot-four strong safety, who ran a 4.62-second 40-yard dash. He was certainly not as fast as Humphrey, so he needed to cheat in to, at least, have a chance of blocking Marlon.

Bobby Williams, the Alabama special teams coach, saw the opportunity. Twenty yards of nice, open green grass was behind Kearse, who was facing the middle of the field and had his back to the Clemson sideline. Alabama placekicker Adam Griffith was a former high school soccer player, adept at different types of kicks. All he needed to do was parachute one into that vacated space, behind Kearse, and let Humphrey beat Kearse to the ball.

Well, there wasn't a clean rep of that "pop" onside kick all week in the practices before the January 11, 2016, Clemson game, Lee said. Humphrey might touch the ball first trying to run under it, but he never caught it cleanly. In practice, Lee said, there would be a scrum for the fifty-fifty ball when it hit the ground or it bounced off Humphrey's pads.

Coach Williams, who is a longtime Saban aide, was not deterred. Several times during the first Clemson-Alabama national championship game, he told the head coach the onside kick was there, that Kearse was cheating in trying to cut off Humphrey. Saban wouldn't do it.

Then, in the fourth quarter, when Williams came back to Saban one last time to tell him the kick was there, Lee heard Saban say, "Do it."

Griffith's kick floated into Humphrey's arms. Two plays later, quarterback Jake Coker and tight end O. J. Howard hooked up on a 51-yard touchdown pass. Alabama led 31–24, and momentum was the Tide's for the rest of the game.

"It never worked when we practiced it, not like it did in the game," said Lee, who was on the forward line of the Alabama kickoff team, three players inside Humphrey on the right side. "The first thing I yelled at Marlon was 'I can't believe you caught it.' He had never caught it in practice."

Alabama won the game, 45–40, and that's a one-score difference. If you take away the last meaningless possession of the game, where quarterback Jake Coker knelt to run out the last twelve seconds, Alabama had 16 possessions. Clemson had 15, a difference of one turn with the ball because of that onside kick. The Crimson Tide also had the ball one more minute than the Tigers (30:31 to 29:29).

"It was crazy," Lee said. "That's thirty reps of him never doing it, and then him doing it when we needed it the most. Right when it was kicked, we didn't know what was going to happen. We might get the ball, we might not. 'Marlon hasn't caught this thing yet,' I was thinking.

"It probably won us the game."

Can you see now? At any time, and anywhere on the field, the resourceful Nick Saban wants to have a remedy. He was that way in Cleveland twenty-five years ago as defensive coordinator with the Browns, and he is that way with Alabama. He rummages through the Toolbox and comes up with a gadget to fix the problem.

Essentially, this is Nick Saban's philosophy:

> I want to be able to run the ball when I need to run it, but I also want to have the capacity to throw it when we need to and strike a balance between the two. I want the explosive ability to make plays down the field and I want to be more than adequate on special teams; I want to win the game there, too, if needed.

The five offensive coordinators who have worked for Saban— Major Applewhite, Jim McElwain, Doug Nussmeier, Lane Kiffin, and Steve Sarkisian—have had guidelines. And parameters will be in place for Brian Daboll, too, in 2017. But Nick gives his offensive coordinators plenty of freedom to build formations and open up the field; he does not demand that they just line up in the I-formation and pound people. Alabama hasn't done that since 2009. Alabama does not even have a fullback on the roster to run that kind of 1970s offense. They spread out, they throw to get a lead, and, typically, run to close the game out.

In the early part of the Saban Era, it was more of a grind-it-out plan because that's what the talent of the squad demanded. Julio Jones was in the program, but the Crimson Tide was still land based and had a stout defense that could suffocate opponents. Even then, Alabama could pop open the Toolbox for a fix. When Alabama's 2009 team hit a midseason rut with 54 points in three games (18.0 ppg), McElwain went to a Wildcat offense with running back Mark Ingram taking a direct snap and becoming an instant runner.

It took some pressure off quarterback Greg McElroy, and it forced teams to prepare for a "running" quarterback. Saban never wants an opponent to have a steady bead on his offense. The Crimson Tide won their last six games of 2009 averaging 32.5 points a game.

Let's go through the Saban Era since I've been there.

McElwain was a formation builder. He did a lot of unbalanced lines, and he would put the tight end out as a wide receiver and the receiver in the slot to create matchup problems for the defense. Mac loved to make the defense work mentally to get lined up.

One of the hallmarks of McElwain's tenure as offensive coordinator was the 2011 national championship game win over LSU. If you remember, the two teams played the so-called Game of the Century earlier in the season, and LSU won in overtime, 9–6. One of the problems the Crimson Tide had in that first game was dealing with the Honey Badger, Tyrann Mathieu, who could play the slot corner in LSU's best defense, their Nickel 4-2.

The Badger—he has since dropped this nickname in the pros— stalked the ball with his quickness and ability to jump short routes in front of him. He was terrific seeing plays and then pouncing when the football was thrown short. Alabama was 5 of 13 on third down, but it could never keep the sticks moving and could not score a touchdown once the Tide reached the "high" red zone, from the +40- to the +20– yard line.

McElwain took care of that in the rematch in the title game by exposing Mathieu's height (five feet nine). First, Bama stayed in its base offense, which forced LSU to use its base defense, a 4-3, not its more disruptive 4-2-5, where the Badger was closer to the football as the slot corner. Then, McElwain had quarterback AJ McCarron throw the football over Mathieu's head to six-foot-two receiver Kevin Norwood with fades and post corners. The idea was to get even with Mathieu, then behind him, so he would have to defend the football in the air rather than playing "downhill."

The Tide kept the Badger busy outside with Norwood (4 catches for 78 yards), then hooked up inside with tight end Brad Smelley (7 catches, 39 yards). Alabama won, 21–0.

Smelley was a gadget that was brought out of the Toolbox. He had sure hands in the middle of the field, and with the Badger preoccupied outside, Smelley made several key plays.

When McElwain left for Colorado State to be the head coach, his friend Doug Nussmeier became the offensive coordinator in 2013 and continued in the same vein. Nussmeier hunted the mismatches and was a better coach than advertised. Alabama won the 2012 national championship with Nussmeier as the OC because he opened up the offense to take advantage of AJ McCarron's passing ability.

But the Bama-Nussmeier partnership did not end well in 2013. The Kick Six, the incredibly painful loss to Auburn on a 109-yard kick return to end the game, did not devastate the program, but the emotional fallout created a palpable tenseness inside the building. Bama had lost its shot at a third consecutive national title, not because of that last play, but because of the lack of execution during the other fifty-nine minutes of play. Saban also had ideas of expanding the Toolbox to match what opponents' offenses were doing to the Tide, which was spreading out and going faster.

Lane Kiffin and Coach Saban share the same agent, Jimmy Sexton, and Kiffin got an invitation to come to Tuscaloosa and watch Alabama tape and assess the offense. In a blunt meeting with the Alabama offensive staff, Kiffin said the offense was too predictable on third down. I wasn't in the meeting, I didn't see Nussmeier's face, but knowing Doug, I'm sure it was upsetting to him.

After the Sugar Bowl loss to Oklahoma, Nussmeier took the hint and packed his bags for Michigan to become Brady Hoke's offensive coordinator. I always liked Doug and respected his abilities as an offensive coach, so I was glad to see him reconnect with McElwain at Florida as his OC.

Kiffin, using his Sexton connection and his obvious skill as a play caller on his résumé, was then named the new coordinator at Bama for the 2014 season.

Not many college coaches have the political capital to pull Lane Kiffin off the scrap heap and convince people that it can work. Saban is one of the few. Kiffin had, after all, walked out on Tennessee and was fired from Southern California, unceremoniously, just off the tarmac of an airport. This was after Al Davis had very publicly fired Kiffin as the coach of the Oakland Raiders.

Kiffin, post-USC, did not have much of a market going until Nick Saban invited him to visit in December 2013. The Alabama coach hired Kiffin and didn't care what you or I thought of the move. Saban thought the hiring of Kiffin could help the program and it was done.

The Toolbox was about to add a few new compartments with the West Coast, sideline-to-sideline flair of Kiffin, who had been an offensive assistant coach at Southern California under Pete Carroll. The installation started in spring 2014, with holdover quarterback Cooper Bateman and an extremely athletic quarterback, Blake Sims. Kiffin started adding to the Toolbox with quick, outside flash passes to wide receiver Amari Cooper and a more horizontal game to create space and spread the field. Cooper was about to become famous because he became a focal point of the offense.

Jacob Coker, a graduate transfer from Florida State, did not fit the style of offense Kiffin was installing. Coker was a six-foot-five pocket passer, and he was also trying to recover from knee surgery. So Sims and Coker battled for the quarterback job throughout the preseason. Sims showed ability to escape the rush and won over the players as the team leader. He could spit the ball out quickly to Cooper, and the Alabama offense could attack the edges of the defense faster than at any time in program history.

Coker, meanwhile, had not recovered sufficiently from a knee injury he'd suffered in 2013 as a backup to Jameis Winston at FSU. Coker had the knee cleaned again before 2014 Alabama summer camp, but it swelled several times throughout July and his throwing suffered. Sims

won the job going into the 2014 season in an upset, because most ob-
servers, including me, had thought that Coker would walk in to Tuscaloosa and become the starter.

The Kiffin offense with Sims included the read-option, and now
Alabama was doing to opponents what offenses had done to Bama:
play up-tempo in what Saban called "speed ball" and put the quarterback to use as a dual threat. Saban's directive to his play callers has
always been to maximize what the squad has in talent, and Kiffin did
that with Sims. Lane's work with Sims and the offense gave Alabama
a dynamic scheme, and the brash OC helped keep Alabama riding
high in the national polls.

Nussmeier did some up-tempo, but not as much as Kiffin. His priority was getting the ball to his best player, the same as it was at USC
when Lane was there. You saw what happened with Amari Cooper in
2014 (124 catches) as he took quick throws from Sims, a six-foot quarterback who was a converted defensive back. Lane, the same coach
who had been cast aside by USC, was a sensation in 2014 as Alabama
made the first College Football Playoff.

Alabama was on a trajectory now: wide-open.

Once you have seen what an athletic quarterback can do to a
defense—Homer Smith's declaration that it was the wave of the
future—it is harder to go back in the other direction. The mobile quarterback can get you out of trouble, and he can sometimes beat the X's
and O's.

Left behind was the Alabama of your father's era. The Crimson
Tide still had 220-pound running backs, but the identity had shifted
as Saban added to his Toolbox.

In 2015, Kiffin tried to stay with the up-tempo spread with Coker
as the quarterback. Alabama beat Wisconsin and Middle Tennessee
State, but then came a disjointed, reckless ride against Ole Miss and
a 43–37 loss. It wasn't unexpected because Alabama had trouble lock-
ing down its identity. Remember there was a six-foot-three-and-a-
half-inch running back named Derrick Henry, and he had not yet
emerged full force.

Kiffin and Saban could not make up their minds about the direction of the offense, or the starting quarterback, by the third week of the season. Coker and Bateman alternated reps, and the practices were a jumbled mess before the Ole Miss game. The quarterbacks would rotate on and off the field in practice, running plays designed for each of them.

"It was one offense with one guy in there, and a different offense with a different guy in there," Coker said. "We did not have a good week of practice. We lacked rhythm."

Two days before the Ole Miss game, Saban called the quarterbacks into his office and said he had still not decided on a quarterback. Coker and Bateman walked out of Nick's office and started down the hall, then Coker stopped and looked at Bateman. "Cooper, I can't stand this anymore. I need to go back in there and talk to him."

Coker pivoted and went back into Saban's office for a showdown. Jake's recollection is that it was not a nice discussion and it got loud. Coker told the head coach he had to make a decision on a quarterback, that the offense was suffering, and so was the team.

Saban held his ground. He would decide when it would be a one-quarterback team.

Linda Leoni, Saban's administrative assistant, looked at Coker with wide eyes as the quarterback walked out, as if to say, "Wow, what just happened in there?"

The Ole Miss game came apart on the opening kickoff with a lost fumble. It ended with a loss as Alabama tried to work with two quarterbacks. Many in the media talked of the Alabama Dynasty being finished.

Alabama was not finished; they were actually just getting started in 2015.

The next week against Louisiana-Monroe, the Crimson Tide regained its traction in a 34–10 win with Coker as the starter. The following week against Georgia, in a driving rainstorm, the wheels were back on the bus. Running back Derrick Henry and Coker established the Alabama offensive identity, and Alabama crushed the Bulldogs, 38–10.

And there it was, the Toolbox popping open.

In the *nick* of time, so to speak, Saban tinkered with his team and

Alabama became a downhill run team with Henry paired with deep play-action passes from Coker to Calvin Ridley and ArDarius Stewart. When the offense needed to isolate a receiver to one side for the catch-and-run, it could do that, too, with quick throws. The Georgia game was the turning point of the national championship season because Bama had an identity, which is always important to Saban.

"When we settled on one offense, we got real comfortable with each other and how we were going to play," Coker said. "It was smooth from then on out."

That Georgia game also gave a glimpse of the Toolbox on the defensive side of the ball. The Bulldogs had some faint offense against the Tide in the first quarter by passing the ball to wide receiver Malcolm Mitchell. Alabama is usually aligned with left and right corners, set positions for Marlon Humphrey (left) and Cyrus Jones (right).

But in the first half, Saban and Kirby Smart huddled in the rain. They decided they would take the veteran Jones and have him guard Mitchell one-on-one. Mitchell caught just one pass in the second half, Georgia's offense lost a weapon, and Alabama rolled to the win.

(We will talk about the evolution of the defense under Saban in chapter 9.)

The diversity of offense showed up again a few weeks after the Georgia game when Coker separated his right shoulder in the second quarter against LSU on November 7. The quarterback crashed into hard-hitting linebacker Deion Jones and two other Tigers at the LSU 3. Coker was dazed. Right tackle Dominick Jackson helped the quarterback to his feet.

"I don't remember a lot, but I think he said, 'The huddle's this way, big guy,'" Coker said. "Man, I was out of it."

Coker played the rest of the game through the pain, but he said he could not sleep that night. "It was terrible," he said. "The next week against Mississippi State we didn't throw the ball too much, and when we did, it was mostly sidearm. There was a play where I was running to my right and I threw it and got hit and landed on the shoulder, and I disappeared into that medical tent on the sideline."

Trainer Jeff Allen hustled Coker into the collapsible tent to work on the shoulder. Receiver Richard Mullaney, one of Coker's closest friends, went in the tent, but it wasn't to check on Coker.

"My girlfriend said, 'I saw Mullaney go in there. Isn't that the cutest thing? He was checking on you.' I said, 'Mullaney went in there to take a piss, he wasn't checking on me.'"

Coker laughed as he remembered it. "The trainers swung open the doors for me to leave, and Mullaney had to turn away and pissed all over himself."

If Alabama ever needed a full Toolbox, it was that Mississippi State game. Its quarterback was seriously dinged up, and Saban and Kiffin had to reach for something else to win besides the deep ball.

Henry rushed for 204 yards and the Crimson Tide won, 31–6.

"We had other options," Coker said. "Thank God Derrick had a good game, because I was hurt. I threw a quick out to Calvin for a touchdown, maybe it was eight to ten yards, and he took it the rest of the way. That's the kind of athletes we have. Playing quarterback is reflective of everybody you have around you. At Alabama, you look good because everybody you are playing with is really, really good."

What is often overlooked is that the people off the field are also really, really good. This is part of Saban's Toolbox, too.

For instance, Jeff Allen's sideline pop-up tent was one of a kind in college football, part of the infrastructure in the Saban Era. The tent was created in a collaboration with the engineering school, and it not only allows some privacy from fans, but also from the opposing team looking on from the press box. The opponent might be interested in whether an Alabama player can return to the game.

Allen and his staff are part of deep and wide organizational structure off the field. The support staff that assists the football program includes academic specialists, nutritionists, life-skills professionals, and strength-and-conditioning experts. Fans think about the stadium and the game, but so much more goes into Saban's operation.

For instance, when players arrive at Alabama, they are handed a nutrition booklet with information on how the team structures meals after practice, on the road and at a bowl site. The booklet instructs them on how they get their meals daily and where.

You have heard of scripted play-calling on the field? Well, the same holds true in academics for the Alabama football player. The Paul W. Bryant Academic Center has forty individual study rooms, a forty-eight-seat computer lab, and a desk where players can check out a computer for when they go on road trips. Just like on the field, the players have certain thresholds and important marker dates to monitor their progress toward a degree under Saban's watch.

Alabama has the highest graduation rate of all football players in the SEC.

The football program is much more than eleven guys on the field. It is also made up of the sixty or so staff members off the field. The medical part of that group managed Coker's beat-up body in 2015 and got the dangerous return man/running back Kenyan Drake back from injury quicker than expected, as the Crimson Tide rolled to the 2015 SEC Western Division championship.

En route to an 11-1 regular-season record, Henry won Alabama's second Heisman in six years. Coker took the pressure off with the pass game because the consistently stout offensive line, led by center Ryan Kelly, kept the pocket clean of pass rushers. The gang-tackling defense was led by captain Reggie Ragland and playmaking safety Eddie Jackson.

Alabama seemed to have every fix in 2015, just how Nick likes it.

Look at the 2015 SEC Championship Game with Florida. Coker said early in the game the Crimson Tide had trouble with the vertical, upfield rush of the Florida defensive ends. The Gators saw no threat of Coker running the ball, so they kept trying to change the line of scrimmage—by penetrating into the Bama backfield—and getting to Henry before he could get started.

The Tide trailed 7–2 when Coker took care of that threat. On the sideline it was decided that instead of handing the ball off for a run outside, or pulling the ball and standing up to throw a perimeter pass,

Coker should read the end, pull the ball from the belly of the back, and run it himself.

In the second quarter, Coker pulled the ball from the back and ran 17 yards. It was the first time all season Coker had pulled the ball on a zone read, and it changed the entire tenor of the game. The same play that had won Blake Sims the job in 2014 and put Coker on the pine, now bailed out the senior quarterback and the Tide a year later in Atlanta.

"We called more quarterback runs that game then we did all season," said Coker. "It slowed them down. It was just something else we could do. Like I said, you have options here."

The Florida defense was less aggressive because of Coker's runs. Henry started finding more room and the Crimson Tide won 29–15.

Coker may not have seen eye to eye with Kiffin all the time over the running of the offense, but the quarterback admired the OC's play calling: "Lane Kiffin is a master at baiting defenses. He will call one play out of one formation and get them looking for it, then he'll use the same formation and run something totally different. He's really good at it."

Coker said he had a voice in the game plan with Kiffin, as long as the quarterback was not "way out there" with how to attack a defense. "You had to get on the same page," Coker said.

The two were synced up in the national semifinal against Michigan State. When they were watching film in the run-up to the game, they both saw clues that the Spartans' deep safety could be suckered inside and then beaten deep.

"We just liked the way the safety was playing," Coker said. "We both saw the same thing with that, I'll tell you."

When Michigan State sold out to stop Derrick Henry in the run game, Coker and Kiffin punished the Spartans deep. With both safeties eyeballing Derrick, any kind of play-action fake to him would get them moving toward the line of scrimmage. Coker, with ample time, could stand in the pocket and find the open receiver racing down the middle of the field. Henry had just 75 yards rushing, but Coker completed 25 of 30 passes for 286 yards and 2 touchdowns.

But even with good players, the Process is not always foolproof. Not by any means. Saban can step on the proverbial rake left carelessly right-side up in the grass and get hit right between the eyes. Auburn was that rake in the 2013 Iron Bowl.

Alabama led 28–21 when it faced a 4th-and-1 from the Auburn 13-yard line with less than six minutes remaining. Having seen two missed field goals earlier in the game, Saban elected to go for the first down instead of trying another kick attempt for a potential two-score lead. The Crimson Tide came to the line quickly. Auburn's defenders were ready and suddenly jumped in and filled every gap on the line.

The ball was snapped, and running back T. J. Yeldon was stopped at the 13 for no gain. Auburn took over on downs.

We'll get to the infamous, if you're a Bama fan, Kick Six in a moment, but one more thing needs to be mentioned about the Process and its vulnerability.

The referees can make mistakes, and Saban has nothing in the Toolbox to fix that.

Alabama still led 28–21 when Auburn quarterback Nick Marshall completed a 39-yard touchdown pass to Sammie Coates to tie the game with thirty-two seconds remaining. On film, the Auburn fullback Jay Prosch is five yards downfield vigorously blocking Alabama linebacker C. J. Mosley on the same side of the field as the pass.

On first blush, many people thought the touchdown should have been disallowed for an illegal lineman downfield. No linemen were illegally downfield. The touchdown should have been waved off because when the ball is in the air, Prosch is making contact with a defender. It was offensive pass interference by Prosch, according to Rule 7-3-8.

So the stage was set for the Kick Six and the ultimate trump card that can beat the Process and Nick's X's and O's. That trump card is the spectacular individual play.

Thirty-one seconds after Auburn scored the tying touchdown, Alabama lined up to attempt a 57-yard field goal by Adam Griffith. Remember, the slowest and least athletic unit of a team is the point-after-touchdown/field-goal-protection team. Those units are assembled to block, not tackle.

During the time-out before the kick, on our radio broadcast I described the dangers of going for the long field goal. One, because of the distance, a low trajectory could lead to a blocked attempt, and two, the kick could be returned against a group of players that are not accustomed to covering in the open field.

When Griffith's kick was in the air, the Alabama blockers watched and then began to move like a herd of water buffaloes. I saw one trying to get his chin strap buckled as he ran. Auburn's Chris Davis caught the ball nine yards deep in the end zone. He ran down the opposite sideline, and the lumbering Alabama "blockers" could not catch him. Ball game.

Alabama quarterback AJ McCarron was typically the holder for field goals by first-team kicker Cade Foster, but Saban put Griffith in to try the long field goal. Punter Cody Mandell was his holder, not McCarron, who is six feet four and more athletic. Perhaps AJ could have saved the day and pushed Davis out of bounds.

It's ironic, isn't it? Two of the most memorable plays of the Saban Era were not on offense or defense, but on special teams: the onside kick that ruined Clemson in the 2015 national championship game; and the Kick Six that denied the Crimson Tide's run to a third consecutive national title in 2013.

Alabama does not often have a breakdown in special teams because the Crimson Tide's devotion to them is a hallmark of the program. Just look at it. Cole Mazza was the best long snapper in the country as a high school senior. He is from Bakersfield, California, and the Tide was able to drag him two thousand miles straight east to Tuscaloosa. JK Scott is from Colorado. Alabama brought him East, too. Scott led the nation in punting in 2014 as a freshman.

Dillon Lee said it is not easy for Alabama to dominate special teams in a game, even with superior athletes, including the backups fighting for a chance to start. Too much space on the field is opened up for a play with too many moving parts for talent to take over. There has to be coaching, and Saban makes sure the special teams get their own periods of work in practice.

I said earlier in this chapter that special teams provided the decisive play in the national championship game against Clemson . . . and I didn't even mention Kenyan Drake's 95-yard kickoff return for a touchdown against the Tigers. I didn't mention, either, that Scott's high punts forced 5 fair catches by Clemson. The Tide also blocked a field goal on the last play of the first half.

"Sometimes, you know, like the Clemson game, our special teams' units were better than theirs," Lee said. "We had good offense and good defense, they had good offense and defense, we just matched up pretty well in the kicking game. So I knew special teams were going to be a deciding factor. It was going to set us apart and it did, with Kenyan Drake's return for a touchdown and Marlon's play on the onsides kick."

Alabama practices special teams every day, Monday through Thursday. Saban not only watches the special teams work, but special teams are taped and reviewed by the coaches just like offense and defense. Sheets are made out on every player's performance on special teams during practice. If you loaf, if you don't execute, it is put on the sheet and then put on the board the next day in the special teams' meeting room for the rest of the squad to see, Lee said.

Saban's eye caught the lack of execution on special teams in practice and games the first two weeks of the 2016 season. There were opportunities for punt returns—it was all blocked up—and the return men were leaving yards on the field. What did Saban do? He put the veteran with vision—Eddie Jackson—back to receive punts, and EJ's touchdown return on the road against Ole Miss sparked a comeback. Jackson had another punt return for a touchdown against Tennessee before suffering a season-ending leg injury versus Texas A&M.

At times teams have poked holes in Alabama's special teams, but it takes NFL talent to do it. T. Y. Hilton, the wide receiver for the Indianapolis Colts who runs 4.3 in the 40, had a 96-yard touchdown return against the Tide in 2009 while playing for Florida International.

In 2010, Albert Wilson, now with the Kansas City Chiefs, had a kickoff return for a 97-yard touchdown for Georgia State.

One of the reasons there was so much consistency with the Alabama special teams was because Bobby Williams served as the special teams coordinator for eight seasons, until moving into a supervisory role in the program for 2016. Special teams does not occupy a remote corner of Nick's Toolbox at Alabama. It is right there, front and center, usually with a trusted veteran coach such as Williams, or Burton Burns in 2016, or currently with Joe Pannunzio, who returned from the Philadelphia Eagles' personnel department to get back on the field as an assistant coach.

The items in the Toolbox that have received the most attention the last three seasons were those of offensive coordinator Lane Kiffin. He was called the Boy Wonder at Tennessee, then the Boy Blunder at USC. Mostly, he was very good for the Tide, especially when it came to catching Alabama up with the rest of college football.

Lane's trademark was that laminated "call sheet" he clutched with two hands on the sideline. He would look at it for down and distance and personnel on the defense and call the play over the headset, and it would be relayed to the quarterback with hand signals. The call sheet was precious to Lane. I'm told the equipment staff would always pack a small printer on game day for Kiffin, so he could tear up the sheet and make changes to it even thirty minutes before kickoff.

Sometimes it was tough translating those plays from the sheet to the field. Blake Sims was an athletic quarterback with virtually no experience as a college quarterback, so Kiffin had to orchestrate a lot from the sideline for his first-year starter in 2014.

The on-the-go training of Sims left Kiffin exasperated in the 2014 season opener against West Virginia in the Georgia Dome. Kiffin shouted over the headset in the first quarter, "Is it always this hard?" in trying to get Sims in the right play. At times during the 2014 season Kiffin yelled the play out to Sims from the sideline. It worked out well enough for Sims to have a phenomenal season in getting the Tide into the College Football Playoff.

In 2015, it took Alabama four games before it found an identity on offense with quarterback Jacob Coker and running back Derrick Henry and a formidable offensive line. The ID was Henry's runs, play-action passes, and quick throws to the outside.

Kiffin was ready with a different scheme when Jalen Hurts became the starter in 2016. Hurts is a supremely talented quarterback with a committed background at the position. Bama added designed QB runs to the Toolbox, and Hurts burned Ole Miss, Arkansas, Tennessee, LSU, and Mississippi State with 100-plus-yards rushing games.

With his remarkable poise and even-keeled presence, Jalen led the Tide to an undefeated regular season and a third consecutive SEC title. He did all of this without being a consistent passer, although he gave flashes of his arm talent and ability to deliver the football downfield.

Unfortunately, his sporadic accuracy caught up with Alabama in the playoff semifinal versus Washington, and then in the rematch with Clemson for the national championship, the Tide only converted 2 of 15 3rd-down opportunities.

Still, he has tons of room to grow as a passer, and the potential is definitely there for him to make a giant leap forward in 2017 as an overall quarterback.

Something else helped expand the Alabama offense in 2016. Kiffin took a trip to the University of Houston in the spring of 2015 to talk offensive shop with Tom Herman, the inventive offensive play-caller and head coach who now leads the Texas program. Herman had schemed and beaten Alabama for Ohio State in the 2014 College Football Playoff. No other team could scatter a defense like Houston when the Cougars were clicking, and they did it with an athletic quarterback.

In 2016, Kiffin visited Texas Christian University to learn about TCU's packaged screens and play-action out of the pistol formation. The Horned Frogs made a living off these plays when they had a quarterback similar to Hurts in Trevone Boykin, who made the Seattle Seahawks roster as an undrafted free agent.

This expansion of plays in the Alabama Toolbox is significant.

The college game has seen a spike in scoring, and the Crimson Tide has remained a championship contender because it could turn to a quarterback-driven offense. All the things that bothered Nick Saban's defense in the past his offense now utilizes to terrorize the opposition: the zone read, the run/pass option, the smoke screens, all at an up-tempo pace.

Look at the NFL quarterbacks other national contenders were running out on the field: Cam Newton at Auburn, Marcus Mariota of Oregon, Jameis Winston at FSU, Dak Prescott of Mississippi State, Cardale Jones of Ohio State, and Deshaun Watson of Clemson. The Crimson Tide dealt with the quarterback-based offenses of other contenders by getting faster on defense and playing keep-away with a run-oriented offense.

Alabama needed to evolve to keep up, and you can see how just by looking at simple statistics. In the 2009 national championship game win over Texas, Greg McElroy completed 6 of 11 passes for 58 yards. In the 2015 national championship game win over Clemson, Coker completed 16 of 25 passes for 335 yards. Both had a Heisman Trophy running back at his disposal, Mark Ingram and Derrick Henry, respectively.

Some programs find an identity doing one thing well. Alabama's identity is doing a lot of things well, which is why Alabama—at one time or another in Saban's reign—has had first team All-American at every position except tight end.

Alabama has total flexibility, whereas when it takes something away from an opponent, most of the time that team doesn't have something to fall back on. Look at Washington in the 2016 national semifinal. The Huskies pass game was smothered after the first quarter and there was no Plan B. Alabama won, 24–7. Opponents don't play well left-handed.

Alabama, meanwhile, always seems to be able to play right-handed regardless of what you do against them. In the same Washington game, the eighteen-year-old Hurts could not challenge UW's superb defensive backs, so the Crimson Tide turned to running back Bo

Scarbrough, and he had a career game against the Huskies with 180 yards rushing and 2 touchdowns. Hurts had similar issues with Clemson, but Scarbrough got hurt in the third quarter and was not available to help take the load off in the second half.

Stay on that thought a moment. Tim Tebow left Florida and the Gators ceased being a national contender. Cam Newton left Auburn and the Tigers backslid for two seasons, regained traction for one year, then slipped back again. Jameis Winston departed FSU and the Seminoles haven't been back to the CFP. Mariota declared early from Oregon, and the Ducks disintegrated by 2016.

This is the full Toolbox. Alabama had different starting quarterbacks in 2014, 2015, and 2016 and made the College Football Playoff all three seasons. That is the hallmark of a complete program with a diversified portfolio.

Nick Saban's season-long approach and agenda is to develop and maximize the entire roster, while being prepared for every eventuality. Bama is either going to run between the tackles or to the edges or throw short, long, or intermediate passes. They can zone-read or dial up a schemed quarterback run. The Tide can play-action, bootleg or naked. In the meantime, Saban's offensive lines always stay healthy and seem to get better and better as the season progresses.

On special teams, Nick wants somebody who can bang the ball out of the back of the end zone on kickoffs or send the football down the hash mark or perform any of the specialized mortar, squib, or onside kicks. He wants a punter who can launch it downfield or direct it to a boundary or pooch-punt it down the middle of the field. With his core special teamers he wants enough bulk to protect on punts and enough speed to cover downfield. Nick likes instinctive returners who are secure with the football, but also explosive enough to score from anywhere on the field.

Nick is like the orchestra conductor. When he points to the horns, he wants the horns. When he points to the bass drum, he wants the bass drum. Alabama is one of the few teams in America, if not the only team, that has developed itself to the nth degree.

Alabama has access to the best prospects because it has expanded its brand into the Washington, DC, and New Jersey areas to get key players, such as Jonathan Allen and Minkah Fitzpatrick. It has volume in recruiting, whereas most schools cannot recruit to that level in terms of height/weight/speed and athleticism.

Here is something else about Nick and his Toolbox. A lot of other coaches are married to a certain philosophy, a certain system on offense and defense. Nick Saban, though, is the ultimate handyman on Saturday. You need something fixed, he has the players and the schemes (tools) to get the job done, whatever it is.

If you think Nick Saban has a full toolbox on offense and special teams, his defense is a twenty-five-year work in progress. He has calls and checks for virtually every formation and motion known to mankind. You walk into the defensive staff room and it looks like Egyptian hieroglyphics on the grease boards and video screens. Alabama's defense, over this decade, has evolved at an even faster pace than the offense.

The defense has especially evolved in the last two seasons, 2015 to 2016, because now the defense is scoring touchdowns. And it's not just dumb luck either, this surge in defensive touchdowns. They are called NOTs, nonoffensive touchdowns, and Nick and his staff started scheming for them in spring 2015 when they made it the newest, most lethal acronym in college football. Alabama is at the top of the mountain as one of the "haves" in college football, but plenty can be learned about the Alabama way from these game-altering NOTs.

9

EVOLUTION OF
A DEFENSE

HARDBALL TO FASTBALL TO MONEYBALL

Alabama's defensive players would shout an alert the first few years of the Saban Era:

"Money, money, money."

It was not kids scrapping for a quarter in the middle of the sidewalk. It was Alabama's call that a football was loose or an interception had been plucked out of the air.

"Money, money, money" was the order for a defensive tackle, linebacker, or defensive back to find an offensive player to block. The Alabama players are drilled to get to the nearest sideline, build a wall of blockers outside the numbers on that side of the field, and knock down or just get in the way of a different-colored jersey.

The Tide uses a more inelegant phrase to call out a turnover these days—one that cannot be repeated here—but it is the same thing as found money.

A lot of this loose change was picked up and cashed in by the Crimson Tide in 2015 and 2016. These turnovers by opponents—fumbles and interceptions—can go for touchdowns. This version of Moneyball is big business for the Tide.

So here is what you should know.

Those NOTs that Alabama kept scoring the last two seasons were not an accident. They were not always caused by the carelessness of the opposing team.

Moneyball was by design, an intentional attempt by Bama to steal points. Sure, every football team preaches to its defensive players to get the ball out and force a turnover. But Alabama's defense made it a part of its identity the last two seasons in practice. It had to.

Alabama had a new quarterback and feature running back for the 2015 and 2016 seasons. The Crimson Tide was not sure what it was going to get in quarterback play and what kind of production was going to come from the offense. The 2016 offense, with freshman quarterback Jalen Hurts, struggled mightily at times, but then the defense would come up with a NOT. If you noticed, Alabama didn't have a NOT in the championship game loss to Clemson.

So a point of emphasis in the spring and summer of 2015 and 2016 in meeting rooms and on the practice field was take the ball. Score points. Get on the scoreboard.

When I was part of the Baltimore Ravens organization when we won Super Bowl XXXV, over the New York Giants, our record-setting defense had the same temperament: "Let's win the game on D." As linebacker Ray Lewis would say to quarterback Trent Dilfer and the offense, "Give us ten and we will win!"

That's right. Alabama and its fearsome roster of defensive players became penny-pinchers. They made getting the football their most important task. Knock the loose change out of the opponent's pockets—reach in and grab it if you have to—then cash it in.

This is part of the evolution of the Crimson Tide defense from 2007 to 2016. Height/weight/speed changes have been made to the roster for ten years as Alabama has slimmed up on the defensive line with lighter and faster players who can still hit like heavyweights. Alabama still developed linebackers that could plug gaps on the run, but now these backers were fast enough to stay in the hip pocket of the tight end running up the seam. Alabama's cover corners, who were used to getting their hands on the football, became safeties in the middle of the field.

It relates to the NOTs because as Alabama became more athletic on defense, it had multiple defenders around the ball quickly. The Crimson Tide could get the runner secured, then go for the ball. On the back end, the safeties such as Eddie Jackson and Minkah Fitzpatrick, cover guys, could break on the ball and steal it.

Alabama scored 11 touchdowns with interception and fumble returns in 2016. That's compared to 8 NOTs by the Alabama defense in the previous three seasons (2013–15) combined.

The Crimson Tide special teams pitched in with touchdowns on three punt returns early in the 2016 season, too. No other team in twenty years had more NOTs than Alabama in 2016.

So while Hurts worked through his freshman season, sometimes in solid fashion and at other times like a rookie, the defense and the special teams gave the kid a hand—a bunch of hands quite literally. The defense had pitched in to help new starter Jake Coker in 2015, as well.

It was all a plot to get the ball out. It started in the spring of 2015. Defensive coordinator Kirby Smart showed up at practice one day with one of those massive belts you normally see hoisted by a prizefighter or WWE wrestler. Kirby was looking for a rallying cry to emphasize turnovers, a message to the defense to be more conscious of taking the ball.

The belt was customized for Alabama with a large *A* against black leather. It has the heft of the real heavyweight belt awarded to a champion boxer. Smart and the staff got the idea because Deontay Wilder, the WBC world heavyweight champion, is from Tuscaloosa.

The belt was awarded to the "turnover champ" in the day's practice. Players were given turnover points, and whoever accumulated the most points would be rewarded in the next day's meeting, where he could sling the belt over his shoulder and strut around the locker room.

Linebackers coach Tosh Lupoi said the belt "emphasizes the importance of getting turnovers."

During games, assistant strength coach Wilson Love is in charge of the belt. Just before the defense goes on the field after a change in possession, the players gather around the defensive coaches for instructions. A maniacal Love circles the crowd of defenders exhorting them, "Who gets the belt?"

"He will let us touch it," said cornerback Marlon Humphrey. "If we get a turnover, when we get to the sideline, we actually get to hold it."

The player forcing the turnover gets to parade with the belt over his shoulder when the defense comes to the sideline. A clamor is made around the player for a few minutes, then it is back to work. Lupoi was adamant that Love was not going to take the belt to Florida Atlantic University, where Love will be the head strength-and-conditioning coach for Lane Kiffin.

"Wilson is not allowed to take our belt to other programs," Lupoi said. "Other programs can do their best to emulate it, but there is only one real authentic belt."

To me, the belt is an acknowledgment that these days in college football you have to score to win. With so many potent offenses and innovative coaches, games can become a shootout if a quarterback is hot. Look at what happened to Alabama at Ole Miss in 2016, when the Rebels jumped to a 24–3 lead. It's hard to contain gifted college teams 100 percent of the time, even if you are Alabama.

So, you take the ball back by force, not on downs. If you look at all the work Alabama does in practice at taking the football, it's not happening by chance.

In a part of practice I call the County Fair, players go from one Ball Out drill to another. In this, the position groups at all three levels of the defense rotate through a series of stations devoted to taking the football. The former Crimson Tide linebacker C. J. Mosley said Alabama consistently practiced five different "strip" drills for getting the football out. This methodical work at practice is why you can't turn your head on Alabama defenders without one suddenly coming out of nowhere to wrestle you for the football.

In one drill defensive linemen, linebackers, and defensive backs ward off a low block, keep their eyes up, and see a football bouncing on the turf. It has been tossed there by a coach.

The drill not only teaches block protection, but emphasizes seeing the football and then getting two hands *underneath* it "to scoop and score." The defensive players are told to look the ball into their hands, as if they were a baseball infielder wearing a glove.

Hands underneath, eyes on the ball, and snatch it. Then you can run. That drill is part of every practice. When the ball is out, or a defensive player grabs the ball, that's when you hear the chorus, "Money, money, money!" Blockers are being assembled up the sideline for the player with the ball, not that Jonathan Allen, the consensus All-American, needs a lot of blockers. At 290 pounds, he is almost able to block for himself by lowering a shoulder and rumbling downfield.

Those of us with a backyard of high grass can practice another drill. Go out to the shed and roll the lawn mower out. Reach down and grab the handle of the nylon chord used to start the mower. Jerk it really hard with a lot of force to start the mower. That's what an Alabama defensive player is taught to do. The first man to the ballcarrier will shoot his arms up and around to the back of the ballcarrier for a perfect-form tackle. The next defender in does the work of ripping at the ball as if starting a lawn mower.

Look back at the national semifinal game with Washington on December 31, 2015, and you will see how Allen came up with a fumble. It was one of those lawn-mower strips.

Dillon Lee, a linebacker on the 2015 national championship team, said that in another drill a running back has a ball tucked high and tight against his shoulder pad with a muscled arm around it. Defenders on either side of the ballcarrier try to strip the ball free.

In yet another drill, every couple of steps the running back has to put his hand on the ground, and then a defender tries to dart in at just that moment when the ballcarrier is catching his balance and tries to poke the ball out of the running back's other hand.

"We really worked on stripping the ball," Lee said, "and the offense really works on keeping it. Our backs hold on to the ball, if you've noticed. They are very consistent with securing it because of the pressure we put on them at practice."

So in a game the Crimson Tide might be leading by one score, 17–10, the strip, recovery, and sudden score can create another touchdown of separation. These can be backbreaking plays to the opponent because now Alabama has a two-score lead.

Look at the Arkansas game in 2016 where Alabama led 42–24 entering the fourth quarter. Arkansas was showing some confidence on offense and was going in for another score. Minkah Fitzpatrick intercepted a pass, going headlong toward the back of the end zone. He stopped his momentum, turned, and yelled to Eddie Jackson, "C'mon, let's go, let's go!" Minkah wheeled out of the end zone, saw the wall set up on the left side, and raced, officially, 100 yards for a touchdown. Alabama led 49–24. Game over.

The Crimson Tide players are absolutely coached that when they intercept the ball on the left side of the field, everyone is going to turn and get blocking set up from the numbers in toward the interior of the field. They are going to try to get you up that sideline. After a certain point the return guy can cut it back and make a play. There is a team fundamental, a team technique, to the business of running with the "money."

Under first-year defensive coordinator Jeremy Pruitt, by nature an aggressive X's-and-O's tactician, the payoff arrived in 2016 with the NOTs. This resulted from Alabama's push starting in spring ball 2013 to be a more nimble defense and to get more defenders around the ball. The transition in recruiting prospects was intentional, from the big, bulky players for the 3-4 defense to more adaptable, speed-based players for sub schemes.

Alabama gradually had more athletic defenders to deal with the spread offenses from Ole Miss, Texas A&M, Tennessee, and Auburn, among others.

Some 70 percent of the time Alabama was finding itself in sub, meaning a situational defense with five (Nickel) or six (Dime) defensive backs. The coaches realized during the 2012 season that they were not going to be in a standard run-look, 3-4 defense that often, so that's when they decided not to recruit the hulking, one-dimensional nose tackles or heavy-footed linebackers anymore.

In a coaches meeting in November 2012, after a loss to Johnny Manziel and Texas A&M, Saban and defensive coordinator Kirby Smart flipped a switch. They told the staff, "We are not in a true 3-4 enough to impact the game against the run. We need to get faster."

Alabama has almost eliminated that nose tackle from their recruiting picture. The Terrence Codys, Darren Lakes, and Josh Chapmans are not being recruited to Tuscaloosa; no more Hippos, only Rabbits. I say *Hippos* because that is a term used for Bama's short-yardage and goal-line defensive package, while *Rabbits* is a four-man defensive-line unit specifically designed to rush the quarterback.

Jonathan Allen, the All-American combination end/tackle, played at 290 pounds. Cody was 365 pounds during his senior season. That's an accurate visual of the evolution.

The other revelation in the 2012 season that made Alabama look at itself in the mirror was the debut of a former girl's high school basketball coach, Hugh Freeze. The Ole Miss coach, fitting to his name, puts skates on his offense, and they played at a hockey pace. *Fastball* is what Nick Saban calls it, and the creative Freeze was a clever designer. No team in the SEC West has annually given Bama more fits since his arrival.

The 2012 season was Freeze's first year. Despite being over-matched in talent, Ole Miss did some things in the spread that bothered Alabama. The Rebels were playing up-tempo and using formations and gimmicks the Crimson Tide had not seen.

Ole Miss quarterback Bo Wallace would be in the shotgun for the snap, then look to the sideline to get a new play, or so Alabama's defense thought. He was not making a check, he was laying a trap. Alabama's defensive players would look to the sideline to get their new defense, a check to the Ole Miss check, and while the Tide players were out of their stance or facing the sideline, Ole Miss would quick-snap the ball.

At times Ole Miss would run two receivers vertically down the sideline to tire out Alabama defenders. The Rebels' receivers would step off, and two different receivers would come in for a new play while Alabama was hustling back to the line of scrimmage for the next snap. Rules have been changed so the defense can now substitute, but these kinds of tactics still take place today.

The week after beating Ole Miss in 2012, Alabama played its annual slobber-knocker game with LSU. It was a lull before the blitz of speed. Manziel and A&M showed up in Bryant-Denny with more fastball. The Aggies won, 29–24.

"We weren't used to the fastball," said Ed Stinson, a defensive lineman on the 2012 team. "The secondary was not getting to its checks; it became a problem for us because once A&M did it to us successfully, other teams started doing it.

"We were backed into a corner, so the next year we started having these fastball practices. No rules for the offense. No rules at all. They played fast and the defense had to keep up."

From that point forward, more conversation occurred in recruiting meetings to get faster players in the house to combat these spread offenses. Also, more effort was made on the practice field to learn how to deal with them. Alabama needed to learn how to hit the fastball.

The following spring, 2013, the Alabama staff had their squad do a period of ones versus ones, first-team offense versus first-team defense. It was unscripted, and that had never before taken place under Nick Saban. Every period of every practice was planned in detail, so this unscripted work was Alabama's call to adapt or stay vulnerable. The defense did not know what was coming. The coaches recalled Saban not liking it at all, but he approved it anyway. It was all hurry-up, no-huddle, and the defense had to be efficient and on point to keep up. Bama had always played a traditional brand of football: huddle up and call the play. This was a real shift for the Crimson Tide's offense to play the game from the line of scrimmage.

Those spring practices were an acknowledgment that SEC opponents were not going to allow Alabama players to buckle their chin strap, tuck in their jersey, and tie their shoelaces between snaps. Nope, Ole Miss, Texas A&M, Mississippi State, Florida, Missouri, among others, were not going to let Alabama get comfortable and tee off at the snap of the football.

Saban saw it. He began adjusting to this sandlot brand of basketball-on-grass and began training his team to play on the fly.

"The fastest team we play? Well, it's our scout team in practice," Dillon Lee said. "We got fast on defense to keep up."

When the team regathered for preseason camp in August 2013, fastball practices got even more intense. At the end of every Tuesday practice a period of ones versus ones had no huddle, no script. It was all reactive, putting the defense in scenarios where it had to adjust to match the offensive formations, regardless of who was on the field for the defense.

"It was Johnny Manziel who helped change us, so we had those fastball periods and you could see us changing the culture of power defense to fast defense and staying physical," said Geno Matias-Smith, who was a freshman defensive back in 2012. "We had to learn how to play against guys like him."

Alabama adapted with practice, but it also adapted with recruiting on all levels of the defense, not just by finding lighter tackles. The Crimson Tide is now recruiting the safety who was 210 pounds in high school and turning him into a 245-pound linebacker who can run sideline to sideline. They are recruiting cornerbacks that may be light, 165 to 175 pounds, and turning them into 190-pound safeties who can support the run and range from the middle of the field to defend the pass. Eddie Jackson, the All-SEC safety, was 149 pounds coming out of high school, and that might have been with rocks in his pocket. He ended up in the 200-pound range with 9 career interceptions and 3 returned for touchdowns.

Alabama sees clearly what the player is when he arrives in Tuscaloosa and what he can possibly be weightwise in two years on strength and nutrition programs. In projecting prospects at all three levels of the defense, the team has a surplus of players who can move and play in space. It gives them great flexibility to adjust from regular to sub defenses. They have linemen that can rush, they have versatile linebackers that can blitz or drop, and they have safeties who can cover and tackle in the open field.

Reggie Ragland was an outside linebacker and they shifted him inside to Mike. Ryan Anderson was a Mike and they moved him outside. Eddie Jackson was a corner; he ended up at safety. A young kid named Terrell Hall is playing an outside, edgy position, but ultimately, I bet he ends up as a defensive lineman. Jonathan Allen is listed as an end, but he is just as much of a tackle.

Minkah Fitzpatrick was recruited as a corner, made freshman All-American at that position, then moved to safety after the season-ending injury to Eddie Jackson in 2016. He is a hybrid that can tackle the running back and cover the wide receiver in the middle of the field.

"I saw Minkah moving to safety at some point," said Matias-Smith. "You could just see the body type and how he played. When Eddie [Jackson] got hurt, that's where they moved him.

"Coach Smart told us in 2015, 'The league is changing. Your safeties have to be able to cover slot guys.'" In 2017, with the departure of Marlon Humphrey to the NFL, the expectation is that Minkah will likely return to his original post as a combination outside and nickel corner.

Rashaan Evans was recruited as an edge rusher, or so we thought. He gained weight so that he was big enough to play inside linebacker, but could also still rush from the outside or "spy" on a dual-threat quarterback. Evans gave the Tide a mixture of blitz and cover ability, so when Bama needed a mirror for Clemson quarterback Deshaun Watson in the 2015 national championship game, Evans was the ideal candidate for the job.

You saw it. When Alabama got a little bit of a handle on Clemson's offense in the second half, Evans was a part of that solution because of his skill in space and acceleration to the quarterback. Watson is a fluid, 220-pound runner who can escape the pocket, but Evans was there to hit him. Five years ago, Alabama did not have this tool in its box.

Look at the versatility now. Offenses today will be in regular "21" (two backs/one tight end) or "12" (one back/two tight ends) personnel and then suddenly shift into "10" (one back/four wide receivers) right before the next snap. You can try to match personnel every time, which will wear out your subs running on and off the field, or you can find linebackers that can stay on the field such as Evans or Reuben Foster or Ryan Anderson, guys that are not too light, not too heavy, but just right.

No program in college football can expand and contract its defense better than the Crimson Tide and be equally as effective in run or pass situations.

Every linebacker Alabama was recruiting for the 2017 class can walk out over a slot, run down the field with a tight end, and stop the run. That's where the game is, so that is what must be defended. These days, the Crimson Tide recruits one Dont'a Hightower type a year, the six-foot-three, 250-pound inside linebacker who is a thumper between the tackles.

This team that does not employ a true fullback, no longer has a nose tackle, and has moved away from the classic Mike linebacker and the run-support strong safety. This is a true, living example of how the game has changed. Most people look at Alabama as being as traditional as any team in America, but only the uniforms have stayed the same.

Here is another look at the retooling of the Bama defense.

Mount Cody went in the second round of the 2010 NFL draft. He was one-dimensional, a run stuffer with little or no pass-rush ability. Josh Chapman was the next nose tackle for Alabama, and he went in the fifth round in 2012. Darren Lake was the next nose tackle in line, and he went undrafted in 2016.

The NFL saw the game evolving, too. The value of the pure run stuffer, the one-down guy, went away. Saban and Co. adjusted their recruiting and have created a totally adaptable unit.

"We could adjust out," said Geno Matias-Smith, a safety for the 2015 national championship team, "so that when somebody like Arkansas might come out in Twelve, or Silver, a back and two tight ends, we would be on the field with our regular defense, a 3-4, and be ready.

"They exploded into an empty set before the snap, nobody with the quarterback. It was spread out, but we didn't have to sub, we just adjusted to the formation with what players we had on the field."

Matias-Smith added, "I don't think many people can adjust like we do. I will peek at defenses from other schools when I'm at a game or watching on TV. It is mental, not physical. It happens fast. We were trained to move fast and adjust out to all formations."

Alabama used to have a column for nose tackles on its recruiting big board. They don't have that column anymore. The nose in the 3-4 is now clumped together with all the defensive linemen recruits. Those nose tackles are at the bottom of the list, if they are even on the list. The value is just not there.

Here is another piece of Alabama's recruiting for defense. Alabama will look at high school wide receivers and then envision them as defensive backs. The coaches covet the exceptional wideout who has played defense in high school. They know he has hit people before, tackled in open space. They try to get a look at him on defense while recruiting and always have a Plan B for that player. If two players have similar receiver skills, Alabama will look harder at the recruit with the defensive background.

Mark Barron was a standout offensive player in high school at St. Paul's in Mobile, but the Alabama coaches understood they were looking at a player with the potential to be an All-SEC safety, which he became. Other programs might have the same forward thinking, but not the volume of athletes to move to the other side of the ball. Alabama has the resources and the depth to take that two-dimensional skill player and find the best home for him.

Always, the Alabama head coach sees players from a defensive perspective. Saban evaluated players at LSU for defense, moved them from offense, often against resistance from their families, then watched them succeed. Corey Webster and Marcus Spears were two Tigers who changed sides of the ball and, literally, set themselves up for long NFL careers.

That's the physical component of the evolution of the defense. What about the mental part?

Dillon Lee thinks about the combinations of coverages, the hand signals, the team meetings, the cohesion needed, and just takes a deep breath before he talks about it. "It was a lot. We might walk in there Monday after a game and have ten new calls for the upcoming game."

It wasn't just learning calls, it was learning the subtleties of playing defense, such as how to disguise what you were doing. Ask Michigan State's Connor Cook how effective Alabama was at putting on a mask before the snap.

"Everything looks the same right before the snap, the way we disguise it, and how the secondary doesn't spin the safeties before the snap," Lee said, referring to the safeties and linebackers, who didn't immediately "flip" their hips and get to their coverage responsibilities. "It all kind of looks the same, and I don't think Connor Cook had seen that. It looked like two deep as the ball is snapped, now it's not, and he's saying, 'I don't know what it is.' It looked like single high coverage, and now it's not.

"You are not moving [on defense] until after the snap. If you are good enough and smart enough, you don't move until the last instant before the play. I don't know if he had ever played against a group like us."

Alabama is connected on defense, eleven players on one string, all pulling in the same direction, almost like an accordion. The ball is hiked to the quarterback before there is one move.

A tight end might see one Alabama outside linebacker standing in front of him, but the linebacker on the other side of the defense is actually covering the tight end going over the middle.

The Crimson Tide gives you a pre- and post-snap look. That's what NFL defenses do.

"Disguise is not everything, but it matters," Lee said. "The more you do, the more you can disguise. You don't panic and think, 'I got to get out there, I got to move.' You are not freaking out. I think disguising really helped take us to the next level my senior year [2015]."

Hootie Jones, a defensive back, said teams became so preoccupied with Alabama's masks for its defense, they overthought the scheme. "We could be showing the look we were actually going to run, but you could tell their quarterback might be thinking, 'Okay, they're not running this. What are they jumping into?' We like disguising things. We really, really work on it."

"It's why you don't see a bunch of freshmen walk in and play right away," Lee said. "It's a bigger learning curve here. A simpler scheme would allow someone to walk in the door and play, but not at Alabama."

If you walked into Alabama's defensive coaches' room and saw the number of calls and checks on the board, it would boggle your mind. The playbook has continued to grow and grow. They have more calls and checks than most pro teams. I mean, this system goes back at least twenty-five years, to those days when we were all in that football think tank in Berea, Ohio, with Bill Belichick, and there is no going backward. The new defenses and the adjustments are pushed out every week to the Bama players on iPads; it's literally another academic course for them when Professor Pruitt stands in front of his unit.

"How can I explain what we do on defense?" Hootie Jones said. "Well, let's say, we do a lot of everything. It is complex." Remember the 1994 quote from Nick to Rick Venturi back at the Browns? "Dammit, Rick, simple is not always better. Sometimes complex is better."

You better be a Grade A football student because when you are playing in this scheme inside Bryant-Denny Stadium, it is extremely loud. There are a lot of moving parts and they have a lot of hand signals. If you can't "signal" the language, you are not going to be out there.

Nick Saban's philosophy has always been to pattern match, which is like a matchup zone defense in basketball. Matias-Smith said the secondary would spend a whole period in practice on pattern matching, I would say it's actually more than that based on what I've seen over the years. It's zone with man principles. I've watched Nick do this a thousand times with the Browns, at Michigan State, LSU, and now Alabama.

"That's his philosophy," Geno said. "It's a zone-match system. As soon as a receiver comes into your area, it's like man-to-man defense. You are not going to let someone come into an area and hook up real easy to catch a pass. If a receiver comes into your area, it's man-to-man, you take him."

Sometimes all the complexity never comes into play during a game. Lee said Alabama practiced super intently for an early showdown in 2015 against Georgia. The staff expected some offensive wrinkles from the Bulldogs and prepared for no-huddle, formation variety, and several gadget plays.

"You go through the whole week of practice, and the game comes and you go, there's no way it's this simple," Lee said. "No way they are going to go Pro Style and use no hurry-up or fastball or zone read. But that's what they did."

Georgia converted 3 of 17 third-down plays. Alabama won, 38–10.

"When we are playing really good, especially last year [2015], it was the best top to bottom with everyone on the defense—corners, safeties, linebackers, and defensive line—being on the same page," Lee said. "Every single person knew what they were doing. It wasn't like, 'I don't know what I'm doing if they line up in this call.' Everyone just knew."

Lee was one of the sheriffs of the defense in 2015, making sure younger players knew assignments. Where are you supposed to be, kid? What's your assignment? Jarran Reed and A'Shawn Robinson were like that, too. Saban would always bark in practice, "Do your job!" As the season progressed, he did that less, and so did his on-field leaders.

"I was always on people with knowing what to do because our defense was so complicated with checks," Lee said. "Communication is so important. You had to stay on people constantly. We had Jarran and A'Shawn, and they mixed it up a lot more than I did. If they had their hand in it, it was going to get crazy."

Serious technique is involved after the snap, at every level of the defense. Opponents are counting on breakdowns in the defense when they spread out on offense. One bust and it is a 20-yard gain.

"When you are talking about playing in our scheme, you have to play technique," said Lee, referring to stance, hand placement, fighting off a block, footwork. "If we are in base defense, our two inside backers are going to two-gap the guards. Everybody is two-gapping. You can't really two-gap a three-hundred-pound-plus guard when you're only two hundred forty without technique. You have to use technique and leverage, and that's what we're taught."

Two-gapping the guards means that when the offensive lineman comes to block you, you brace to take him on, stripe to stripe. Then you shock and shed the blocker and make a tackle no matter which side the runner chooses.

"It's complex, so you have to trust the man next to you when we build that wall," linebacker Ryan Anderson said. "Don't try and do nobody else's job, that's when big plays happen. It's trust and relationships."

Alabama's goal is to build a wall inside, then have sideboards to prevent the back from bouncing to the outside. If the running back can get through the first line of defense, the secondary is right there to stop a long run. In the 10–0 win over LSU in 2016, All-American running back Leonard Fournette had two runs where he thought he was going to take it to the house. The secondary closed fast because of their disciplined fits in support of the run defense and their willingness to tackle.

"There are fundamentals on how to break on the ball, and angles to the ball, which minimize big runs," Lee said. "All that's coached on how to stop a back like Fournette from breaking a big run. If the front seven breaks down, it's all about how the safeties are coached to run to the ball and take away his angle. That's how explosive runs are contained. Eddie Jackson is good at it; they are all good at it."

Fournette had 31 yards rushing in the 2015 Alabama win and 35 more in the 2016 Alabama 10–0 victory. I would argue that those two games were as worthy of a "clinic" for total run defense as any in Nick Saban's tenure.

Alabama's "hardball" defense has never been doubted, but the Tide has become elite in its "fastball" defense. At every level of the defense, everyone got faster and more athletic, but never lost attention to techniques in tackling and coverage.

The 2016 season under Pruitt/Saban was not just a culmination of the new look of the defense; some old-fashioned re-recruiting had gone on the previous January. Just look at the five defensive guys who came back for their senior seasons: defensive end Jonathan Allen, linebackers Reuben Foster, Ryan Anderson, and Tim Williams, and safety Eddie Jackson.

All five could have entered the NFL draft as early entrants, yet every one of them returned for one more season. No one inside the building could have predicted that all would come back, but that's what happened, and it was the main reason why Alabama looked untouchable most of the year.

No one else gets that kind of boost from juniors coming back. Ohio State had nine underclassmen declare for the 2016 NFL draft, and LSU has lost thirty players over the past nine off-seasons, the most in the country.

Williams and Anderson seemed logical to come back because they were part-time players up until their senior seasons. They had to wait behind talented upperclassmen while playing a certain role. They also needed to learn the entire scheme, from base to sub.

Who better to learn from than Nick Saban and his cadre of defensive coaches?

Last November, I talked to Steve Sarkisian, who served as Pete Carroll's offensive coordinator during a historic run with the Trojans in the early 2000s. Carroll, like Saban, is considered a defensive mastermind. Sarkisian had a chance to work with both men.

Sark said Pete and Nick have very different methods, but they are trying to get to the same place with their players and program. They handle their players differently off the field, but there is also a significant on-field difference. Carroll keeps the game plan simplified for his defense, so his players can play as fast as they can. Saban wants to disguise and scheme and have a variety of calls and checks. Both men have a similar goal: to defend every blade of grass on the field.

When the Crimson Tide started to evolve on defense five years ago, they were able to maintain their hardball tactics on that grass inside the tackles. When they morphed into a unit that could defend fastball, too, they could defend the grass growing out near the sidelines as well.

In 2015 and 2016, Alabama then added a dose of Moneyball. The Crimson Tide not only defended every blade of grass, they made the other team pay for coming onto its turf.

And while it was evolving on defense, the Alabama football program kept looking for ways to diversify the offense. The Crimson Tide majored in the run game. It could be physical at the point of attack and crack some holes in the defense for its running back. What the Tide needed was a better passing game. The great receiver Julio Jones showed the way. Then came Amari Cooper and Calvin Ridley and ArDarius Stewart.

After fifty years of being a program built on a foundational run game, Alabama started to emerge outside the hash marks with receivers who could make the program complete in every way.

10
ALABAMA JOINS THE MODERN GAME

JULIO LEADS A PARADE OF RECEIVERS INTO T-TOWN

Thomas Dimitroff, the general manager of the Atlanta Falcons, called me the morning of the 2011 NFL draft. He wanted my opinion on Alabama receiver Julio Jones.

I was a player-personnel executive for the Philadelphia Eagles and did a good amount of college scouting for them in 2010 and 2011. I was between jobs as general manager of the Browns and executive director of the Reese's Senior Bowl. I knew SEC football.

I was downstairs in one of the position meeting rooms when Thomas's number showed up on my phone.

I knew the draft order—the Falcons were picking twenty-seventh—so my first thought upon seeing his incoming call was "He's getting ready to make a big-time leap to get Julio."

Julio was being projected as a top ten draft pick along with Georgia wide receiver A. J. Green. One or the other would be gone by pick no. 5. The Cleveland Browns were looking for extra draft choices to overhaul their roster, and the Falcons needed a trading partner for their proposed bold move.

"What do you think of him?" Thomas asked me.

I told Thomas, "First of all, you don't realize how big he is until you get up close to him; he is an imposing figure. Second, he's a worker. He doesn't just show up and catch passes. He practices like an offensive lineman. And third, a large percent of the guys who get overhyped in high school never live up to the billing. Julio delivered from day one in Tuscaloosa. And on top of all that, he's tough and totally opposite of the diva, look-at-me wideout."

I thought back to the 2010 Tennessee game when Julio caught 12 passes with six pins and a plate in his hand to support a broken bone. Thomas hung up after hearing what he wanted: that Julio was a special player.

That night, with the first round being televised in prime time, Atlanta traded five draft picks to move up to no. 6 to take Julio. They made a deal with my former team, the Browns. I was happy for Julio because he would be closer to home and, more importantly, the Falcons had an established quarterback in Matt Ryan.

It was the most-talked-about trade of the first round, and Thomas's head has been on the chopping block several times because of this deal. When Julio played only five games in 2013 because of injuries, Thomas said he would be spinning through the stations on the radio and hear the Paul Simon song "Me and Julio Down by the Schoolyard." He knew he was being ridiculed for the trade because the Falcons were having a miserable season (4-12).

But, overall, Quintorris Jones has been a spectacular player for the Falcons. He had 104 catches in 2014 and 136 in 2015. In 2016, he helped get the Falcons to their second Super Bowl in franchise history. Julio is a consistent Pro Bowl–level performer. He is everything the Falcons wanted: a team guy, a go-to target for Ryan, and a receiver who takes pressure off the rest of the offense.

What's important for Alabama football fans to know is that Julio created a mold for the Crimson Tide to follow. He was the guy the coaches could hold up in a recruiting meeting and say, "Julio is what we are looking for, this is the benchmark. Hands, feet, speed, desire, willing blocker, team-first. Find a receiver like this one."

During his three seasons from 2008 to 2010, the assistant coaches and analysts in the program could watch Julio's work ethic closely in practice. They measured him in every way and captured a mental picture of what a major league receiver looked like. When they watched tape of high school receivers or visited the school of a receiver they were recruiting, they had a picture of what they wanted.

Then they went out and got Amari Cooper, who had an All-American season for Alabama in 2014. Then ArDarius Stewart and Calvin Ridley came along and gave the Tide two more pass catchers who helped win a title in 2015. In between they had a quality receiver in Kevin Norwood, who wrecked LSU in the 2011 national championship game. Marquis Maze was a capable receiver and is playing in the Arena League. You know about Brad Smelley and his workmanlike contributions in 2011. O. J. Howard came up big in the postseason for Alabama in 2015 and 2016 and will likely go on to a significant NFL career.

So it was not just the defense that evolved at Alabama under Nick Saban, it has been the offense, too. Bama started bringing in good receivers who could help the team keep up on the scoreboard with all of these spread offenses. Julio was the first wide receiver at Alabama in forty years (the great Ozzie Newsome was a tight end in the NFL) to get picked in the first round of the draft. Cooper caught a school-record 124 passes in 2014 and he was a first-round pick, too.

Ridley and Stewart thrived with quarterback Jake Coker in 2015, but then the passing game was up and down as Alabama tried to bring along freshman quarterback Jalen Hurts in 2016. The downfield passing game wasn't the same with a running quarterback such as Hurts, who did not see the field as cleanly as a six-foot-five veteran such as Coker. Hurts wasn't given a chance to develop that downfield passing in 2016 as Bama played it safe and used him more on the run. We'll see more of the receiver skills in 2017 as Hurts develops into an accomplished passer under new OC Brian Daboll, a former assistant from the New England Patriots.

One thing is certain: the mold is there to follow at receiver thanks to Julio.

The Crimson Tide was not responsible for the natural-born, God-given physical gifts Julio possessed. Those were already apparent when he was in the eighth grade. I got a call from one of Julio's Foley middle school coaches in June 2004. He said, "I know you run a high school camp, but we have this phenom down here and we would like you to look at him. He's only in the eighth grade, but can we bring him over?"

Camp Savage was that high school summer camp we did for nineteen years when I was at the Ravens and the Browns. We had practice sessions in Mobile and across the bay in Fairhope. They brought Julio to the Eastern Shore with the other participants from the Foley High School area.

He was already six feet two, 190 pounds, and better than kids three to four years older than him. He went through one afternoon session and looked like a grown man. He had a freakish combo of size and speed.

In high school Julio was recruited by programs all over the country. Oklahoma and Bob Stoops thought they had him, then Alabama hired Nick Saban and Julio became the signature player of Nick's first full signing class in 2008, a class that changed the landscape in Tuscaloosa.

What was so impressive about Julio after three seasons at Alabama was that he wasn't just overpowering defensive backs or running past them with no technique or separating from man coverage off raw ability. He was coachable, and the UA staff pushed him to be great. He had a disciplined stance, stemmed his routes, and improved his hands technique. He also blocked, learned multiple wide receiver spots, and expanded his overall game.

Alabama requires its receivers—Julio to ArDarius—to come in as freshman and learn to work. Some young receivers pout because they don't get the ball. Alabama receivers are stripped of the selfishness from the moment they walk on the practice field, and that included Julio.

Stay on that thought for a moment. Practices have no sliding scale where one player can relax because he is a star and another player has to go full speed. Nick does not let his guard down in that regard. If he ever did, he risks losing the very foundation of Alabama football, which is effort and detail on the practice field. I saw it with my own two eyes as Julio Jones went from celebrated five-star recruit to a diligent, no-nonsense practice player. He elevated his work ethic and passed it on to the receivers who came after him.

You need to know something about the development of Alabama receivers because it gets at the core of Saban's coaching, which is to teach fundamentals, but also to adapt and change. Ask any successful CEOs how their companies survive and they will tell you it is because they are not afraid to change. Alabama has morphed from a conservative, traditional offense to one that can be wide-open with a myriad of formations and motions because of their bona fide receivers.

In the 2014 SEC Championship Game against Missouri, Alabama had 504 yards of offense with a mix of a no-huddle and spread alignments for three quarters, followed up by a physical ground game led by running back Derrick Henry in the fourth quarter. The 42–13 win propelled Alabama into the first-ever College Football Playoff.

"It's been very, very beneficial to us," Saban said of the fastball offense, which he used to loathe as being bad for the game. "If we didn't do it, I don't think we would be where we are right now."

It takes receivers to make the fastball game hum, and making a legitimate receiver at Alabama is as subtle and incremental as collecting loose change. Consider those dimes, nickels, and pennies you dig out of your pocket and toss into a mason jar. Those coins represent the receiver's fundamentals of stance, route technique, and hands. The assistant coach is the keeper of the jar, and he collects, collects, and collects. One day you glance over and it is not a mason jar with a jingle, it's a vault holding enough treasure that it takes two hands to pick it up.

For Alabama, it's not merely skill, it is the drip, drip, drip of development through drills. Nothing is prearranged. It's how Julio, Kevin Norwood, Brad Smelley, Amari Cooper, O. J. Howard, ArDarius Stewart, and Calvin Ridley became top-notch receivers in the Saban Era. One coin at a time.

So here is a glimpse of what receivers have to learn at Bama.

- Proper stance (nose over knee over toe of front leg) and alignment (exactly two yards outside the numbers as a split end, for example).
- Precise releases, either stemming to break down an "off" defender's leverage, or if a defender is jamming at the line of scrimmage, how to jab and accelerate with the feet, while using the hands to "swat and stroke" the opponent's hands off the receiver for a clean getaway.
- Dropping their weight—not weight loss, but bending their knees and cutting at the apex of the route, allowing for separation from the defender either laterally or vertically.
- Catching the football; the coaches teach thumbs in to catch a ball above the waist, thumbs out below the waist, and where it is okay to make a body catch (in a crowd with imminent contact or in the end zone).

These early lessons have nothing to do with making acrobatic catches. It's all about learning those things that lead up to the great, game-changing play. When camp opens in the baking summer sun, the coaches are the wardens of fundamentals, and they can make even Julio Jones and Amari Cooper feel months away from serious stardom.

Ridley was no different. Here is part of his story.

Calvin did not just show up and suck passes out of the air. Freshmen have blank stares, just like every other school's first-year prospects, and that was Ridley, even though he was a twenty-year-old freshman when the 2015 season started. Ridley wasn't even on the top line of the depth chart that August. Sophomore Robert Foster was the starter ahead of him.

When camp opened in 2015, people were nervous about the Alabama receiving corps. It was shiny new. All three starters from the season before, Cooper, Christian Jones, and DeAndrew White were gone. Projected in their place were sophomores Foster (6 receptions in 2014), ArDarius Stewart, and a new graduate transfer from Oregon State, Richard Mullaney.

Stewart was the leading returning receiver with a mere 12 catches.

With too many new puzzle pieces in the receiving corps, second-year offensive coordinator Lane Kiffin took some shears to the playbook. He decided during the 2015 spring drills to put the new guys in one spot, on one side of the field or the other. By the opening of preseason camp, Foster would be the left-side wideout with Stewart to the right and Mullaney in the slot. This was vastly different from the 2014 season, when Kiffin moved Cooper all over the place and had him play all three wide receiver posts.

The first three games of the 2015 season made it apparent that Alabama's offense had lost some luster with the downsizing.

Kiffin couldn't manipulate the players inside a game plan as he wanted to. Things were too restrictive, and a tactical edge had been eliminated. Alabama had pressed the reset button hard with the new guys so as not to overwhelm them, but the Crimson Tide looked too vanilla and couldn't regulate the distribution of the football to get their best players in their most advantageous roles with the ball.

Nick Saban cherishes versatility in his offense, and his most dynamic receiver, Ridley, was not only a backup the first month of the 2015 season, he was easy to find on the field as a left-side wide receiver. Opponents knew how good he was, and coverage rolled right to him for three games when he was on the field.

Kiffin and Saban decided the Sunday night after the Ole Miss loss to take off the kid gloves. With 70 to 80 snaps a game available to the Alabama offense, Ridley was going to get 8 to 12 touches a game with some specific "shot" plays. That's all there was to it.

All along, wide receivers coach Billy Napier had been coaching up Ridley, preparing him for a starring role. Understand, Napier is not just any assistant coach. He was once the youngest offensive coordinator in Clemson history (twenty-nine, in 2009). Napier has an extraordinary background and quietly did a tremendous job for Alabama after he returned from Colorado State, where he followed Jim McElwain in 2012. It should be noted that near the conclusion of the 2017 recruiting cycle, Napier accepted the offensive coordinator position at Arizona State.

Nevertheless, Ridley was ready for Cooper's role, but to get that kind of manipulation, Kiffin needed to go back to the traditional X (split end), H (slot), and Z (flanker) arrangement of receivers. He had to teach Ridley all three receiver spots, which is what Bama had done with Cooper to turn him into a star.

The freshman Ridley was thrust into Cooper's role as the playmaking split end with the capacity to move around the field and get into the other spots (H, Z) for his special, dialed-up routes. He would become the guy who made the defense debate whether to put eight in the box for the run to stop Henry and play single coverage on the outside, or to play safe against the deep ball with seven up front and four defensive backs deep.

Alabama suddenly regained the ability to move checker pieces around and cater to Kiffin's noteworthy abilities as a play caller. Kiffin game-planned with Ridley, and the Tide started to get the matchups it wanted.

That Ridley was a gracious teammate when he wasn't starting the first month of the season made the coaches' decision to turn him loose easy. As a reserve, Ridley was still vocal and positive with his teammates, as he toiled away learning the fundamentals.

"My mom has fun, she taught me to have fun and have some personality," Ridley said. "I just don't want to be sitting around. I wanted to work and enjoy myself. I didn't start when I got here, but I had fun in practice and kept my confidence up.

"I had a blast, really."

While Cooper was quiet and reserved, Ridley was not afraid to do what his mom said. He was the enthusiast who tried to beat everyone else in the receiving corps to practice. Giving him a bigger role in the offense was a reward for his positive attitude, as well as his skill.

In his reserve role at the start the season, Ridley caught 3 passes for 22 yards in the opener, a 35–17 win over Wisconsin. He had 4 catches for 37 yards against Middle Tennessee State in the second game, a 37–10 victory. His numbers were even more modest in the only loss of the season, on September 19, to Ole Miss (6 catches for 28 yards).

When AL.com reported Foster had suffered a season-ending shoulder injury September 19 against Ole Miss, Ridley became a starter.

Look at what the freshman was stepping in to. After that loss to the Rebels, 911 calls were made all over the state, with a firestorm in the media. Alabama was unsettled on offense because the quarterbacks, Jake Coker and Cooper Bateman, were still trading snaps. Alabama had no dynamic playmaker outside the hash marks. The dynasty was dying, or so many people thought.

Wishful thinking, it wasn't crumbling. It was about to get some new juice from Calvin Ridley, a Florida-bred receiver just like Cooper.

Ridley became the starter in that Monday practice, September 21. He was fifteen pounds lighter than Amari Cooper, but his footwork was superb and he could avoid the defense's strong-arm tactics at the line.

Alabama's coaches had Ridley watch video of their previous All-American wide receivers, Jones and Cooper. The rest of us watch video for highlights. Players watch video for oracles. There was no mystery of what the Tide coaches thought Ridley could become: a mixture of Jones and Cooper. Ridley soaked it up.

The staff analysts cut up plays for him and said, "Here are all of Cooper's tunnel screens, here are his takeoffs. Study these." Calvin Ridley could see for himself that "this is what playing wide receiver at Alabama is supposed to look like."

It's how steady, winning programs stay established. They make a player watch the guy who was in that job before him. They have a prototype, a standard, at each position, and they can say this is the goal, this is where you should be striving to be. Instead of Billy Napier teaching Ridley from scratch, well, a picture is worth a thousand words.

Alabama was still seeking an identity on offense when Ridley became the starter in week four. One issue still had to be worked through: there was no film for him to watch of quarterback Jacob Coker spitting balls out to Cooper on those quick horizontal passes to the outside. Coker didn't play in 2014; Blake Sims did.

Alabama went from a shortstop in Sims, in 2014, to a first baseman in Coker, in 2015. Sims could make that throw seamlessly as if he were "turning two" at second base and throw what they call smoke to the outside receiver. Coker's feet were not as quick, and his delivery on that pass, which is a staple of Lane's offense, was more deliberate. The timing was different for Calvin. I don't remember seeing Amari Cooper drop a ball until his sophomore season. Ridley had some drops as a freshman, but I think the contact from the defensive backs was quicker than with Cooper because the ball wasn't out there as fast from Jake, which created a timing issue for the blocking as well.

When Ridley got his chance to start in 2015, he caught 4 passes for 38 yards and a touchdown against Louisiana-Monroe, the fourth game of the season. The breakthrough on offense came against Georgia. Ridley had as much to do with Alabama's finding an identity on offense in 2015 as Derrick Henry.

By that October 3 game in Athens, Georgia, Ridley was not just a stationary target at X for the defense, he was in motion, split wide or in the slot. The defense was going to find it hard to roll toward Ridley because it didn't know where he would be when Alabama came to the line. Ridley was nowhere and everywhere. He was Julio. He was Amari.

On the third series in the soaking rain in Athens, Georgia, Coker faked a handoff to Henry and threw a pass for a 50-yard gain to Ridley. It set up a field goal.

In the second quarter, Ridley was split out just a few steps from the left tackle. He ran right up the left hash marks past cornerback

Aaron Davis and caught a 45-yard touchdown pass. Look at the camera frame as the ball is being snapped. Ten Georgia defenders are standing within seven yards of the line of scrimmage waiting for Henry to be handed the ball. The motion from left to right in the Bama backfield is to distract the safety in the middle of the field. Coker turns left as if to hand off to Henry, Ridley bolts down the left side hash marks.

Easy touchdown, with nothing circumstantial about it. It was all set up, from Henry's plowing runs to draw a crowd near the line, to Coker's fake, to Ridley's learning over the first month of the season how to play from different spots on the field.

That was a coming-out party. It was against a defense with speed on the field. People said Ole Miss was the turning point of the season because it was the only loss, but Georgia was the turning point to me because Alabama figured out what their identity would be.

It was "we're going to run this big tailback, then we're going to fake to him and take our shots downfield or to the edges with our new receiving star; they cannot defend both."

Opponents kept creating these eight-man fronts to slow Henry, and it left receivers one-on-one, which made things clearer and easier for Jake to read. Alabama's skill advantage comes into play then because the Crimson Tide can say, "Our wide receiver is better than your cornerback."

Alabama suddenly had strength right down the middle of the field—the six-foot-three, 242-pound Henry; the six-foot-five, 236-pound Coker; and the six-foot-five, 303-pound center Ryan Kelly—and then the separators on the outside, such as Ridley and Stewart.

Suddenly, Alabama was dynamic. The receivers could be trusted, and they showed it when they bailed out the Tide against Tennessee. A late drive featured Stewart catching a pass for 29 yards, Ridley grabbing another toss from Coker for 15, and a Derrick Henry 14-yard run for a touchdown with 2 minutes, 24 seconds, to play. Alabama won, 19–14, and stayed in the national championship race.

Ridley showed his worth catching the ball, but he became endeared to the coaching staff in game eleven against Charleston

Southern. Prone to taking plays off on the back side when Bama ran the other way, Ridley suddenly woke up to the full duties of an Alabama wide receiver. He came all the way across the field to make a block that set Henry loose for a long touchdown run.

After that block, Ridley could join the Parade of Receivers behind Julio and Amari.

ArDarius Stewart was next in line. He blocked like a lineman, then caught passes like a featured receiver.

Following Alabama's win over Florida in the 2015 SEC Championship Game, Coker was sitting on a small wooden podium by himself outside the locker room talking with a reporter about the so-far-triumphant season. He didn't want to talk about himself. He wanted to talk about Stewart and his selflessness and his work ethic.

A year later, in 2016, as Coker sat in my office at the Reese's Senior Bowl, he still wanted to talk about Stewart. Derrick Henry had won the Heisman. Calvin Ridley had emerged as the next great receiver. But Stewart was a folk hero to Coker.

"He's a different kind of guy," Coker said. "He's tougher than anybody on that team. In the Mississippi State game, a perfect example, team attitude. Calvin catches this out route and Kenyan blows a guy up near the line. As soon as I let the pass go to Calvin, I see ArDarius hauling ass from the other side of the field to get to Calvin's side, and he is knocking people down all the way to the goal line. You can watch a lot of film and you don't see a lot of guys do that.

"Wide receivers just watch when they don't catch the ball. A lot of other guys would not handle it the same way. That was one of the things that won a national championship last year, that mentality. He's awesome."

Coker said the first part of 2015 he tried to connect with Stewart on the deep ball. They couldn't click. Coker said his timing was off as the Crimson Tide was still trying to figure out its deep threat.

"Then Calvin became a starter after Ole Miss and he started catching balls. Not once did ArDarius come to me and say, 'Hey, why is the freshman [Ridley] getting all those passes?' Not once. ArDarius did not complain and say anything negative about some freshman coming in and catching balls."

Coker chuckles as he recalls the devastating blocks thrown by Stewart on unsuspecting linebackers and corners and safeties. "He plays angry. You tell him to block somebody, well, that somebody is going to pay for it."

In the 2016 SEC Championship Game against Florida, Stewart ran a deep out to the back of the end zone. Gehrig Dieter ran a shallower out route in the end zone. Quarterback Jalen Hurts floated a pass to Dieter. The ball hung in the air, but Stewart kept bodying up the Florida defender who was trying to intercept the ball by keeping himself between the ball and the defender, and Dieter came across the end zone to catch it for a touchdown.

"Boxed him out like under the glass in basketball," Stewart said with a big smile. "It's what you do when you don't catch the ball."

Stewart said he watched tape of Julio and Cooper and how they played away from the ball. He is a sturdy guy at six feet one, 204 pounds, and will block all day. "There is not a receiver here who wouldn't do the same for me," he said.

Late in the 2016 season, Stewart, the Hines Ward–like blocker (remember how he would de-cleat defenders when playing for the Pittsburgh Steelers?), became the trusted pass catcher. He had 8 receptions for 156 yards and 3 touchdowns against Mississippi State. He had 10 catches for 127 yards and a score against Auburn. In the SEC Championship Game, Stewart had 3 catches for 42 yards, continuing his big-play trend of averaging almost 15 yards per catch.

Alabama's receivers not only blocked and caught passes, they made defenses second-guess their defensive substitution packages.

For instance, look at what Alabama did with Mullaney, the wide receiver in 2015. Alabama goes by colors when it comes to their personnel groupings on the field. They can take Blue and make it Silver just by simple motion.

Blue is one back, one tight end, three wide receivers. Silver is one back, two tight ends, and two wide receivers. When Mullaney, who

would be split wide in Blue, would motion in back toward the formation and line up off the hip of the tackle, Alabama was suddenly in Silver, because he was big enough as a wide receiver to perform the
back-side blocking duties of a tight end.

In other words, with Mullaney on the field as a third wide receiver,
most defenses would counter with their Nickel or five-defensive back
package. Once he motioned to the hip of the tackle and became part
of the offensive "core," now Bama would be running against a "light"
box of defenders with only a front six to combat seven blockers.

If a defensive coordinator decided to stay in his base defense with
Mullaney on the field, then Alabama would keep the receivers split
away from the core and get a favorable matchup with Mullaney or
Ridley running a route against a linebacker or a safety.

Kiffin and Alabama have also mastered putting Ridley in the slot
with O. J. Howard, the tight end, outside as a wide receiver. Now the
corner is covering the tight end and the bigger safety is covering a
skilled wide receiver. Jim McElwain was proficient at that, and Alabama continued doing it with Lane.

Understand that Alabama's offense, whether it be with Kiffin or
Daboll calling plays in the future, always wants to run the football and
is always looking for the mismatch. It may take a half to get the defense "scattered" before Bama rolls up its sleeves and decides to go
north-south with the run, but ultimately, running the football is their
statement of dominance to an opponent. The other thing they do is
"formation" against the defense to get a wide receiver on a linebacker
or safety in the slot. Again, McElwain was the coach who brought this
concept to Tuscaloosa.

In the second quarter of the Michigan State playoff game in 2015,
Ridley was in the slot and came flying at safety Demetrious Cox, who
is twenty pounds heavier. Calvin spun Cox around with a fake inside,
then went straight down the field to haul in Coker's pass at the 1. The
other safety, Montae Nicholson, was late in getting over the top of
the defense. Alabama had a touchdown shortly.

In the third quarter, Ridley, again in the slot, got matched up with the slower Cox. This time it was a post route and a 47-yard touchdown pass from Coker to make the score 31–0.

Ridley finished the 2015 season with Alabama's all-time record in catches (89) and receiving yards (1,045) for a freshman. He broke Cooper's freshman records.

Alabama's passing game is not a system, such as you saw for instance with the San Francisco 49ers' Bill Walsh and the West Coast Offense. With the 49ers, their passing scheme would have an answer for every defensive coverage. At Alabama, they are looking to create certain matchups by formations and motions and then to exploit the weakest player or vulnerable area of that opponent's defense.

In other words, the Tide wants to dictate the action rather than react to what the defense shows. The passing game looked a little rough around the edges in 2016 with freshman quarterback Jalen Hurts, but even Alabama is going to struggle in the passing game with an eighteen-year-old playing the most important position on the field. A freshman has not quarterbacked a national championship team in thirty years for a reason. Hurts will be coached differently in 2017, and I believe his vision of the field is going to improve. Plus, just like everyone else on the team, another talented prospect, freshman and midyear enrollee Tua Tagovailoa, will be on the scene and competing through the spring and summer.

The receivers are there in Tuscaloosa, and they are complete players in every way.

The receiver who blocks, catches passes, and moves around the formation all started with Julio Jones. In November 2016, in the middle of his sixth season in the NFL, Julio was asked about his legacy at Alabama. His answer was understated, as usual, and he knew whom to credit.

"The coach," he said, when asked what sparked this run of terrific Alabama receivers the last nine seasons. "It was the coach. He let us play."

That's right. The receivers were "let" in at Alabama. The physical culture, running the football, is still the sharp end of the stick for the

Crimson Tide, but this stick can fly like a javelin, too. Defenses with eight players eyeing the running back are susceptible to the streaking Alabama wideout or tight end.

Alabama had some good receivers before Saban—Don Hutson, Dennis Homan, Ray Perkins, Ozzie Newsome, Freddie Milons—but now it has a framework and a demonstrated devotion to getting the football to the receivers.

In my view, Julio will always be remembered as the signature signing for Nick Saban because Julio thrived in the program and demonstrated to future prospects that Tuscaloosa was a viable destination for wide receivers.

And Thomas Dimitroff? He can whistle "Me and Julio Down by the Schoolyard" all day long, knowing he made the right call.

11

MY EYES TO
YOUR EARS

IN THE PHILM ROOM FOR NICK SABAN

4th and Goal Every Day is my textbook on Nick Saban's way of doing business at Alabama. The recruiting, development, practice, evolution of the defense, and build out of the offense are all elements of the program that I have observed since 2009.

But what about the opponents' approach to competing against Alabama?

The last eight seasons (111 games), I have watched hours and hours of film on opponents, from Wisconsin to Southern California to Ole Miss to Auburn. It was all to prepare for my radio broadcasts on the Crimson Tide Sports Network on Saturdays with play-by-play man Eli Gold.

I write a ten-to-twelve-page report off this film study every week to prepare for my listeners. I also e-mail the report to Nick every Monday morning. It is included as an introduction to the Bama game plan each week. I'm humbled, yet motivated, knowing that my work is included by the coaches as a very, very small piece of the weekly preparation puzzle.

Here is an example I'm proud of, from the report I wrote for the 2016 game against Texas A&M:

The A&M guards are "down" in three-point stances, while the tackles are "up" in two different two-point stances. Once again, Bama's defensive front will need to reestablish a new line of scrimmage and control the action in the trenches.

As mentioned, the tackles play from "squared" or "staggered" stances. When they are "square" or "level," it's almost always a run or RPO action with the back going across the bow of the QB. When "staggered," it's a drop-back pass or a designed QB draw.

Alabama linebacker Reuben Foster would see the A&M offensive tackle stances and anticipate run or pass. He was totally disruptive in the game with 12 total tackles. The Aggies ran for just 114 yards on 38 carries (3.0avg) and Alabama won, 33–14.

So, you see, I do not just wander into the radio booth before kickoff and guess. I break down opponents' schemes and search for match-ups Alabama might exploit. I look at what a team did one season against Bama and what they might do the next and how an opponent's personnel has changed from a year ago.

My film study stays in line with the whole theme of the Alabama program, which is to be prepared. Nick Saban would not expect me to show up on Saturdays without a game plan. Everybody around the team is expected to perform his or her job, even in a part-time role like mine.

I was in the NFL for twenty years and learned how to dissect opponents from great coaches such as Bill Belichick and Nick Saban. I wanted to put that skill to work. So I wrote reports off the film study with the intent of sharing the notes with listeners.

I happened to share the first report with Nick, too, just on a lark. I thought the notes on Virginia Tech in 2009, which would be my first broadcast, would be nothing more than "bathroom reading" for Nick.

The notes are included in the weekly game-plan book for the coaches—eight years running now. I have done 111 of those reports, one for every game. A few seasons ago, I asked Linda Leoni, Nick Saban's administrative assistant and the "gatekeeper" of the program, if he still read my reports. She walked me into his office and said, "See, there they are, right on top." Sure enough, they were front and center and opened on his desk.

The assistant coaches read them, too.

I was trying to get into the Alabama football facility at 7:30 a.m. the morning of the 2016 Iron Bowl so I could do our *Tailgate Show* for SiriusXM College. Mario Cristobal, then the tackles and tight ends coach, punched in his security code and let me walk in with him.

"Hey, you must put a lot of work into that report," Mario said. "It helps us out. Thanks."

Typically, over the summer, I will watch two games of offense and defense on every Alabama opponent for the upcoming season. I will put together a skeleton or template on each team before the season ever starts. I send the first report about ten days ahead of the first game, and from that point on, I operate a full week ahead of the game schedule. In other words, while Alabama's next game is LSU, I'm already working on Mississippi State.

I usually watch three to five games on each side of the football on Tuesday and Wednesday nights. On Thursday, I begin to add to the summer skeleton by writing the overviews for offense, defense, and special teams.

What's in these notes I put together for the listeners and Nick?

First, I have factual information on each team for use on the radio broadcast and during the week for my interviews as a guest on stations across the state. It includes an overview of the opponent's offense, defense, and special teams with statistics.

Then I get specific on the opponent's personnel and schemes: the X's and O's. I give an opinion on what the opponent might try to do against the Crimson Tide defense and where the yardage might be available for the Bama offense.

Let me tell you, back in 2009, I didn't want to just dive into the radio job blindly. I called several friends from the broadcast industry and got some sound advice about being a color analyst.

Todd Blackledge, the former Penn State and Kansas City Chiefs quarterback, who works as a top game analyst for ESPN/ABC, told me the "play-by-play announcer sets the scene and tells what happened on the play. The color man needs to explain how and why it happened."

Randy Cross, a longtime analyst for CBS, told me, "Preparation is important, and make sure to put your points on paper or you will forget about them during a game."

Rich Gannon, the former Oakland Raiders quarterback and NFL MVP, is an excellent broadcaster for CBS and SiriusXM. Rich said I needed to take a theatrical approach to the game: set the stage, introduce the characters, fine-tune the story as it progressed, then circle back and nail my opening points.

David Norrie, a former UCLA quarterback who has been doing games for ESPN for over twenty-five years, said, "Allow the game to come to you and react to what happens."

Incidentally, he played for Homer Smith, the ultimate authority on clock management, and no other analyst out there goes through the intricacies of the two-minute offense more than David and I do on our respective radio broadcasts.

Here are some more samples of the reports and some insight into opponents during the Saban Era:

TENNESSEE, 2009.

Alabama went against Lane Kiffin and the Tennessee Volunteers at Bryant-Denny Stadium. Here is what I wrote about the UT offense ahead of the "Third Saturday in October":

Offense: Kiffin hired Jim Chaney as his offensive coordinator, but Kiffin calls the plays himself. Chaney had a successful run under Joe Tiller at Purdue before going to the NFL for a few seasons, but this is Kiffin's simplified version of the West Coast Offense. #8 QB Jonathan Crompton had his best game as a Volunteer against Georgia when he completed 20 of 27 passes for 310 yards and 4 touchdowns. They utilized a number of bootlegs and misdirection play-action passes which seemed to fit his abilities more than dropping him straight back in the pocket.

Prior to the Georgia game, Crompton looked uncomfortable in this scheme, inaccurate with the football and stiff in the pocket. Expect a similar Georgia-like game plan for him vs. Alabama.

Alabama won this game, 12–10, when Terrence "Mount" Cody blocked a Tennessee field goal at the end of the game. The Vols scored just 10 points, but I think Kiffin's schemes on offense stuck with Nick. Tennessee used a lot of shifts and motions and made Alabama uncomfortable, and Coach Saban did not forget it.

Crompton was not a great quarterback, but Kiffin worked with him and developed his skill, and he became a fifth-round pick in the NFL draft. I think Nick had some respect for Lane because of that, and it played into the decision to hire him as offensive coordinator in 2014.

LSU, 2011 (BCS NATIONAL CHAMPIONSHIP).

I was accurate in my forecast of the scheme Alabama needed to use to beat LSU in the 2011-season national championship game, 21–0.

The best option to move the football on the Tigers is to keep them in Base personnel, so that Sam linebacker No. 23 Stefoin Francois stays on the field and No. 7 Tyrann Mathieu plays as an outside corner. For an offense trying to attack this defense, No Huddle has to be a consideration for the game-plan, so that their Base can be dislodged by multiple formation shifts and motions.

I got this right.

LSU's best defense in building a 13-0 record was a Nickel (five defensive backs) with Mathieu playing a hunter inside the hash marks over the slot receiver. From that spot the Honey Badger was disruptive with pass breakups and interceptions all season. Alabama had to keep him to one side of the field and limit his playmaking. That's exactly what happened. Bama's play calling on first down—passes—kept LSU in its weaker Base defense and simpler coverages. The Badger was not a big-play factor in the game as Kevin Norwood had a memorable night with 4 catches for 78 yards.

Here is one more tip from the LSU/Alabama rematch film study report:

> The running game has to go North/South because lateral perimeter runs cannot escape their team speed. LSU had no less than 4 pivotal tackles-for-loss against the Tide in the first meeting. The overall length and speed of the LSU front four and defensive secondary is the best in the nation and the Tigers have ridden that ability to a 13-0 record so far.

Trent Richardson and Eddie Lacy combined for 139 yards rushing. Alabama went inside against the Tigers and did not test the Tigers on the flanks.

Here is another sample from 2011 and the national championship game with the Tigers:

> Bama has a decided matchup advantage with its tight ends against the undersized LSU linebackers, so that is an avenue to be explored.

Brad Smelley, the Crimson Tide tight end, had a career game with 7 catches against the LSU linebackers. Smelley's route running and sure hands proved to be a difference-making aspect of Alabama's 21–0 win.

NOTRE DAME, 2012.

Here is an example of some football-speak I put into every report. The Alabama coaches know exactly what I'm talking about with this lingo.

> Notre Dame begins in a 3-4 front with Quarters coverage in the secondary. With OLB Prince Shembo's versatility, they can easily morph from Odd to Even looks and confuse the opponent offensive line. In addition to Quarters, they will play a form of Cover 2, send the Sam and play Cover 3 or rush the Jack and support it with Cover 6. They will also jump into a Double Eagle (46) and play Man Free. When ND goes to Sub, it is usually a basic Nickel (4-2-5) package. They like to twist and stunt the line and will also stand everyone up in a "Psycho" look, bring 6 rushers and play Cover 0 with both safeties in MM.

MM is man-to-man. Odd is a five-man front with the offensive center "covered," while Even is a four-man front with no one over the center.

Here is another example from the Bama-Irish game report/film study:

> In long yardage situations, the Irish like to use an 8-man drop and roll into C-3 Cloud. ND has shown two different Short Yardage/Goalline structures in the way of a Double Eagle (46) front and an old-fashioned 6-1 that was particularly effective in the USC game.

Ahead of Alabama's SEC, bowl, or playoff opponents, I like to compare the other team's starters with the Crimson Tide's and then count up how many players, if they showed up on Nick Saban's doorstep in Tuscaloosa, could get on the field and contribute wearing the crimson and white. I think this can tell you where the game is going, usually.

For Notre Dame, I counted seven starters on the Fighting Irish squad that could switch uniforms and help the Tide.

Alabama won easily, 42–14.

Two years later, against Ohio State in the first College Football Playoff, I felt the Buckeyes had at least sixteen, if not eighteen, starters who could compete for a role in Tuscaloosa. Indeed, this was bad news for the Tide as we would find out in New Orleans.

Mississippi State, 2014.

The Bulldogs were ranked no. 1 on November 15 when they came to Tuscaloosa. By the fourth quarter the front seven had only allowed 124 rushing yards for Alabama, but Blake Sims had thrown for 211 yards and had two clutch third-down scrambles to move the sticks, which helped the Tide take a 25–13 lead.

> The reality here is that their front seven has size and strength, is relatively airtight in terms of gap responsibilities and plays extremely hard, but their secondary is vulnerable because they simply don't have similar talent back there. Despite the fact that MSU has given up a bunch of yardage, they rank #1 in Red Zone defense by allowing only 18 scores in 31 trips inside the +20 (10 touchdowns/8 field goals) and that has been a huge improvement for them from a season ago (t-80th in 2013).

So what happened? The Tide went 4 for 5 in the red zone with 3 touchdowns and a field goal. The point of emphasis going into the game for the Alabama coaches was to make things happen in the red zone. They did, and the Crimson Tide won, 25–20.

OHIO STATE, 2014.

> These Buckeyes are, in essence, the Florida Gators wrapped in Scarlet-and-Gray with an abundance of sizable linemen on both sides of the line and plenty of speed at the skill positions. Meyer runs a demanding program and will have his

team convinced that they can out-physical Alabama at the point-of-attack and run away from the Crimson Tide on the perimeter.

The Buckeyes rushed for over 200 yards that night and victimized Alabama in the passing game on the edges.

On the other side of the football, OSU was rather basic in their Base 4-3, but more sophisticated on third downs in their Nickel 3-3.

The reality is that their Base defense is fairly simple, while their Sub package is quite a bit more complicated. For Alabama, the idea of putting Regular people on the field and then expanding and contracting formations to keep Ohio State in their vanilla looks and coverages is much more attractive than trying to play Blue personnel, monitor DE No. 97 Joey Bosa and try to block all of their exotics from the 3-3-5. Therefore, it will be crucial for the Crimson Tide offense to have success on early downs, stay ahead of the sticks and keep the Buckeyes at bay with their Sub packages off the field.

Alabama played behind the sticks much of the game, and DE Steve Miller dropped off in a Fire-Zone and QB Blake Sims hit him between the 8s for a pick-six in the third quarter that essentially sealed the deal for the Buckeyes to win and advance.

Ohio State, more evenly matched with Alabama than Notre Dame, beat the Crimson Tide, 42–35.

MICHIGAN STATE, 2015.

In this report I wrote regarding where the Spartans' defense might be vulnerable. It was rewarding to see this one come to life:

Where is the yardage? The biggest question in this game: can MSU control Derrick Henry with their safeties "back"? If Alabama can put together a play-action plan to get the safeties to react towards the line-of-scrimmage, the 1-on-1's should be there on the outsides for Calvin Ridley and ArDarius Stewart.

With Richard Mullaney as the slot receiver and backside blocker on runs away, cannot imagine the Spartans playing anything other than their 4-3. With No. 45 Darien Harris deployed as a pass defender, Alabama can create a mismatch for the inside receiver when in three-wides.

Sure enough, Michigan State built a nine-man box and held Henry to 75 yards rushing. Alabama quarterback Jake Coker picked apart the Spartans with a vertical passing attack., Lane Kiffin and Co. knew that MSU would be tough to run on, so they adjusted and threw the football downfield.

As a slotted receiver with the tight end set to the outside, Calvin Ridley made it look easy as he ripped MSU down the seam and raced past their flat-footed safeties in Bama's 38–0 shutout win.

CLEMSON, 2015.

The strategy in my report turned inside out from Michigan State to Clemson. The Tigers were better on the perimeter than in their front seven, so the Alabama game plan needed to start between the hash marks with the run and then over the top with the pass.

This is from the Clemson report I sent Nick:

Where is the yardage? Michigan State gave the invitation for Alabama to attack the perimeter and test their Base 4-3 in coverage. In contrast, Clemson's strength is on the edges, so the Crimson Tide might start on the inside first with a package of Regular, Silver and Green runs designed to go straight at their undersized linebackers.

Because of all the communication on D, the Tigers are often late lining up, so an up-tempo approach in the run game might be in order. Get up there and go, and keep punching them in the mouth (both Florida State and Oklahoma found early success running the football). Alabama must stick with their blocks, and with all the reaching/grabbing tackles from the secondary, the potential is there to break off some big gains.

On Alabama's second possession of the game, Henry ran straight up the gut for a 50-yard touchdown run.

(Of course, I didn't write that Clemson was vulnerable to the onside kick because of how they lined up for kick return. That was the brilliant work of Bobby Williams, the Alabama special teams coach.)

Here is more from the Clemson report:

In the passing game, crisp shifts/motions into and out of stacks/bunches will likely create confusion, and again, if it's done from Regular or Silver, outside linebacker No. 11 Blanks can be exposed in space.

Mixing in a QB run can help take some pressure off Derrick Henry and when the safeties get "nosey" as a tandem creating a 9-man box, that's when the Tide must take their downfield shots.

Jake Coker went upstairs for big gainers to ArDarius Stewart and tight end O. J. Howard when Clemson's safeties tried to sniff out the run too early or just outright blew their coverage assignments.

The 2015 Clemson team, in my estimation, had fifteen starters who could make an impact in T-Town under Coach Saban. The Tigers took Alabama into the fourth quarter and lost, 45–40.

WASHINGTON, 2016.

About ten days before the Crimson Tide faced Washington in the 2016 CFP semifinals, wide receivers coach Billy Napier sent a text to me: "Have you completed your scouting report yet? We start practicing for UW tomorrow and I usually read your report before we get going."

You talk about encouragement. It's why I have kept writing these weekly reviews of the Bama opponents over these past eight seasons.

Although the Alabama offense struggled against the Huskies, the real story of the game was on the other side of the football. Here is what I wrote the week of Christmas:

> Offensive Line: Arguably, the place where Alabama should win the game is here along the OL. This UW unit is just okay and will need their play-callers to keep the Crimson Tide off balance with their run-pass mix. No. 72 Trey Adams (6080/309) is the left tackle and their best offensive lineman. He has obvious height and length and is sound against an initial pass rush due to his agile feet and arm length. However, he struggles with counter or 2nd moves and will consistently give up the edge when facing quality players.
>
> Their tandem of right guards can be breached by the Tide as these are the two weakest links in the lineup. No. 60 Shane Brostek (6040/289) and No. 56 Nick Harris (6010/270) are both undersized and lack the overall physical strength to win at the line-of-scrimmage vs. Bama's front seven. Attacking the A- and B-gaps on their right-side is a must in order to affect and harass QB Jake Browning in the pocket and directly in his sight lines.

Other than on one scoring drive on the second possession of the game, the Crimson Tide defensive front, led by Jonathan Allen, dominated the action up front, held the Huskies to 44 yards rushing, and sacked Browning 5 times.

While this book is my eyewitness account of Alabama under Nick Saban, there is no manual on how to defeat the Crimson Tide. I've learned that from being on the practice field and inside the film room.

So how do you beat Alabama?

You have to win the turnover margin. You can't give away easy points to Alabama. You almost have to get a fluke big play, such as the tipped pass Ole Miss got in a 43–37 win over the Crimson Tide in 2015.

The opponent needs its quarterback to be razor sharp. South Carolina's Stephen Garcia completed his first 9 passes in the 2010 game when USC won, 35–21.

Oklahoma's Trevor Knight was on fire in the Sugar Bowl following the 2013 regular season in the Sooners' 45–31 win.

You have to try to pull Alabama into a frenetic, fast-paced, hair-on-fire kind of game. The Tide needs to feel jittery, where it doesn't quite have a grip on the game. You know you are getting something done against Alabama when you see Nick Saban over in the defensive huddle rather than pacing the sidelines during a game.

It helps to be unconventional, too. In 2011, only one team scored 21 points against Alabama. That was Georgia Southern, which ran the triple option. The Crimson Tide won, 45–21.

I have to tell you about the setting where I put these reports to use and the complete professionalism of all the people involved in the radio broadcasts.

Eli and I do not have a pregame meeting on Saturday to discuss his background work on the depth chart or my pregame study of the opponent. On a given Saturday, the only thing I send him is a "Star to Watch" for one of our sponsored segments before the kickoff. Otherwise, we have great trust in each other's preparation. His depth-chart boards are meticulously put together with all sorts of statistics and biographical information, plus the pronunciations of any unusual names. I admire the research and homework he puts into every single broadcast and no one can say, "Touchdown Alabama!" quite like Eli.

I was at the Masters in 2009 just before my audition with the network when I ran into Mike Tirico, one of the signature broadcasters for ESPN who is now with NBC Sports. I told him about my new assignment and he said, "Eli is a pro's pro, you're in good hands, he will set you up."

Eli gave me two basic instructions to follow in the booth when we worked together for the first time at A-Day in 2009. He said,

"When the ballcarrier is tackled or the pass is incomplete, that is your cue to take it and explain what happened. You can have it until they break the huddle for the next play, then give it back to me."

His other directive was "When I ask you a question, you cannot just nod. It's radio, you have to speak!"

Eight seasons later, almost everyone in college football runs the no-huddle offense, so we have had to modify and adjust just like the coaches in trying to call the games. If it's true "fastball," as Nick Saban refers to an up-tempo attack, we find places between snaps or I will go back a down or two to describe a key play that might have just occurred.

If the offense is at the line with everyone looking to the sidelines for instruction, then we have time to do our normal routine.

And, after one hundred wins and four national titles, I'm happy to say that I have never just nodded when Eli asked a question.

We have expert help, of course. Chris Stewart is our proficient sideline reporter. Engineer Tom Stipe keeps the mics on, and spotter Butch Owens makes sure we are accurate with our calls. Brian Roberts, the son of our former leader and game host, Tom Roberts, is our regular statistician, and when he is not available, Jimmy Bank is the man putting the numbers together.

It is a terrific crew and we work well together. We have hand signals in the booth, just like on the field with the team, as we get synced up. We point to each other and we absolutely can execute a handoff from Eli to Chris on the field, or Eli to me in the booth.

Speaking of working together, I have noticed the same thing about the relationship between Alabama fans and Nick Saban. They work well together. The state loves football and pours itself into the sport. Nick returns the favor by pouring himself into the sport and the university. If you have noticed, there is very little talk or speculation about his leaving for another coaching job and that has not always been the case during his tenure in Tuscaloosa.

The state of Alabama and Nick Saban have found their bliss. It took a tragedy to help cement the relationship, but it looks like a permanent partnership for the foreseeable future.

12

A PERFECT MARRIAGE

NICK SABAN AND ALABAMA CONNECT

The University of Texas job came and went in late November 2016. Head coach Charlie Strong was fired, but there was no Texas two-step with Nick Saban, no rumors involving a $10-million-a-year deal. No whispers were fed into the media mill by agents to get the merry-go-round started around college football's king.

You never say never, but Nick Saban and Alabama appear to be in lockstep, perhaps permanently.

One day—April 27, 2011—as tragic as it was, was the impetus for a marriage that would last between Nick Saban and the state of Alabama. On that day catastrophic multiple-vortex tornadoes roared through Tuscaloosa and Birmingham, killing fifty people and doing $2 billion in damage.

Nick rallied his team. The players helped rebuild the town. At the same time, their head coach built a relationship with the community and the state.

The tornadoes developed an emotional connection between Nick and his wife, Terry, and the city of Tuscaloosa and small towns across northern Alabama. People saw his compassion after the disaster, a side of him that had rarely been shown over the years. The state's pain was more glue to hold him in place versus taking the next big college job or seeking another NFL challenge.

The rumors of Nick's leaving for Texas—or returning to the NFL—did not subside for several more years after the tornadoes. It took time for the glue to dry. Now that it has, Nick Saban is a part of this state, and Alabama football has become more than a job; it's a lifestyle for him and his family. He is sixty-five years old and home as a coach, I believe.

Here is something else I think is true about this marriage: the culture of Alabama suits the West Virginia–bred Nick Saban better than that of any other state that has a football colossus to feed. Florida is not rustic enough. California is not conservative enough. Texas is too big. Ohio and Michigan, too cold.

Alabama is ideal, in temperament for football and the mentality of its people. Nick is a squared-away guy working in a state where people appreciate and admire the disciplined leader of their team. He keeps the nonessential stuff to a minimum and gets down to coaching his team.

Might a devoted Catholic such as Nick suddenly bolt for Notre Dame? I suppose, but I think it is a better bet that Nick retires after Alabama or becomes the "commissioner" of college football. There will be a random rumor about his leaving for another job—fake news is alive and well—but something tells me he is here to stay.

It has been a ten-year exercise to compare Nick to Coach Bryant. Here is my shot at it.

Nick is still not as sentimental and spontaneous as Paul "Bear" Bryant, but the Alabama fans respect Nick's process and the approach. Many fans are intimidated by his success—How does he do this?—but they marvel at his devotion to his craft.

So while he might not have that seemingly personal Bear touch, Nick has built that same rapport with the state—albeit slowly—that existed with Coach Bryant. They are two different men. The Bear was more congenial and homespun. Some of you may remember the advertisement he did with South Central Bell:

"Have you called your mama today? I sure wish I could call mine."

I don't see Nick doing that kind of commercial, but he is tight enough with the citizens of the state that some folks here take it personally if you try to mess with Nick. The folks from my adopted hometown of Fairhope, Alabama, serve as an example.

I relayed this story to Bill Belichick at Bama's 2017 Pro Day when he asked me, "So, how much is Nick loved in this state?" He thought it was funny and I hope you do, too.

We had a new chief parachute in from South Florida to run our Fairhope police department. He was an outsider. He didn't understand that Nick Saban is appreciated by people here, and the chief found that out to his detriment.

In 2013, when we had a Tuesday practice for the Reese's Senior Bowl at the Fairhope Municipal Stadium, Nick arrived nearby in a helicopter and needed a police escort to get in and out quickly because it was in the height of recruiting season. He was doing the city—and its economy—a favor. When Nick Saban is in Baldwin County, gas stations, convenience stores, you name it, become more profitable because more people drive in from the surrounding area to get a glimpse of "their" head coach.

I was told that when our police chief was asked about the escort and road closures to get Nick to practice, the chief deadpanned "Fuck Saban."

The city leaders found out about the alleged remark. This police chief had plenty of other missteps—he had his officers issue tickets for jaywalking, they set up "speed traps" all over town, had cars towed at the local hospital on Christmas and from churches on Easter, and placed armed officers in security "towers" to survey the crowds at the annual arts festival among them—all to the point that the Fairhope people wanted him out almost immediately after his arrival. But, to make such a statement about the Alabama football coach, well, that was crossing the line and would not be tolerated.

Two weeks later, the chief, who was a purported Miami Dolphins fan, was finally fired. Translation: You don't have to love our coach, but you better respect him.

I suppose some people outside Alabama feel Saban doesn't deserve the reverence. I know what they are thinking: Nick has made some mistakes and allowed players into the program many felt should never have been let in. I know all about those stories and criticisms.

I thought I would bring up some dealings with players you might not know about.

Here's one:

Saban will defend his players, even to his assistant coaches who get out of line in the heat of a game. In the 2016 game against Western Kentucky, the backups were in the game working with a 38–3 lead. Offensive coordinator Lane Kiffin called too exotic of a play considering Alabama was merely trying to run the clock. Western recovered an Alabama fumble, and Kiffin said into the headset for all the coaches to hear on the sidelines, "Dumb players make dumb plays."

One of the coaches told me that Saban barked back through his headset, "No, dumb offensive coordinators call dumb plays."

Remember when Saban surprised the WKU postgame press-conference gathering by saying, "That was an ass chewing," on the sidelines with Kiffin? It was about the OC's unfortunate remark about one of their own players. It made headlines.

That's why the team responds to Nick Saban.

Here is another Saban story players will rally around.

Brad Smelley, a Tuscaloosa native, was an H-back/tight end from 2008 to 2011. He was athletic and had good hands. He could separate himself from the defensive backs and catch the football in traffic. But Smelley tried to make himself into a brawler, a bigger tight end that could block anyone and still catch passes. He put himself on a heavy weight-lifting regimen before the 2010 season.

"I tried to change my body and be an every-down guy," Smelley said.

Smelley had a postseason assessment meeting with Saban. "In our meeting Coach told me, 'Be your own guy, do what you do best, and let it shine,'" Smelley said. "Coach told me my strength is to get open on anybody and catch everything thrown to me. I'll never forget him telling me as I left, 'Don't forget who you are and what got you here.'"

Smelley put it all together his senior season at Alabama in 2011. He remained a versatile tight end, not a blocking behemoth. Smelley paid attention to detail and understood defenses and made that his forte. He was going to be an accomplished receiver, not a dominating blocker. He got back to being who he was, a skill athlete with some degree of size, and it paid a big dividend with 34 receptions for 356 yards that season, which culminated in a national championship win over LSU.

Smelley learned something valuable along the way: Saban wasn't the only Alabama coach players could believe. Smelley said longtime assistant Bobby Williams was knowledgeable in his own right, and it was Williams who taught Smelley hand placement and footwork. The assistants were an extension of Saban and they could be trusted, too.

Brad was drafted into the NFL, spent some time on practice squads, and played in four career games, which puts him in select company (only 0.08 percent of high school players ever get drafted).

In the late spring of 2015, Smelley was working out in the UA football facility when Saban came hustling through the weight room on his way to Coleman Coliseum for a pickup basketball game. Saban loves basketball and religiously plays every day from signing date until the start of spring football. This time frame is part of "his" process during the off-season, an outside interest that gets his mind away from football.

Saban saw Smelley out of the corner of his eye. The head coach stopped and came over to Smelley. "How are you? How are your folks? Good to see you, Brad."

"I had not seen Coach in four years," Smelley said. "Four years. He remembered my name and he stopped his ritual to come say hello.

"He gets this knock that he is not personable. I don't agree with that criticism."

Smelley's story gets at the heart of Saban's Process for players.

Publicly, a whole billboard has been erected about Alabama's being "team first," but I absolutely believe Nick has an individual, precise game plan for each player. How does the player project in the weight room? How does he forecast for us: starter, backup, or a "program" kid, a guy who deserves to be part of the team because of his attitude? Nick knows these things. If you are on his team, he knows who you are and where you are headed on the depth chart.

Michael Nysewander, an H-back on the 2015 national championship team, could draw the tender emotion out of Saban. Nysewander was a walk-on from the Birmingham area who was not considered a Division I prospect. He wanted to play for UA. He practiced with Alabama and regarded it as a privilege, even though he was paying to play when his college career started.

Nysewander's work earned him snap after snap in 2015, and he became an escort blocker for Heisman Trophy winner Derrick Henry. Nysewander was nicknamed Highway 46 for his bone-crushing blocks. Saban would become emotional just talking about Nysewander's career path at Alabama.

Here is another reason the Alabama fan appreciates Saban. In the 2016 season opener against Southern California, sophomore safety Ronnie Harrison got into a verbal confrontation with a USC player. When Harrison got to the sideline, senior safety Eddie Jackson was waiting for him and said that Alabama stays out of jawing contests with the opposing team. Saban demands this on the field. Harrison understood.

From the top down, Alabama has a consistent message and a consistent method of dealing with players. Football players appreciate Saban's consistency. They appreciate how he treats them. Can he screw up? Sure, but his batting average is pretty high in his interpersonal relationships with these teenagers who join his team.

"He doesn't care where you come from or what coach recruited you. At end of the day I found out it does not matter to him if you are a Mike Shula or a Mike Price guy, you are my guy now," Smelley said. "'I'm here to make you a better player.' That's his message.

"Smart guys who play hard and are consistent in what they do and do the right thing all the time, they can be a Saban guy. We all know that."

The six players who returned for the 2016 season certainly know that. O. J. Howard, Jonathan Allen, Ryan Anderson, Reuben Foster, Tim Williams, and Eddie Jackson were eligible for the draft and returned not just because they wanted to improve their draft status. They wanted to stay in the "brotherhood" of the Crimson Tide program and play for Nick Saban one more year.

Some of them returned because Saban had convinced them of the importance of completing school and polishing their skill. The NFL covets players who are determined and can finish. The players made their own decisions to come back and get themselves 100 percent prepared for when they left Alabama, but Saban had something to do with those decisions.

Do you see what those decisions did for the program? Those players—typically, half would go pro—were not in the picture for the 2016 season. In my opinion, they were the secret sauce to another run at a potential national championship.

Did Saban worry over losing those six players? Probably. He is a worrier, no doubt about that, but he also does his homework and tries to provide the best info for these aspiring pros and their families. Nick has a pretty good idea of whether a player is ready for the NFL, but he always outsources a number of people, including me, to take a look at his underclassmen and give a neutral assessment.

Rick Venturi, who coached with us at the Browns in 1994, told me he picked up Nick at the airport after Saban went to Michigan State to interview for the head coaching job. Nick got in the car and Rick asked him how it went.

"I don't know, maybe not so good, I think they are going to hire somebody else," Saban said.

Michigan State hired Nick. It is Saban's personality to overthink and "know" the answer to things, such as his interview at Michigan State. The worry over the Michigan State job is because Nick understands other capable coaches are out there. He does not stand on a mountaintop and proclaim himself king of anything. The man is pure blue-collar, as befits his upbringing.

It is why he has a driven personality. He takes that "work" personality with him all over campus.

In the pickup basketball games in Coleman Coliseum, the Alabama football coach is as stern as the Alabama basketball coach when it comes to movement. If you are not running the baseline to get open on down screens, Saban barks at you. If you don't pass and cut, he will get annoyed. He is a terrific teammate, especially when it comes to knowing what's a good shot and making the open shot.

"At the elbow, he doesn't miss his shot much," Smelley said.

What about putting a taller defender on the coach and making him shoot "out of a well," just as his defensive linemen make shorter quarterbacks throw out of a well?

"Uh, nobody does that to Coach," Smelley said. "I wouldn't try to pack him, I know that. I think everybody is scared to get up in his grill."

Saban's drive—on and off the field—holds off the swing of the pendulum. He understands better than anyone else that the pendulum does not swing and stick to the winning side on its own. It can swing back to negative—from winning to losing—in an instant, just as it did on Joe Paterno, Bobby Bowden, Pete Carroll, and Les Miles. So Saban does not take any chances with his approach.

He puts off the swing of history and losing momentum with aggressive recruiting and the teaching of fundamentals. He puts off a downturn in his program with an adherence to details, just as his friend Bill Belichick does with the New England Patriots, who are also perennial contenders, in the NFL. Belichick does not win every title and neither does Saban, but they win more than their share.

You think Saban sweats the details? You should get a load of Belichick.

In preseason camp before the 1991 season, Bill asked me to conduct a tryout with some new guys. "Great, that's what I'm here for," I thought. "Run some free agents through drills and see if they are good enough to add to our roster."

It wasn't a tryout of players. It was a tryout for ball boys!

Bill wanted ball boys who could throw and catch. I'm not kidding you. He didn't want some kid who couldn't throw the ball ten feet holding up his practices by running the ball to the spot for the next play. Bill didn't want some kid who couldn't catch letting the ball hit the ground and roll around and stopping practice while the ball was tracked down.

Bill said, "I don't want twenty-two guys ready to scrimmage and we can't get the football spotted."

Bill gave me that signature ultimatum of his in his now legendary tone: "I don't want to be talking about this on July twenty-first. They got to be able to catch the fucking ball, okay?"

It's what he would say on Tuesdays as we game-planned for the next opponent: "I don't want to be talking about this on Sunday."

So I got twenty kids on a back field in Berea and tried them out. Most had some connection to the organization such as being the nephew of the team doctor or the neighbor of the marketing director. I scouted them, watched them throw and catch. I put some as ball boys and I put some on the chain gang. I reported back to Bill, "Hey, I think we have a decent crew ready to go."

Every scenario was accounted for. There are no gaps. Details were rehearsed.

Saban has the same mind-set. In his mind he has an answer for everything . . . even those seconds between plays when a ball bouncing around on the practice field could halt a scrimmage.

You think there would be some downtime, one miss of Saban's eagle eye. You think he would let just one thing get away from him. Maybe by accident he won't see something that needs to be addressed, but only by accident.

In the 2016 game with Mississippi State, a 51–3 Alabama win, the Crimson Tide kicked off 9 times. The Bulldogs returned one of those kicks 50 yards. Running backs coach Burton Burns, one of the best assistant coaches in all of college football, had taken over the unenviable task of handling the special teams from Bobby Williams. Burns

is the only assistant left from Nick's original staff in 2007. Nevertheless, this gentle, wise man felt the sting of Nick and his never-ending
strive to coach a perfect game.

During the review of the special teams against MSU, where the
Bulldogs had one long kickoff return to the other side of the 50, that
kick return came up on the video.

Burton blurted out, "Well, we were close to making the play, we
almost got him."

Saban barked (with some colorful language omitted), "Oh, yeah,
we almost got him. They had one return and ran it to the plus side of
the field."

As the staff left the meeting, Burton said with a chuckle, "I've been
here long enough to know better, I was just trying to be positive."

Nothing escapes the man, not even one lousy play in a 48-point
demolition of an SEC rival.

Nick tries to think of everything. Just look at Lane Kiffin.

Nick figured Kiffin's shelf life as an assistant coach was going to
be two or three years. When it got to three years, Nick started looking
around for Lane's replacement. Standing off in purgatory, just as Kiffin had been before he came to Tuscaloosa, was Steve Sarkisian, the
ousted coach of USC, who would need a second chance to get his
career going again.

Sark was hired in September 2016 as an "analyst." A good football coach, he appeared to be the ideal hire as the offensive coordinator to replace Kiffin. And sure enough, after Lane was named head
coach at Florida Atlantic and it became obvious that his balancing of
both jobs was not going to work, Sark was promoted to OC for the national title game against Clemson. It should be noted that several
weeks later when the Atlanta Falcons needed a new offensive coordinator, head coach Dan Quinn reached out to Sark and he left for the
NFL. To say his career got restarted in Tuscaloosa would be an un-
derstatement in my estimation.

Is Nick always thinking football? Not always.

Saban's Kentucky Derby parties in Cleveland were always on

everyone's calendar. Pat Hill, who coached tight ends and was later the Fresno State coach for fifteen years, said Saban was the life of the party at his house the first Saturday in May.

"The best time, the best party," Hill said. "He was a lot of fun to be around that day. He would take a hat around with the numbers of all the horses, and we would all take a number out of the hat and that was our horse. He threw a great party."

All kinds of stories are told about the personality of the Nick that we don't see.

Remember when I wrote that Alabama was years behind in the technology of football, and that the program had some catching up to do in the digital age?

Well, he meant everybody but him. If he doesn't want to catch up, he doesn't have to.

The technology staff tried to get him up to speed with using the iPad like the rest of the coaches. He doesn't like the iPad. He prefers his laptop, which reminds me of the time his friend Bill Belichick took the newfangled Surface tablet by Microsoft and flung it to the ground and said it was just too "undependable" on the sidelines.

Nick didn't sync up with the iPad and one day muttered, "I've won plenty of games with Beta tapes."

When Terry Saban's home computer developed a bug, the staff went to the house to try to repair it. They figured they would have to replace it, so they took the computer from Nick's office—which he never used—and set it up for her. He would never miss it, right?

Nick came in that night after practice and said, "Hey, where's my computer? I sit my [straw] hat on that thing."

His children gave him a portable music player one year for Christmas. He had some Beats headsets. They thought he might like to listen to music while he worked. A coach walked into Nick's office one day and music was blaring, but the headset wasn't attached correctly.

"Hey, I can't get this 'music machine' to work the right way," Saban said.

The music was Jim Morrison and the Doors, from the era of Saban's college days at Kent State. A staffer plugged the headphones in correctly. Saban smiled, gave a thumbs-up, and went back to work.

Nick does not need the next gadget, or the more modern iPad. He prefers a notebook computer he can flip open and get to work on watching tape.

When he gets on the plane after a game, Nick eats his dinner and immediately opens that notebook and starts grading the game and taking notes. In the middle of the night flying back from LSU or Texas A&M to Tuscaloosa, after another win, he is right back at it, truly a film junkie.

Everything is in sequence with him, he's always been like that. This is what's supposed to be happening at night after a game, and that's what happens. It's not time for a nap. That's when he watches the game tape and gets it done.

Think about it. The man goes through the whole game, then talks to his team, then addresses the media, and you get on the plane and think, "It's time for some shut-eye." Not with him.

Here is what I have learned about Nick Saban after twenty-five years.

He does not have to be the smartest man in the room every single day. Venturi, who worked in the NFL for three decades and worked with us in Cleveland, told me that Nick has invited him to talk to Nick's coaches about X's and O's. That's right, Nick will bring in an outside voice if he thinks it will make a difference in his program. That is significant in this day and age because football is full of bright minds and you can never have enough brainpower. That's why Lane Kiffin ended up at the University of Houston in spring 2015, and TCU in spring 2016: to learn for the UA staff.

One of the things Saban is smartest about is the hold football has over kids from Alabama.

He could recruit nationally and pull in a class of twenty-five five-star players from around the United States. But he is wedded to the state, and the South, and he counts on that allegiance and state pride to add something extra on game day. Nick gets that from kids who played high school football in Alabama. Sure, he has added players from New Jersey, Texas, Pennsylvania, the DC area, and California, but he understands that the players from the state provide an extra layer of passion.

That's one of the balances that Saban has to juggle. If you have seventeen starters from other parts of the country, it may not mean quite as much to put on that Crimson helmet and jersey.

Just look at Jake Coker. A Mobile native, Coker willed Alabama to a national title in 2015. He dislocated his shoulder against LSU and continued to play for three weeks with pain. His knee ached from two surgeries in 2014 and he never complained. Coker was never 100 percent healthy, but center Ryan Kelly said Coker was the toughest player on the 2015 team.

It had to do with state pride. It is difficult to see how a player from Mississippi or California or Texas could have the same determination as Jake.

Coker is a disciple of Coach Saban's because of Nick's devotion to his players, no matter where they are from.

"Once you are done at Alabama, you're not done," Coker said. "You can come back and work out for free, like you never left. You can go in the training room and they will fix you up. They will treat you like they did when you played there. I can call Jeff Allen, the head athletic trainer, right now.

"For instance, Jeremy Sell, one of the trainers, worked with me on my toe when I was there. Well, I needed some insoles for my shoes before the draft, and the next day I had insoles. They are willing to do anything for anybody that played there."

Coker said that some programs might have smooth sailing for three or four years, but one hiccup and the whole thing collapses, the program drops from the top ten. Saban's consistency, once again, keeps Alabama humming. Within twelve hours of Alabama's last-second loss to Clemson in the 2016 national championship game, the

Las Vegas oddsmakers had already installed the Crimson Tide as the favorite for the 2017 title.

I saw the consistency in training camp with the Browns in 1991 when Nick coached the defensive backs. When the rest of the team came out for practice, shirttails were out, loose bits of tape dangled from their arms. Shirts might have been cut off, and because it was training camp, players stopped to chat with fans. When the defensive backs came out on the field, they marched right to their appointed spot, with Nick and me waiting for them. Their shirts were tucked in, socks were the same color, and nothing about them was scraggly. In training camp they did not sign autographs on the way to the field like players at other positions might do. They went to work.

Nick says that's why it's called a uniform; it represents the team with everyone wearing it the same way. Even now, the Alabama players are required to tuck in their jerseys with no outward signs of individualism.

"The leadership he has and the way he handles himself is so infectious," Coker said. "Everybody buys in. A lot of programs have that for four years maybe and they are really good, but then they lose a couple games and then all of a sudden it falls apart.

"You remember what happened in 2015 when we lost to Ole Miss. People said the dynasty was over and we had no chance. The foundation is there and it is never going to change as long as he's there. One game was not going to crack the foundation. It's lasted ten years because of him."

These Alabama-bred quarterbacks, these native sons, fear failure, a pressure that might not register with quarterbacks from other parts of the country. When the Alabama quarterback goes home, he is looked at as "Did you win or lose?" That was a driving force for Coker, it was something he had to do, he had to win a championship. He persevered through all those injuries to what looked like an unlikely title after that early-season loss to Ole Miss in 2015.

For quarterbacks who have transferred out of Alabama and have come from other parts of the country, it is a little easier for them to go home and say, "I didn't get a fair shake" or "They just didn't like me." You don't have that option if you are from within the state because the natives are always going to side with the coach. It's hard to leave the program if you are from the state of Alabama.

Bama dealt with it when backup quarterback Blake Barnett (California) left the program during the 2016 season, and then, after the year ended, Cooper Bateman (Utah) and David Cornwell (Oklahoma) departed for other schools.

"Alabama football is more of a lifestyle than a hobby," Coker said. "It's definitely different at Alabama than anywhere else." There's that word, *lifestyle*, the same one I used earlier to describe Nick's current situation in Tuscaloosa. It's not a hobby for him or his family; they embrace the program and the players.

"I think that's why there has to be a lot of Alabama guys on the team. I think Coach Saban does a good job of finding guys who really care and put everything they have out on the field."

Saban has won four national championships at Alabama. When he hoisted that first trophy in January 2010 in Bryant-Denny Stadium, he said, "This is not the end, this is the beginning."

Saban was just getting started with his Process of recruiting and development and practicing. He modified his offense, adapted his defense. More important, Saban installed a mind-set. One person—that's all it takes—can set the tone for an entire program. That's him. Nick will set a tone for 2017 as Alabama tries to get back on top.

There are some things I need to close with about this mentality of 4th and goal every day.

Steve Spurrier made this dig at the Alabama coach when the "Head Ball Coach" was at South Carolina:

He's got a nice little gig going, a little bit like [John] Calipari. He tells guys, 'Hey, three years from now, you're going to be a first-round pick and go.' If he wants to be the greatest coach or one of the greatest coaches in college football, to me, he has to go somewhere besides Alabama and win, because they've always won there at Alabama.

It was ridiculous and off the cuff with no basis in fact. Saban had already won a national championship at LSU, and the Crimson Tide had not won it all since 1992.

To further the point, the Crimson Tide went from 1978 to 1992 without a national championship. Spurrier made it sound as if titles fall off the trees for Alabama. Perhaps the HBC should have said, "They've always won there at Alabama . . . when they have had the right coach."

Bear Bryant was the right coach. Gene Stallings was the right coach. Nick Saban is the right coach.

Here is another attribute to highlight: Nick Saban's inherent hustle.

On the team's flight to the White House in June 2010 to receive their congratulations from President Barack Obama for winning the 2009 season national championship, Saban did not bask in the glory of meeting the most important person in the world. He pulled out his computer. The Crimson Tide staff had loaded tapes of the upcoming 2010 opponents. Nick Saban, on his way to the White House, was breaking down tape on his laptop.

Finally, I need to tell you about a phone call I had in January 2007 with Alabama legend Ozzie Newsome. Ozzie was the GM of the Ravens, I was the GM of the Browns. Nick had just been hired at Alabama.

I said, "Ozzie, this is either going to be the quickest, ugliest divorce you have ever seen, or an incredible marriage."

Ozzie just laughed. "You're right."

The both of us knew how strong willed Nick is, and we knew the Alabama fan base was just as strong willed. Nick was certainly going to take heed of the legacy of Coach Bryant, but Nick was going to the University of Alabama with his own ideas of how things were going to be done, and it was going to be the Saban way or the highway.

Nick was going to implement the Process with his set of rules, and everyone would bend to his system or Nick would be out of there in a flash. The regents, the governor, the president of the school, they all were going to let Nick right this ship in his own manner. And right the ship he did.

The Nick Saban that Alabama has gotten is the culmination of what a head coach is supposed to be. He has, through trial and error, figured out what works and what doesn't work, on and off the field. He has a plan for strength and conditioning, the weight room, and the off-season program. He has a thick playbook for academics, recruiting, dealing with alums, and addressing the media. The man has dedicated his life to football, and Alabama—the state, the university, and its people—have enjoyed the fruits of his labor.

Nick brings forty-plus years of experience to every meeting, practice, and game. Virtually no situation can arise that he doesn't have a solution for, situations that might trip up another coach with less of a pedigree.

Alabama fans have accepted that Nick is of the same pedigree as Coach Bryant. The job is too big for many coaches. It was not too big for Coach Saban and Coach Bryant. They both came into challenging situations—at a school where football really matters—and they succeeded. Why? They were brave.

I have to tell you one last story.

On the Saturday before Alabama played Clemson for the 2015-season national championship, I invited one of my best friends, T. J. McCreight, who is the scouting director for the Indianapolis Colts, and his son, Matthew, to attend the Crimson Tide practice. Matthew plays high school football in the Phoenix area for Jeff Rutledge, the former Alabama quarterback from the 1970s, who was a childhood hero of mine. I asked T.J. to invite Jeff, too.

When Jeff came on the field in Arizona to watch the Tide, it was the first time he had been back to an Alabama practice since the day before the 1979 Sugar Bowl, where Bama beat Penn State, 14–7, for the national title and preserved the win with an unforgettable goal-line stand in the fourth quarter.

Jeff began to reminisce about playing for Coach Bryant. He said that on Saturday mornings after the team meal, Coach Bryant would take a walk with his starting quarterback, just the two of them, one-on-one. Coach would say simple things like "We need to throw when they think we will run, and run when they think we will pass. When we need a yard, let's run the ball with our best back behind our best lineman."

At the end of the talk, Coach Bryant would look Jeff in the eyes and before turning to walk away, the Bear would grumble, "Be brave."

Man, I get chills down my spine and tears in my eyes just thinking about that day inside Arizona State's practice bubble, when Jeff relayed what it was like to be the quarterback for Coach Bryant.

Two days after Rutledge told me this story, Alabama played Clemson for the 2015 championship, and another Alabama quarterback, Jake Coker, whose career—to say the least—was riddled with injuries, gave a truly brave performance. Another brave performance came when Nick Saban called for the surprise onside kick that proved to be the difference for the Tide. Alabama won its sixteenth championship, 45–40.

In the meantime, my wife, Dorothy, and I were expecting our second child in late February. We had chosen Ever as a first name, but had yet to settle on his middle name. At dinner the night before Ever was born, the Coach Bryant/Jeff Rutledge story hit me between the eyes. Be Brave.

The boy, born on February 25, 2016, would be called Ever Brave Savage. He was born with a name that has a story behind it, and a name that carries some responsibility in front of it.

My final impression to leave you with is this: Alabama football is a matter of being brave. So continue to go for it, fellas. Embrace the responsibility and expectations. Understand the pressure and treat the game with respect. When you play for the Crimson Tide, it is 4th and goal every day.

EPILOGUE

We use the phrase *windshield time* in scouting because scouts/re-cruiters are in their cars frequently staring through a windshield. They are driving from town to town looking for players. Alabama re-cruits the entire state thoroughly, and its coaches bump along back roads, sometimes to the most remote of places.

No spotlight shines on this part of the process. It is solitary work. Most of the time scouts sit alone in the stands or in the end zone and just watch a player. That is the way it should be. Scouts are trained to evaluate players with their eyes, not their ears. Do not listen to the chatter, the hype. Look. See. Study.

I scouted in the NFL and continue to do so in identifying pros-pects to invite to our annual Reese's Senior Bowl in Mobile. I have been to schools from coast to coast, from the biggest to the smallest, and other than Iowa State, have stepped foot on every major univer-sity in the country. I have been on NAIA and Division III campuses as well as visited Division II and FCS-level programs trying to find players who can make a successful leap to the National Football League.

I don't know if scouts have a motto or a creed. I guess this will do as well anything: "We go where there are players." It's not flashy, but scouting is not flashy. It is a grind, and sometimes it can be exhilarating.

In 1994, I was sent by the Cleveland Browns to scout players at every HBCU (historically black colleges and universities) from Prairie View A&M in Texas to Delaware State in Dover. It was a long road trip. I learned about the solitude of scouting and trusting your ability to evaluate players.

Years later, my mother, Carol Savage, went on a scouting trip with me when I was the player-personnel director with the Baltimore Ravens. On the final day of our week together, we went to Jackson State in Jackson, Mississippi, during the afternoon and then a Southern Miss game that night. As we drove back home to Fairhope, she wrote a poem about the sojourners of the football industry, the scouts.

ODE TO THE SCOUT

A cool afternoon, the sun starting to set, the shadows long
    on a grassy field,
the scout takes his position at yet another college football
    practice.
He's greeted by the coaches, noticed by the players and
    causes excitement amongst the small gathering of fans.
He finds the numbers he's looking for, watches a few series
    of plays, all the while keeping an eye peeled for an
    unknown, undiscovered gem.
He has spent the last month grading players with the eye
    and the ear, trying to separate athletes who look the
    same to the common man.
What appears to be a simple standing around, watching
    and listening endeavor, will later that night be recorded
    into a detailed, calculated scale written in his own words
    from his own thoughts.

All of this information is discussed and re-discussed over
  and over before draft day.

In the meantime, the scout moves on down the road to a
  night game, this time to take up another post in the
  stands of a big university stadium.

With a watchful eye and the pad in hand, he's always
  looking, always searching for the best of the best, which in
  turn makes his team, the Ravens, the very best of the NFL.

—Carol Savage,
November 2002

ACKNOWLEDGMENTS

When you have a ten-acre farm, seven horses, four jobs, and a family with two children under six, writing a book is certainly not a one-man project, so I have many people to thank.

On the home front, my wife Dorothy did not know a single thing about football back in December 2001 when we met for the first time. She fell in love with me, not football, and that has been revealed through all of the ups and downs of our "football life" together. She is an amazing combination of love, beauty, and toughness wrapped in a spirit of resolve that is immediately recognized by everyone who knows her. Babe, I love you!

To Honor and Ever, the two greatest gifts a father could ever receive, I hope, as you get older, you will be 1/100th as proud of me as I am of the two of you.

Major thanks to my parents, Phil and Carol Savage, for providing such a foundation of education, common sense, and opportunity for me. You sacrificed many of your own dreams to give Joe and me every chance to have success in life.

To Joe and Pam Savage, thank you for always keeping me grounded as it relates to the work you are doing in Moldova and Ukraine. Those orphaned children make a given football Saturday seem trivial in comparison to the mission set before you in rescuing and saving their lives.

My good friend, Ray Glier, not only broached the topic of writing a book, but became the primary engine in producing the 80,000-word manuscript that resulted in *4th and Goal Every Day*. I knew about his devotion to writing and his desire to tell a good story; what I did not know was the supreme work ethic and passion he would bring to this endeavor. Thank you, Ray, a job well done, indeed.

In 1972, Bob Gouthiere "scouted" me on his way home from work as I passed the football with my father in our front yard in West Mobile. At seven years old, I became his quarterback for the next seven seasons, and it was during those days as a member of the Mims Park Redskins that sparked my love of sports and football.

Ruth Welborn, thank you for giving me that Bible verse, Romans 8:28, it changed the direction of my life.

Coach Horace Moore, thank you for paying a visit to Murphy High School and giving me a shot at college football. Coach Dewey Warren, you became one of my lifelong friends, but thanks for first bringing your BYU offense to Sewanee.

I am so appreciative of the head coaches whom I've worked for over the years: Bill Curry at Alabama, Terry Donahue at UCLA, Mike Riley with the San Antonio Riders, Bill Belichick with the Cleveland Browns, Ted Marchibroda and Brian Billick with the Baltimore Ravens, Romeo Crennel with the Cleveland Browns, and Andy Reid with the Philadelphia Eagles.

I've had the good fortune of learning from and working with some incredibly savvy talent evaluators. Michael Lombardi and Dom Anile welcomed me to the "other" side of the building in player personnel back in 1994. Ron Marciniak, Ernie Plank, and Jake Hallum are three veterans who always gave me sound scouting advice. And Gil Brandt, the godfather of NFL scouting, thank you for sharing the genesis of what has evolved into the business of modern-day player personnel at both the collegiate and professional levels.

After a Hall of Fame playing career with the Browns, you can argue that Ozzie Newsome deserves recognition as a Hall of Fame general manager, too, after twenty-plus years heading up the Ravens. He opened the door for me to be a decision maker at a young age, which put me in position to emerge as a GM candidate. Those were awesome years in Baltimore, thanks Wiz and Roll Tide!

I'll always be thankful to Howie Roseman, GM of the Eagles, who reached out to me in 2010 with a chance to get back into the NFL.

To all the coaches and scouts I've been associated with over the years, thank you. Much of what is in this book came from your knowledge in evaluating and coaching players.

To Mal Moore, thank you for taking my call in late January 2009 and giving me an audition with the Crimson Tide Sports Network for the A-Day game that spring. No one represented and loved Alabama more than Coach Moore and we think about him every broadcast.

To Jim Carabin, your phone call in mid-May 2009 is one of those that will never be forgotten. The chance to be the color analyst for Alabama games changed our lives and opened up another window of opportunities.

Thanks to our radio crew at CTSN: Eli Gold, Chris Stewart, Tom Stipe, Tom Roberts, Brian Roberts, Butch Owens, and Jimmy Bank. The Bama Nation could not have a more dedicated group of individuals bringing them the action every Saturday.

Thank you to the coach himself, Nick Saban. First, for showing me what it means to be totally committed to football; second, for granting me the freedom to write this book and; third, for giving it the credibility needed with your opening words.

To Linda Leoni, you have been a dear friend since those early Berea days. My thank-you would never be sufficient enough to convey how much my family and I appreciate you and all of your efforts over these many seasons.

A special thank you to former players Greg McElroy, Dillon Lee, Brad Smelley, Geno Matias-Smith, and Jake Coker for their insights into the program.

For all of the assistant coaches and staff members who have worn the scripted "A" since 2009, congratulations on your success and thank you for letting me inside your world from time to time. Roll Tide!

For all my SiriusXM counterparts on the College and NFL channels, from top to bottom, thank you for indulging me in regard to the Reese's Senior Bowl, Alabama football, and now *4th and Goal Every Day*.

I appreciate the support received from my friends at ESPN, too. Thanks to Rece Davis for the Foreword and everyone in Bristol who has and will help promote this book.

We have a special group at the Reese's Senior Bowl and they have allowed me the flexibility to work on radio and TV, write a book, and help raise two little ones at home. Thanks Rob Lehocky, Lauren Fleming, Julie Jeter-Hicks, Sonya Wakefield, and Patrick Woo for your work in putting on a tremendous event each year.

To the good people at St. Martin's Press, wow, so thankful for your efforts in making this book a reality. Pete Wolverton, for your belief in this project, Jennifer Donovan, John Nicholas, Joe Rinaldi, and all the staff in putting forth such an extended effort.

As a follower of Jesus Christ, I believe the Lord does order our steps and I thank Him for the journey that has included all of the people mentioned here and put me on a path that I could have only dreamed of as a child.

SELECT SCOUTING REPORTS

FLORIDA, 2009 SEC CHAMPIONSHIP

Head Coach: Urban Meyer (5th) (56-9 at Florida) (39-8 at
  BGSU and Utah)
Offensive Coordinator: Steve Addazio (OL background)
Defensive Coordinator: Charlie Strong (four different staffs
  at UF)

STRENGTHS

OFFENSE
- the "power of Tebow" (former Heisman winner, 34-5 as starter,
  84td's to 15int's, 50.0% conversion rate on 3rd downs)
- spread system in place with variety, misdirection plays and options
- overall size at skill positions (QB, TE, WR's)
  #15 QB Tim Tebow (accounted for 30td's in '09 and 140td's
  for his career)
  #81 TE Aaron Hernandez (athletic player with 51 receptions
  in '09)

DEFENSE

- statistically dominant with depth and experience
- 3rd downs (26.2% conversions allowed)
- only allowed 20+points in one game (23–20 win vs. Arkansas)
- #8 DE Carlos Dunlap (9.5 sacks in '08, 7 sacks/6pbu's in '09)
- #49 DE Jermaine Cunningham (11.5tfl/7 sacks/6 qb hurries)
  #51 IB Brandon Spikes (53tt/4.5tfl/3 sacks/2int/2pbu)
  #41 OB Ryan Stamper (leading tackler with 71tt/5.5tfl/2.5 sacks/2int)
  #5 DC Joe Haden (boundary corner with 4int)
  #35 SS Ahmad Black (57tt/1int/3pbu)

SPECIAL TEAMS

- only 4 punt returns allowed all season for 13 total yards (3.3avg)
- #25 KR/PR Brandon James (handles both duties)

WEAKNESSES

OFFENSE

- 81st in the nation for sacks allowed (26 total)
- 81st in the nation for Red Zone offense (44 scores in 56 drives with 28td's)
- lost 11 fumbles in 12 games

DEFENSE

- rarely has to play from "behind" (don't know how much they like a physical offensive approach)

STATISTICAL COMPARISON

2008		2009
10th	Rushing Offense	6th (236.7)
61st	Passing Offense	64th (214.7)
15th	Total Offense	12th (451.3)
4th	Scoring Offense	10th (36.5)
15th	Rushing Defense	8th (89.9)
20th	Passing Defense	1st (143.2)
9th	Total Defense	1st (233.1)
4th	Scoring Defense	1st (9.8)
2nd (+22)	Turnover Margin	17th (+8)

OTHER KEY STATS

3rd Downs	t-5th (50.0%, 77/154 conversions)
3rd Down Defense	2nd (26.2%, 43/164 conversions allowed)
Sacks Allowed	81st (26)
Sacks For	18th (34)
Red Zone Offense	81st (44 scores in 56 drives including 28td's)
Red Zone Defense	12th (17 scores in 23 drives including 7td's)

GENERAL OVERVIEW

Florida comes into the SEC Championship game riding a 22-game winning streak. Head Coach Urban Meyer has enjoyed unprecedented success at Florida and brings a gaudy 56-9 record into this matchup with Alabama and a résumé that includes two national championships. QB Tim Tebow is the spiritual and physical leader of this team and spearheads their offensive "Spread Option" system. The Gators' defense returned their entire two-deep from 2008, and they have statistically dominated their opponents this year. This is a team that has innumerable strengths and very few weaknesses. By outscoring their competition 109–16 in the first quarter, they are able to take control of the game and methodically squeeze the life out of their opponent throughout the remaining three quarters.

OFFENSE

After spending the past four seasons as the Gators' offensive line coach, Steve Addazio took over as the offensive coordinator when Dan Mullen left UF to become the head coach at Mississippi State. Their offense has virtually the same rankings as last year's unit, yet there is a feeling that this team is not as explosive overall. Tebow is the most decorated player in college football history, and he triggers the entire operation. With the loss of WR/RB Percy Harvin and WR Louis Murphy, Florida has turned to their talented tight end, #81 Aaron Hernandez, and two size receivers in #11 Riley Cooper and #83 David Nelson to change the dynamic of this offense from a "fast-break attack" to more of a "half-court" type approach. On the ground, Tebow has 193att/796yds/4.1avg/13td's. Through the air, he has 162comp/244att/66.4%/2,166yds/17td-4int. Hernandez is extremely talented and has 51rec/654yds/12.8avg/4td's. He is utilized down the field and as the Shovel option runner. Cooper has caught 41 passes for 703yds, a 17.1avg and 8td's. Nelson is used to block off the back side like a 2nd tight end, but has chipped in 19rec for 201yds, a 10.6avg and 1td. Both utilize their height to body position defenders down the field on underneath zone routes or over-the-top shots. #2 RB Jeffrey Demps (95att/729yds/7.7avg/7td/lg62) and #3 RB Chris Rainey (83att/541yds/6.5avg/4td/lg76) share reps as in the backfield, but both provide the speed element to this offense. #25 Brandon James is utilized in the Harvin-like role as a combination runner/receiver from the backfield or the slot position. The Gators stress a defense because of their diversified talent at the skill positions; when a team tries to match their size, they counter by getting the ball into the hands of their speed players and vice versa.

Florida uses Blue, Regular, and Pony (#25 Brandon James with another RB) as their primary personnel groupings. They will use an extra offensive lineman (as a 2nd TE, almost like Silver) and Red personnel on a rare occasion. They are excellent on 3rd down because of the run/pass ability of Tebow. He is too strong to contain on 3rd and 4 or less, so it's imperative to win defensively on 1st and 2nd downs.

DEFENSE

Charlie Strong is the defensive coordinator and he is surrounded by a group of veteran assistant coaches. This unit returned all 22 players on their two-deep coming into the 2009 season. They are a 4-3 team that mostly plays an Under front. Whereas most SEC teams have a "player" at each level of the defense, the Gators have multiple players in the defensive line, at the linebacker positions and in the secondary. #49 DE Jermaine Cunningham and #8 DE Carlos Dunlap are the bookends of this front four in Regular. Dunlap, at 6-6/290, will slide inside on Sub downs. They have combined for 20tfl's and 14 sacks. The entire defensive line does an outstanding job of "compressing" the pocket and batting down passes at the line of scrimmage. Overall, this defense is characterized by fast flow linebacker play. #51 IB Brandon Spikes is their spiritual leader. He will slide outside and rush from an End position in Sub. He is bothered by direct runs and his stiffness shows in space when trying to change directions. #41 WB Ryan Stamper is their most productive tackler, and he is generally protected on the backside of their Under front. He likes to be in air where he can run and pursue to the football. He will rotate to the middle LB position when Florida substitutes their depth. #16 OLB A. J. Jones (currently injured) or #40 OLB Brandon Hicks are the formation adjusters and will walk into space. #5 DC Joe Haden plays into the boundary and has recorded 4 interceptions this season. UF uses three safeties for two spots: #35 Ahmad Black, #21 Major Wright, and #10 Will Hill. #14 Markihe Anderson or #10 Hill appear to be the Nickel/Star.

On early downs, UF plays C3, Man Free, and C5 (two-deep/man-under). From a C2 umbrella look, they will "fire" the boundary corner and play Man Free, "fire" the Sam and Mike and drop a DE into a C2 (8-man zone), or "fire" the Sam and vacate a zone in C3 (with 3-under).

In Sub, the Gators play Nickel with a 3-3 front (Odd). As a changeup, they will move to a four-man front with #51 Spikes as a DE. From the Odd look, they like to play Man Free and "fire" a combination of the Star, Mac, or OLB to create their 4- and 5-man pressures with Man Free or C5 behind it. In long-yardage situations, they will drop 8 and play C2. Since they are ahead in most games, they force an offense to "drive the ball" and execute at a high level on a down-to-down basis. They have only recovered 3 fumbles, but have forced 20 interceptions. It is critical for the QB to negotiate the football around the dangerous hands in the pocket, for the outside receivers to win, and for the offensive unit to take a PHYSICAL approach regardless of run or pass.

RADIO BROADCAST NOTES

PREGAME/OPENING
- pointing toward this matchup of #1 vs. #2
- all the elements of a classic game: "competitive character" of both teams
- SEC Championship/Georgia Dome: most electric atmosphere in college football

OFFENSE ("IN ONE STEP," FIELD IS THREATENED HORIZONTALLY AND VERTICALLY)
- #15 Tebow (193att/796yds/4.1avg/13td) (2166yds/66.4%/17td-4int)
- #2 Demps (95att/729yds/7.7avg/7td)
- #81 Hernandez (51rec/654yds/12.8avg/4td)
- #11 Cooper (41rec/703yds/17.1avg/8td)

DEFENSE (4-3 FRONT, "A PLAYER," UF HAS MULTIPLE "PLAYERS" AT EVERY LEVEL OF THE D)

- #49 Cunningham (11.5tfl/7sacks)
- ***#8 Dunlap, suspended***
- #51 Spikes (53tt, missed essentially 4 games) (4int returns for td's)
- #41 Stamper (71tt)
- #5 Haden (boundary corner with 4int's) and #1 Jenkins (2int's)

SPECIAL TEAMS

- #19 Caleb Sturgis (19/26fg's, 15/19 inside 40)
- #25 James (SEC all-time leader with 3999yds and 5td's)

LOWE'S REPORT CARD

- convert on 3rd downs, offense and defense (maintain possession and get off field)
- win turnover margin (UA = +15) (UF = +8)
- special teams: get a return (4pr/13yds) and make kicks (Tiffin: 27/31fg's)

BAMA OFFENSE

- value football (keep away from hands at LOS)
- convert on 3rd down (win on the outsides)
- stay physical and make UF "uncomfortable"

BAMA DEFENSE

- win on 1st and 2nd downs (force 3rd and 7+) (since '07: 6.1avg per rush on 1st down)
- tackle well! (get Tebow, Hernandez, and RB's on the ground)
- no big play scores!

TIDBITS/ITEMS

- SEC tug-o-war (big plays, turnovers, and special teams)
- UF: 43-1 when scoring first (13-8 otherwise) (opening-drive scores in 7 games)
- 7th meeting between UA/UF in SEC title game
- UF senior class: 47-6 (winningest in SEC history)
- Meyer: 11-2 vs. AP top 10 teams (6 in a row)
- Charlie Strong rumored for Louisville job
- 4th quarter: UA 102–24, UF 91–27

Next Opponent: BCS Championship (Texas), Sugar Bowl (TCU, Boise, Cincinnati)

PENN STATE, 2011

Head Coach: Joe Paterno, 46th year/402-135-3 (885 changes since '66)

Offensive Coordinator: Galen Hall, 8th year (Florida head coach '84–'89)

Defensive Coordinator: Tom Bradley, 33rd year (12th as DC)

2010 Record: 7-6/4-4 Big Ten

2011 Record: 1-0 (Indiana State, W 41–7)

Returning Starters: 7 offense/7 defense

STRENGTHS

- size/speed WR corps (stats from 2010 season)
    - #6 Derek Moye (6050e200e440e) 53rec/885yds/16.7avg/8td
    - #19 Justin Brown (6030/214) 33rec/452yds/13.7avg/1td
    - #20 Devon Smith (5070/155) 27rec/363yds/13.4avg/1td
- talented running backs
    - #25 Silas Redd (5100/205) 77att/437yds/5.7avg/2td
    - #26 Curtis Dukes (6010/237) 6att/47yds vs. Indiana State

- defensive line overall size and experience
  #81 Jack Crawford DE (6050e265e) 14tt/4.5tfl/2sacks (missed 6 games with fx foot)
  #71 Devon Still DT (6050e305e) 39tt/6tfl/4sacks
  #47 Jordan Hill DT (6010/297) 36tt/2.5tfl/0.5sacks (7tt vs. Ala)
- solid secondary (six players return with 6+starts in '10)
  #8 D'Anton Lynn DC (6000e210e) 75tt/3int
  #2 Chaz Powell DC (6010/206) (moved to corner for final six games of '10)
  #28 Drew Astorino DS/Hero (5100e200e) 70tt/1int/5pbu
  #1 Nick Sukay DS (6000e210e) 29tt/3int

WEAKNESSES

- inconsistent quarterback play
  #1 Rob Bolden QB (6030/216) 112comp/193att/58.0%/1360yds/ 5td/7int (8 starts)
  #11 Matt McGloin QB (6010/211) 118comp/215att/54.9%/1548 yds/14td/9int (5 starts)
- new placekicker
  #4 Evan Lewis PK/WO (5100/173) (scout team WR)

2010 STATISTICS

Rushing Offense	74th	Rushing Defense	74th
Passing Offense	52nd	Passing Defense	16th
Total Offense	68th	Total Defense	35th
Scoring Offense	81st	Scoring Defense	50th
Sacks Allowed	t-10th	Sacks For	101st
3rd Down Offense	48th (41.8%)	3rd Down Defense	6th (31.7%)
RZ Offense	67th (39/48, 27td/12fg)	RZ Defense	117th (34/37, 26td/8fg)
TO Margin	75th (-4)		
Penalties	3rd (4.08 per game)		

Vs. Alabama: The Tide holds a 9-5 series advantage over Penn State, including a 3-2 mark in Beaver Stadium. In 2010, the Nittany Lions suffered a 24–3 loss on a hot, humid evening in Tuscaloosa when their offense turned the ball over four times and their defense was left staggered by an effective no-huddle attack orchestrated by senior QB Greg McElroy.

GENERAL COMMENTS

The incomparable Joe Paterno returns for his 46th season as head coach in hopes of improving on last year's 7-6 record. With seven starters back on each side of the football and two quarterbacks with significant game experience, the Nittany Lions are expected to challenge for divisional honors in the newly expanded Big Ten. Paterno passed the 400-win mark last season, but the Lions also lost four games by 20+points for the first time in school history. Alabama beat Penn State in Tuscaloosa by the score of 24–3; however, the home-and-home series now shifts to State College, where the Lions are 53-17 over the last ten seasons and have won 23 straight nonconference games (2nd-longest streak in the nation).

OFFENSE

Primarily a Blue, Regular, and Gold team in the past. Galen Hall begins his 8th season as offensive coordinator with the goal of getting better overall quarterback play in 2011. Last year, #1 Rob Bolden became the first true freshman to start at the position for PSU since 1992, while #11 Matt McGloin became the first walk-on to start during the entire Paterno era. Both proved to be inconsistent in spite of being able to hand the ball off to the Lions' all-time leading rusher, Evan Royster, who has since moved on to the NFL. #25 Silas Redd is expected to become the lead back this year with #37 Joe Suhey and #9 Michael Zordich sharing the fullback position. Redd rushed for 104 yards and two touchdowns in the opener vs. Indiana State. Another runner to keep an eye on will be #26 Curtis Dukes (6010/237), who had 6att/47yds in the first game and is considered to be extremely talented by Penn State insiders. The strength of their offense will be at the wide receiver position, where #6 Derek Moye returns after grabbing 53 passes a year ago. #19 Justin Brown also returns, and both of them have tremendous size on the outside. #20 Devon Smith is their gadget/reverse specialist and has the ability to catch and run the football. PSU returns three starters up front with #74 LG Johnnie Troutman and #67 LT Quinn Barham both being NFL "suspects." This has been the weakest part of the Penn State team over the last decade with only 8 offensive linemen drafted in the last 11 years and only one of them being a 1st-round selection.

DEFENSE

The Lions employ a 4-3 system under longtime assistant Tom Bradley, who returns for his 33rd season overall and 12th as the defensive coordinator. They have classic size on the defensive line anchored by DT #71 Devon Still, DT #47 Jordan Hill, and DE #81 Jack Crawford. DE #56 Eric Latimore (6060/277) also returns from a season-ending wrist injury a year ago and played but did not start against Indiana State. The Lions lost two starters from their linebacking corps, but return #42 Michael Mauti, who will line up on the outside in 2011. OLB #34 Nate Stupar had 73tt/6.5tfl's last year and was expected to be a starter; however, in the game against Indiana State, Stupar was a backup with #40 Glenn Carson (6030/239) and #6 Gerald Hodges (6020/234) opening as the MLB and OLB, respectively. The strength of their defense will be in the back end, where six players return who started at least 6 games last year. #8 D'Anton Lynn is a three-year starter at boundary corner and brings excellent size to the table. #2 Chaz Powell is also a bigger corner, who doubles as a kick returner. #12 Stephon Morris is athletic, but undersized as their third corner. #28 Drew Astorino comes back as the strong safety (Hero) and will pair off with free safety #1 Nick Sukay, who missed six games with injury a year ago. #10 Malcolm

Willis stepped in for those six games and made an impact with 54tt and 4 passes defensed.

SPECIAL TEAMS

Overall, Penn State improved from #115 to #34 in special teams after a horrific showing in 2009 (all areas). #4 Evan Lewis made his debut vs. Indiana State and missed a PAT and two field goals (38 and 47 yards). KR #2 Chaz Powell averaged 24.0 yards per return last year, including a 100-yard TD vs. Youngstown State. He took the first kickoff of the season back for a 95-yard touchdown last weekend. #20 Devon Smith returned 12 punts for a 12.9avg, but has excellent quickness and make-miss ability.

CONCLUDING REMARKS

Penn State will be a challenging road test for Alabama in the second game of the year. With their experience (7 seniors on both sides of the football) and NFL-looking defensive unit, the Lions have enough front-line talent to compete with the Tide. For Bama to win, the Crimson Tide must take advantage of Penn State's inconsistent QB play, their underwhelming offensive line, and a shaky field goal kicker by dominating the LOS, forcing turnovers, and scoring touchdowns in the Red Zone (PSU was 117th in the nation in Red Zone defense last year).

RADIO BROADCAST NOTES

TAILGATE/PREGAME SHOWS
- storied rivalry between two traditional powers (both have 800+)
- different environment than a year ago (stadium, weather, QB experience)
- improvement from game #1 to game #2 (run ball, eliminate turnovers)

FUTURE STAR OF TOMORROW

QB/RB Blake Sims (Wildcat package)

DE Jesse Williams ("pack your defense")

FOR BAMA TO WIN

- offense: solid start, run the football, ball security
- defense: stop the run, affect the QB's, force turnovers
- special teams: win field position, create a turnover

BAMA NOTES (#2 COACHES/#3 AP)

- 15th meeting with Penn State (9-5, 3-2 in State College)
- 15-9 vs. Big Ten
- Nick Saban/5th season (44-11) (135-53-1) (11/14 bowls, 2 BCS)
- 2nd most wins since '08 (37) (Boise State has 38)
- 14-5 vs. Top 25 and 9-3 vs. Top 10
- 25-1 with a 100-yard rusher
- 39-3 when leading at halftime (LSU '07 and '10, Auburn '10)
- 41-8 when forcing a turnover
- Players of the Week: Kent State
    offense: Barrett Jones, Eddie Lacy
    defense: Courtney Upshaw, DeQuan Menzie
    special teams: M Maze, W Lowery, Trey DePriest, Vinnie Sunseri
- new coaches: Jeff Stoutland/OL, Chris Rumph/DL, Mike Groh/WR
- 11 players already graduated: Hardie Buck, Josh Chapman, Nick Gentry, Brandon Gibson, Barrett Jones, Phelon Jones, Alfred McCullough, Morgan Ogilvie, Chris Underwood, William Vlachos, Alex Watkins

2010 BAMA STATISTICS

Rushing Offense	29th	Rushing Defense	10th
Passing Offense	27th	Passing Defense	13th
Total Offense	22nd	Total Defense	5th
Scoring Offense	18th	Scoring Defense	3rd
Turnover Margin	11th		
3rd Downs/Off	32nd (44.7%)	3rd Downs/Def	12th (34.0%)
RZ/Off	3rd (48/57, 36td/12fg)	RZ/Def	4th (20/30, 10td/10fg)
Penalties	24th (5.08 per)		
Scoring:	123–43/160–47/ 112–41/ 69–45= 464–176 (35.7–13.5)		

PSU NOTES

- 125th season (819-357-42) (Bama 803-319-3/120th season)
- 43,998 enrollment
- Beaver Stadium (106,572/2nd largest in nation)
- Joe Paterno (62nd year on staff, 300 faster, college HoF, 4-9 vs. UA)
- 17-18 vs. SEC (14-16 under Paterno, 8-5 in bowl games)
- #2 Miami in 2001 season opener
- 59-19 since '05 (11th best win % in nation)
- 23-game nonconference home winning streak (Boston College, 9/6/03)
- Big Ten is 20-13-1 at home vs. SEC since 1933 (only 3rd trip since '81) (LSU-OSU '88, Vandy-UM in '06)

- Big Ten expands to 12 teams (Nebraska), Lucas Oil Field, Indianapolis
- Captains: Drew Astorino, Quinn Barham, Derek Moye, Devon Still
- fathers/sons: (26 fathers/sons in 46 seasons) (Hull/Mauti/Stupar/Suhey/Zordich)
    D'Anton Lynn/DC (father, Anthony, RB coach at NY Jets)
    Ryan Scherer/WO (father, Rip, OC in '87, now at CU)
    Michael Zordich/FB (father, Mike, DB coach at Eagles)

GEORGIA, 2012 SEC CHAMPIONSHIP GAME

Head Coach: Mark Richt (12th season) 117-39 (FSU)

Offensive Coordinator: Mike Bobo (6th year) (all UGa)

Defensive Coordinator: Todd Grantham (3rd year) (MSU)

2011 Record: 10-4/7-2 SEC East (L SEC title to LSU, 42–10)

Top Players Lost: OT Cordy Glenn, TE Orson Charles, DC/
RS Brandon Boykin, K Blair Walsh, PT Drew Butler

2012 Record: 11-1/7-1 SEC East (L @ South Carolina, 35–7)

Returning Starters: 7 offense/9 defense

Best Players Returning: QB Aaron Murray, WR Tavarres
King, WR Malcolm Mitchell, DT John Jenkins, LB Jarvis
Jones, LB Alec Ogletree, DS Bacarri Rambo, DS Shawn
Williams

Tapes Viewed: VU, Tennessee, South Carolina, Florida,
GSU

STATISTICAL HISTORY (NATIONAL RANKINGS)

	2011	2012
Rush Offense	49th (164.0yds)	39th (190.1yds)
Pass Offense	48th (244.5yds)	35th (273.6yds)
Total Offense	39th (408.5yds)	24th (463.7yds)
Scoring Offense	33rd (32.0pts)	17th (38.0pts)
Rush Defense	11th (101.2yds)	67th (163.4yds)
Pass Defense	10th (176.0yds)	9th (174.4yds)
Total Defense	5th (277.2yds)	22nd (337.8yds)
Scoring Defense	23rd (20.6pts)	16th (17.7pts)
Turnover Margin	t-26th (+7)	19th (+9)

OTHER NOTEWORTHY STATS

3rd Down Offense	27th	46.0%
3rd Down Defense	32nd	35.6%
Red Zone Offense	t-23rd	35 for 41 (33td/2fg)
Red Zone Defense	13th	27 for 38 (18td/9fg)
Sacks Allowed	56th	22 total
Sacks For	60th	24 total
Penalties	t-89th	6.8 per game

GENERAL COMMENTS

The Georgia Bulldogs closed out an 11-1 regular season with a 42–10 demolition of archrival Georgia Tech last Saturday. Having already secured the SEC Eastern Division title, the Dawgs head to Atlanta for the 5th time under head coach Mark Richt in search of their third conference championship in his 12 seasons. After a controversial summer that included several high-profile dismissals and a number of season-opening suspensions, Georgia managed to win their first five games before getting physically whipped 35–7 at South Carolina. They survived on the road against Kentucky (29–24) the following week, but since that time have played their best football down the stretch as their offensive and defensive lineups have stabilized. Guided on offense by a veteran quarterback in Aaron Murray, the nation's passing efficiency leader, and anchored by an extremely talented 3-4 defense, Georgia has outscored its last five opponents by a count of 179–43 (35.8–8.6). With Alabama coming off its best performance of the year vs. Auburn, this SEC title matchup will feature two teams that are similar in style and ability. The battle at the line of scrimmage, the turnover margin, special teams' play, and the in-game coaching adjustments will determine the outcome of this contest, which will prove to be the most physical college game of the season, with the winner advancing to the BCS National Championship Game.

OFFENSE

Richt turned over the play-calling duties to Mike Bobo for the last game of the 2006 season, and he has been the offensive coordinator ever since. The Bulldogs are a traditional, I-Formation team with the capability of using multiple personnel groupings. #11 Murray (6010/210) is the triggerman, and he is the first QB in SEC history to pass for more than 3000 yards in three different seasons. His stats are more impressive on paper than on tape. He has completed 213 of 320 attempts (66.6%) for 3201 yards, 30 touchdowns, and 7 interceptions. He has an easy motion, and the ball is clean off his throwing hand. He is more like a six-footer and seems to play "small," especially when the pocket is squeezed and big people get around him. Most of his success comes on quick throws to the perimeter or play-action timing patterns outside the hash marks. When he tries to pass between the numbers, his attempts get batted or tipped at the line on a regular basis, and he seems to struggle seeing around the wall of pass-rushing defenders. Murray is nimble enough to slide and escape pressure, but he is not a significant runner and is not a creative ad-lib-style quarterback. In the run game, the Bulldogs use #3 Todd Gurley (6010/218) and #4 Keith

Marshall (5110/216) in combination to form the "Gurshall" backfield in tribute to legendary Heisman Trophy winner #34 Herschel Walker. Gurley has rushed 176 times for 1138 yards (6.5avg) and 14 touchdowns, while Marshall has gained 720 yards on 107 attempts (6.7avg) and scored 8 touchdowns of his own. Gurley is a fluid runner who is strong through his hips and thigh pads. Marshall has a flowing style and has a 75-yard TD run to his credit. Both can catch the football as well and have accounted for 20 receptions between them. Their lead blockers include both #43 Merritt Hall (5110/238) and #46 Alexander Ogletree (5100/225), who have touched the football 10 times on the season (5 runs/5 receptions).

#88 Arthur Lynch (6050/258) is the tight end, and he has registered 18 catches for 344 yards (19.1avg) and 2 touchdowns. #87 Jay Rome (6060/265) will also see play time, and he has grabbed 10 passes for 133 yards (13.3avg) and a touchdown. Georgia's receiving corps has lost two players to season-ending injuries (#82 Michael Bennett and #15 Marlon Brown), but they still have quality athletes in this group, led by #26 Malcolm Mitchell (6010/192). He actually started three games at cornerback in the early part of the season when the secondary was depleted due to the suspensions. He has since moved to offense full-time and has recorded 36 receptions for 532 yards (14.8avg) and 4 touchdowns. The Bulldogs rotate a number of wide receivers, but when Mitchell is in the game, he is a priority performer for them. They will isolate him as the single receiver and throw hitches, slants, take-offs, and back-shoulder fades to try and get him the football. He will motion and carry the ball on a Jet sweep, or they will bring him around on a reverse after a hard run-fake into the line. He will arguably be the best athlete on the entire Georgia Dome field on Saturday afternoon. #12 Tavarres King (6010/200) is a senior and he has had a very solid career. He has outstanding vertical speed, and in 2012, this linear-built prospect has 34 catches for 704 yards (20.7avg) and 8 touchdowns. #31 Chris Conley (6030/205) is their biggest receiver, and his reps have increased after the injuries to Bennett and Brown. He has totaled 16 receptions for 195 yards (12.2avg) and 4 touchdowns. #17

Rantavious Wooten (5100/179) and #27 Rhett McGowan (6000/190) will both spot in and together have 24 catches. As good as the Bulldogs are skill-wise, they may be just as bad in the offensive line.

They had to replace three starters from the 2011 team, and despite their offensive production, this is a unit that is not overly gifted. They generally play six linemen across five positions, with #72 Kenarious Gates (6050/318) seeing time as the left guard and at left tackle. When returning RG starter, #68 Chris Burnette (6020/322), went down and missed a few games, #64 Dallas Lee (6040/300) was inserted at that position after subbing in as a LG earlier in the season. He is a player that Bama must take advantage of in the individual matchups when he is in the game. #61 David Andrews (6020/295) is the first-year center, and #71 John Theus (6060/309) is a true freshman starter at RT. #79 Mark Beard (6050/302) is the LT when Burnette is out of the lineup. As a group, they are position blockers in the run game and rely on a quick passing game to help them protect the QB.

As stated, Georgia will utilize Regular personnel and play I-Formation football from Pro and Slot sets. Their runs include the Zone Extra, Power O (Toss), Toss G Lead, Weak Iso, Counter OF Weak, and Flip outside. They will lead the fullback to a play-side linebacker or Cut block them to the back side. The Bulldogs will play-fake and throw mirrored routes to the outside or take a Post shot when they expect Quarters coverage. Their other personnel groupings include Silver, Blue, Red, and Purple. In Blue, they will go 2x2 and 3x1 (Trips and Trey) and run the Zone or a Rim G sweep. And they can fake both with a complimentary Bubble or Now screen off of that action. Speaking of screens, they have a basic RB, Door, and WR Tunnel in their package.

In most every game, they will jump in Red or Purple and play an entire series with Murray in the Gun and throwing the football. All of the standard patterns show up like the Double Seam, Seam-Cross, Seam-Hitch, Double Smash, China, Hawk and D-Curls from 2x2 and Dallas, Slants, Choice, and a 4-strong swing to the 3x1 side. In short yardage and GL, they will put in Black with both fullbacks leading the tailback or try and sneak Murray, who is not a courageous or strong ballcarrier. And, one final note, the Dawgs will use the Freeze snap count to grab a free 5-yard offside penalty at least once per game.

For Bama to win defensively, the Tide must:

• physically win the 1-on-1 OL/DL matchups
• control the run game
• push and squeeze the pocket on Murray/get hands up
• be alert when #26 Mitchell is in the game.

DEFENSE

Former Nick Saban assistant Todd Grantham (at MSU) is the Georgia defensive coordinator, and in three years, he has not only transitioned the Bulldogs from a 4-3 to a 3-4, but has upgraded their size and strength and transformed their toughness and overall temperament on this side of the football. After a slow start to the season due to player suspensions, the Bulldogs finally have all their pieces in place and have virtually no weaknesses from a personnel standpoint. They have NFL-quality prospects at every level of their defense. The Bulldogs are huge across the front line with four players now manning three positions. Alabama should expect to see #6 John Jenkins (6030/358) at defensive end, with #99 Kwame Geathers (6060/355) inserted as the Nose. After DE Abry Jones went down with a significant injury, #56 Garrison Smith (6030/297) moved into the other starting DE spot. Jenkins has 44 total tackles, 1 tackle for loss, no sacks, but 12 QB hurries. He is massive with athletic feet and is rarely on the ground. Geathers is a giant and has recorded 31 total tackles, 5 tackles for loss, a sack, and 6 QB hurries. Smith has 52tt, 2 tfl's, a sack, and 5 hurries and brings legitimate quickness to the table. #83 Cornelius Washington (6040/268) is listed as a starter and plays regularly in their Sub packages as a DE and DT. He has 21tt, 3 tfl's, a half sack, and 11 pressures. He is very active with his hands and plays hard, but is not very instinctive when reading run/pass.

The linebacking group has two big-time playmakers in #29 OLB

Jarvis Jones (6030/241) and #9 ILB Alec Ogletree (6030/232). Jones missed the Florida Atlantic and Kentucky games due to injury, but has still posted 71tt, is 2nd in the nation with 19.5 tackles for loss, and his 10.5 sacks lead the SEC. He will slice through a gap or race around the edge with his missile-like speed and then finish the play by tracking down the football with his relentless pursuit. Ogletree is an angular, long-limbed defender who leads the team with 87 total tackles after missing the first four games due to breaking university behavior policies. He also has 7.5 tfl's, 2 sacks, 5 pass breakups, 5 pressures, and an interception. He plays with low hands and is not a technician at all when taking on blockers; however, with his length and range, he can affect passing lanes and chase the football from sideline to sideline. #52 Amarlo Herrera (6020/245) and #35 Michael Gilliard (6020/230) share the Mike position and have 111 total hits and 4 tfl's; however, neither is a difference maker. #59 Jordan Jenkins (6030/257) is the other outside linebacker, and he quietly has accumulated 28tt, 7 tfl's, 4 sacks, and 20 pressures rushing from the opposite side of Jones.

Once safety #18 Bacarri Rambo returned from suspension and allowed #19 Sanders Commings to shift from safety to corner, the Bulldogs' secondary settled down and has played extremely well in the final month of the season. In eight games, Rambo (6000/210) has registered 59tt, forced 3 fumbles, and intercepted 3 passes from his "field" safety position. He is a smooth, one-speed athlete who likes to try and strip or rake the football from runners as they are being tackled by other defenders. He is ball aware and has excellent hands, as evidenced by his school-record 16 career interceptions. #36 Shawn Williams (6010/217) is the "boundary" safety and is 2nd on the team with 78 stops, 5.5 tfl's, 4 pass breakups, and a forced fumble. He is the spiritual leader of the defense and plays with an aggressive demeanor, but he has lateral tightness in space and is not a cover safety. Commings (6020/216) is the "boundary" corner, and he has 40 total tackles with only 1 pass breakup; however, he did record 2 interceptions to close out the Tennessee victory. In a confined area, he is a "zone" corner who can support the run, but may not run well enough to defend the deep part of the field. #5 Damian Swann (5110/189) moved from the boundary to the field corner position after Rambo returned. He has 59tt, a pass breakup, and 3 interceptions. He is a key figure in the back end, because he is a far better player than their Nickel corner, #1 Branden Smith (5110/182). Smith has a sprinter's build and is light when tackling or playing man-to-man against bigger receivers.

Georgia will match their packages with the offensive personnel, but the starting point is the 3-4 with amoeba-like coverages in the back end. They begin with a Quarters concept, but can play Cover 2, Three-Deep, and various forms of Man Free. When they play Nickel, the Dawgs go to a 2-4-5 arrangement with #29 Jones and #59 Jenkins as the DE's and #6 Jenkins and #83 Washington on the inside. On some occasions, Jenkins will slide inside and Washington will rush from outside. #9 Ogletree is the coverage linebacker, and #45 Christian Robinson (6020/235) is alongside. He is their weakest linebacker and the most finesse-oriented player in their front seven. They will slide from Even to Odd looks, and they like to pressure with 5 and play Man Free with "floaters" behind it.

For Bama to win offensively, the Tide must:
- consider going No Huddle/Up Tempo to simplify pass defense
- use motions/shifts/unbalanced formations (UGa late lining up)
- run directly at #29 Jones and #9 Ogletree rather than away
- try to isolate #1 Smith in coverage and target him (in Nickel)

SPECIAL TEAMS

The Bulldogs graduated two NFL-caliber specialists a season ago in PK Blair Walsh (Minnesota Vikings) and PT Drew Butler (Pittsburgh Steelers). As their replacements, true freshmen PK #13 Marshall Morgan and PT #32 Collin Barber have started all year. Morgan has made 8 of 12 field goals with a long of 52 yards in addition to converting on 54 of 58 extra points. Barber has averaged 41.2 yards on 51 punts with 24 fair catches and 16 landing inside the -20. In

Net Punting, the Dawgs rank 79th in the national NCAA statistics with a 36.1 yard average.

#99 Jamie Lindley has shared kickoff duties with Morgan and has 21 touchbacks on 48 attempts (44%). Morgan has landed 12 of 32 kickoffs (38%) in the end zone. Their kickoff coverage unit gives up 19.8 yards per return, and that is good for 34th in the nation. #26 Mitchell is the primary kickoff returner, and he has 15 runbacks for 347 yards (23.1avg) with a long of 48, while #3 Gurley has also hauled back 7 kickoffs for a 34.7 average including a 100-yard TD vs. Buffalo in the season opener. Georgia's 23.0 yard KOR average places them 42nd in the overall stats. Mitchell has also been the main punt returner with 10 attempts for 50 yards (5.0avg) with #27 McGowan (6000/190) chipping in 7 returns for an 8.1 yard average. Those numbers equate to a ranking of 84th in the nation.

RADIO BROADCAST NOTES

TAILGATE SHOW/TOM
- SEC Championship = National Semifinal/BCS Berth
- 21st SEC Title Game/Bama's 8th appearance (all against UF)
- evenly matched/similarly built teams (QB, run game, 3-4)

PRE-GAME SHOW/ELI
- electric atmosphere of Georgia Dome (13-5-1/5-2 under NS)
- most physical game of the year
- coaching matters

HARDEE'S FUTURE STAR OF TOMORROW
UGa: Cyrus Kouandjio

FOR BAMA TO WIN
- off: most physical game all year/dictate tempo/no huddle
- def: dominate LOS/control run/push pocket
- st: hidden yardage/experienced specialists

BAMA NOTES (#2 BCS) (HARRIS, *USA TODAY,* AND SIX COMPUTERS)

- 8th SEC Championship Game appearance (3-4 all vs. Florida)
- going for 23rd SEC Championship (most in league history)
- 66th meeting vs. Georgia (36-25-4) (W 41–30 in 2008)
- five common opponents (FAU, Miss, Mizz, Tenn, Aub) 32.8–25.8
- 59 bowl games in school history (33-22-3)
- 32 10-win seasons/15 11-win seasons (2nd most/OU-20)
- five consecutive 10-win seasons (4 out of 5 with 11 wins+)
- 79th consecutive week in AP poll (leads nation)
- NS (66-13)/6th season (157-55-1 overall) (3 BCS titles)
- 1st most wins since '08 (59) (most in SEC history over 5-year span)
- 21-7 vs. Top 25/12-4 vs. Top 10
- 37-1 with 100-yard rusher/48-0 when rushing for 150+yards
- 60-3 when leading at halftime (LSU '07 and '10, Auburn '10)
- 28 straight tied or leading at half (489-97)******ended vs. A&M
- 57-8 when forcing a turnover******none vs. LSU or A&M
- 26 nonoffensive touchdowns since 2007 (12int/2fr/3kor/7pr/2blks)
- six with college degrees (58 graduates competed in last 5yrs)
  Barrett Jones, Damion Square, Robert Lester, Carson Tinker, William Ming, Michael Williams
- 4th fewest scholarship seniors in country (9)
- 10 true frosh and 11 RS frosh have made debuts in '12
- 21 players on both '09 and '11 championship teams
- 11 consensus A-A's since '07 (most in nation/Oklahoma 9)
- only turned ball over 70 times in last 66 games (since '08)
- 51 turnovers in 52 games (since '09) (75 int's vs. only 16 thrown)
- points off turnovers: 146–24 (73 int's for UA vs. 16 for opp's)

- 154 consecutive games scoring (longest in school history)
- since MSU/Capital One: 946-175
- Coaches' Players of the Week:
    offense: B Jones/AJ/Cooper/Lacy
    defense: Pagan/Lester
    special teams: L Collins/Ragland

UA STATS

Offense		Defense
22nd (214.2yds)	Rushing	2nd (77.0yds)
77th (218.8yds)	Passing	3rd (156.7yds)
43rd (433.0yds)	Total	1st (233.7yds)
15th (39.0pts)	Scoring	1st (9.3pts)
18th (47.9%)	3rd Downs	18th (32.4%)
t-9th (48/53) (39td/9fg)	Red Zone	1st (14/23) (11td/3fg)
49th (20 total)	Sacks	t-26th (30 total)
Penalties	t-7th (4.0 per)	
Turnovers	t-9th (+14)	

BAMA OFFENSE (7 OFFENSIVE STARTERS)

- 155 career OL starts
- balance in 2012: 2570yds rushing/2626 passing
- QB AJ McCarron (31td's in last 15 games)(44td's–2nd UA)
- AJ:
    #2 nationally in pass efficiency/23-2 as starter
    67.2%-2507yds-25td-2int
    streak of 292 broken (A&M)
    most TD's (20) to open season
- RB (two-headed monster)(321 yards/5 td's vs. Mizz)
    Lacy: 164att/1001yds/6.1avg/12td/lg73
    Yeldon: 129att/847yds/6.6avg/10td/lg43

- WR (16 different receivers have caught a pass)
    Cooper: 45rec/767yds/17.0avg/8td/lg54
    Norwood: 26rec/395yds/15.2avg/4td/lg47
    Chr Jones: 24rec/306yds/12.8avg/4td/lg34
- TE Michael Williams (19rec/3td)/Kelly Johnson/B Vogler
- OL B Jones/Warmack/Anthony Steen/Cyrus/DJ Fluker
    Jones: NFF National Scholar-Athlete

BAMA DEFENSE (5 DEFENSIVE STARTERS) (KIRBY SMART-AFCA ASST)

- less than 300 total yards in 23/26 games (GSU/LSU/A&M)
- under 200 yards on 14 occasions
- under 100/2 times (Kent State and LSU/BCS)
- 2nd nation in 3-and-outs (64 of 143=44.8%)
- 10 points or less 40 times in 79 games (3 shutouts in '12)
- less than 300 yards offense in 52 of 79 games (65.8%)
- 26 under 200 yards in last 66 games
- allowed only 39 rushing td's since 2007 (Ohio State, 54)
- DL Jesse Williams/Square/Ed Stinson/Q Dial/Pagan/Ivory
    J Williams: 31tt/2.5tfl/1sk
    Stinson: 26tt/8.5tfl/3sk
    Square: 31tt/3.5tfl/3.5sk
- LB Nico Johnson/Trey DePriest/CJ and Hubbard/Dickson
    CJ: 92tt/6tfl/4sk/2int
    Nico: 52tt/2tfl
    DePriest: 52tt/4tf
    Hubbard: 35tt/9tfl/5sk
- DC Dee Milliner/Deion Belue/Geno Smith/John Fulton
    Milliner: 47tt/16pbu/2int (finalist for Nagurski award)
    Belue: 31tt/6pbu/2int
- DS Robert Lester/Nick Perry/Vinnie/Haha Clinton-Dix
    Sunseri: 51tt/6tfl/3pbu/2int
    Lester: 34tt/3pbu/4int (14 career int's)

BAMA SPECIAL TEAMS (ALL SPECIALISTS RETURN)

- PK J Shelley (60/60 XP's and 10/10 FG's) (only PK in NCAA)
- KO Cade Foster (4-8/3 50+FG's) (37tb's/79ko's/43%)
- PT Cody Mandell (44.1avg/14 in -20/4tb/12 50+)
- PR/KOR Cyrus (7.6/26.8)/Christion (10.7/30.3)

GEORGIA

- 5th SEC Championship Game appearance (2-2, all under Richt) ('02, Ark 30–3 W; '03, LSU 34–13 L; '05, LSU 34–14 W)
- 2nd SEC East division championship in a row
- only other meeting with both in top 3 (Oct 31, 1942)
- Head Coach Mark Richt (Miami grad/Jim Kelly's backup)
- 2-3 against Saban-coached teams
- 89-14 when scoring first/27-26 when opp scores first
- 106-16 scoring 18+/11-23 when scoring less than 18pts
- 102-22 rush 100+/only 15-17 when rush less than 100
- only 17-17 when allowing 100-yard rusher

OFFENSE (MIKE BOBO)
- traditional I-Formation with 4/5 WR versatility
- QB: Aaron Murray (leads in pass efficiency/psychology grad) three straight 3,000-yard passing seasons (213/320/66.6%/3201yds/30td/7int)
- RB: "Gurshall" backfield (10 of 12 games over 97yds combined) Todd Gurley (176att/1138yds/6.5avg/14td) Keith Marshall (107att/720yds/6.7avg/8td)
- WR: lost two receivers to injury Michael Bennett/Marlon Brown Malcolm Mitchell (36rec/532yds/14.8yds/4td) Tavarres King (34rec/704yds/20.7avg/8td) Chris Conley (16rec/195yds/12.2yds/4td)
- OL: three new starters

LT Kenarious Gates/RG Chris Burnette

take advantage LG Dallas Lee and RT John Theus

DEFENSE (TODD GRANTHAM)

- installed 3-4 in 2010/transformed mentality
- DL: big across front

    John Jenkins/Kwame Geathers/Garrison Smith
- OLB: outside speed rusher

    Jarvis Jones (19.5tfl/10.5sks)

    Jordan Jenkins (7tfl/4sks)
- IB: POA and range

    Amarlo Herrera (65tt/int); Alec Ogletree (87tt/7.5tfl/2sks/int)

    (missed first 4)
- DB: 4 of top 5 are seniors/experienced

    FS Bacarri Rambo (59tt/3ff/3int)

    BS Shawn Williams (78tt/5.5tfl/sk)

    BC Sanders Commings/FC Damian Swann

SPECIAL TEAMS (EXCELLENT SPECIALISTS)

- PK: Marshall Morgan (8/12 FG's and 54/58 XP's)
- KO: Jamie Lindley (44%)/Morgan (38%)
- PT: Collin Barber (41.2avg/16 in -20/3tb/24fc)
- KOR: Mitchell (15ret/23.1avg)
- PR: Mitchell (10ret/5.0avg)

LSU, 2015

Head Coach: Les Miles/11th year (138-50/110-29 at LSU)

OC: Cam Cameron/3rd year

DC: Kevin Steele/1st year

ST: Bradley Dale Peveto/2nd year (2005–8 previously)

2014 Record: 8-5/4-4 SEC West

Top Players Lost: RB Terrence Magee, OT La'el Collins, DE Danielle Hunter, LB Kwon Alexander

2015 Record: 7-0/4-0 SEC West

Returning Starters: 6 offense/6 defense/1 specialist

Best Players Returning: RB #7 Leonard Fournette, WR #83 Travin Dural, WR #15 Malachi Dupre, OC #77 Ethan Pocic, RT #74 Vadal Alexander, LT #65 Jerald Hawkins, DT #91 Christian LaCouture, DT #57 Davon Godchaux, IB #52 Kendell Beckwith, SS #33 Jamal Adams, CB #18 Tre'Davious White, PT #38 Jamie Keehn

Tapes Viewed: 2015—MSU, Syracuse, Auburn, USC, Florida

NCAA STATISTICAL RANKINGS

Rushing Offense	5th (309.1)	Rushing Defense	6th (93.7)
Passing Offense	116th (156.9)	Passing Defense	64th (222.1)
Total Offense	28th (466.0)	Total Defense	18th (315.9)
Scoring Offense	14th (38.9)	Scoring Defense	39th (22.6)
Turnover Margin	t-13th (+7—9 gained, 2 lost)		
3rd Down Offense	25th (44.4%)	3rd Down Defense	39th (34.4%)
Red Zone Offense	20th (90.3%)	Red Zone Defense	t-121st (94.1%)
Sacks Allowed	t-13th (8.0)	Sacks For	t-49th (18.0)
Penalties	t-97th (7.4 per gm)		
KOR	110th (18.3)	KOC	100th (23.1)
PR	42nd (10.7)	Net Punt	119th (33.1)

Upcoming Schedule: Arkansas, @ Ole Miss, Texas A&M

GENERAL COMMENTS

Despite the fact that LSU has recruited extremely well during the Les Miles era, the departure of more underclassmen to the NFL than in any other college program in the country finally caught up to the Tigers in 2014, when they finished 8-5 with a very inexperienced roster. Lots of "raw talent" revealed itself, but subpar quarterback play and, subsequently, an ineffective passing game derailed their chances of winning 10-plus games or more for a fifth consecutive season. The silver lining to this situation, of course, was the fact that they were able to get a number of gifted athletes on the field and begin to reintroduce their identity as an athletic, physically imposing team. With that said, LSU added Ed Orgeron as the defensive line coach and Kevin Steele as the defensive coordinator to replace the departed John Chavis, who bolted to Texas A&M during the offseason. Still, the Tigers had major QB questions coming into 2015, but after Anthony Jennings was arrested over the summer, Miles and offensive coordinator Cam Cameron opted for Brandon Harris as their starter. He had a disastrous outing vs. Auburn last year and was less than impressive in the first month of this season. Now, after three dependable showings against South Carolina, Florida, and Western Kentucky, the Tigers believe they have enough passing to complement their dominant run game, led by super sophomore RB #7 Leonard Fournette. Fournette is having a spectacular, Heisman Trophy–winning type of campaign, but their overall squad has taken care of the football, and they have a slew of quality players. After winning the first "Game of the Century" in Tuscaloosa during the 2011 regular season, LSU has lost four straight to the Crimson Tide, but Miles thinks this group is special and will point to the fact that the Tigers actually have an all-time record of 8-7 in Bryant-Denny Stadium.

OFFENSIVE OVERVIEW

Cam Cameron is in his 3rd year as the offensive coordinator, and he orchestrates their run-first system. In 2014, they ran the football 69% of the time, and that number has actually increased in 2015 to a 72%/28% run/pass ratio. Fournette (6010/230) gets all of the national attention, but they have a very impressive offensive line, and their top two wide receivers both have length and playmaking ability. Typically, LSU will come out of the Bye week with a couple wrinkles for Alabama from a personnel/formation/blocking-scheme standpoint, so the Crimson Tide will have to adjust on the fly once the game begins.

PERSONNEL
Quarterbacks: #6 Harris (6030/206) has completed 75 of 128 passes (58.6%) for 1098 yards, 9 touchdowns, and zero interceptions. He has also run 41 times (including sacks) for 136 yards (3.3avg) and 3 touchdowns. He has a fluid passing arm, and the football comes off his hand

very cleanly with lots of spin, but he is not inherently accurate. Harris has deceptive speed and can run for more than a 1st down with his legs. He is at his best on boots/nakeds for shorter throws and will launch the football downfield in hopes of letting his receivers make a play. On the intermediate reads and throws, he is very ordinary in terms of getting off coverage and delivering the ball with any real consistency.

Running Backs: #7 Fournette is a physical beast and he shoulders a heavy load for this offense. He combines quick feet with explosive strength in his hips and a lethal off arm that he uses as a weapon on pursuing tacklers.

He has shredded defenses for 1352 yards on 176 carries for a 7.7-yard average and 15 touchdowns, while also catching 7 passes for 58 yards (8.3avg).

#5 Derrius Guice (5110/220) and #34 Darrel Williams (6000/232) will spell Fournette at times, and both of them can play. Guice has excellent quickness and balance and has run for 316 yards on 34 attempts for a gaudy 9.3-yard average and 2 scores. Williams has power in his body and has carried the ball 50 times for 265 yards (5.3avg) and 3 more touchdowns. #44 John David Moore (6040/235) is the starting fullback, but was hurt vs. South Carolina, and his status for Alabama is not known at this time. #47 Bry'Kiethon Mouton (6010/255) is a true freshman and has done a solid job of filling the role since Moore's injury.

Tight Ends: #85 Dillon Gordon went down vs. Florida and is out for the season, so #81 Colin Jeter (6070/244) will likely get the most snaps. He has 5 receptions on the season for 40 yards and has split time with #84 Foster Moreau (6050/261) and #89 DeSean Smith (6050/243) when they use their multiple-TE sets.

Wide Receivers: #83 Travin Dural (6020/203) leads the team with 24 receptions for 426 yards (17.8avg) and 2 touchdowns. He is the most accomplished of their receivers and can operate short, medium, and deep. #15 Malachi Dupre (6030/190) has a lean build and long arms with a large catching radius. He adjusts to the football in the air and has 21 grabs for 397 yards (18.9avg) and 5 scores. No other wide receivers have more than 4 catches on the season.

Offensive Line: Arguably the best line in the country, they are anchored in the middle by OC #77 Ethan Pocic (6070/309), who handles much of the communication and does steady work in getting to his assignments and staying on his feet. #65 Jerald Hawkins (6060/305) played RT in 2014, but is the left tackle this year. He can move his feet and uses his extremely long arms to protect the edge. RT #74 Vadal Alexander (6060/320) was the left guard last season, but is on the power side in 2014. He is the one senior on their offense and a legit NFL prospect as a RT or OG.

SCHEME

LSU will use an assortment of personnel groupings including Regular, Silver, Green, Blue, and Gold by situation and Black (Wildcat) in SY/GL. Everything centers around the run game that features the Zone (Extra and Away), Zone-Read, Lead Iso (weak), and Toss Power. They have a Counter OY as a changeup and will call a Jet Sweep (or Tap Pass) on occasion. Their goal is to line up and pound the interior of the defense before play-faking and taking shots downfield when they get single coverage outside. The passing game is simplistic for the QB in terms of mirrored routes, Nakeds, Bootlegs, and "hard" play-actions designed to fool the defensive backfield. They love to line up in Green and throw the fade when 1-on-1 coverage shows up. They will Dash the QB and, again, cut the field in half for him, too.

The Tigers will give a dose of paired run/pass plays, but it's not what they do best.

In Sub, Cameron appears to like Gold this year for protection purposes and also because their RB's are obviously more threatening than the TE's as pass receivers.

ANTICIPATED GAME PLAN

Alabama should expect a "surprise" formation or some alternative run-blocking scheme with LSU coming off the Bye. Otherwise, it's strength vs. strength with the Tigers being 1st in the SEC in rushing and the Tide being #1 in the league against the run. Although LSU is +7 in the turnover margin, they are t-97th in penalties per game (7.4 per) and have a history of being sloppy with line-of-scrimmage infractions, fumbled snaps, and ill-advised passes. When they make a mistake, Bama must take advantage of the "free" yardage and keep them behind the sticks as much as possible. Playing field position and making them convert consecutive 3rd downs will be a huge key in the game.

DEFENSIVE OVERVIEW

Chavis spent six seasons in Baton Rouge before moving on in a controversial transition to College Station as one of the highest-paid assistant coaches in college football. Miles tabbed Steele, the former Alabama linebackers' coach, as the new coordinator, and he has stayed with the 4-3 and a split-safeties concept as their foundations. Steele has a vast background in coaching, but he has definitely taken more than a few pages from his time in Tuscaloosa as this defense is very reflective of the scheme employed by Alabama.

PERSONNEL

Defensive Line: This unit is characterized by their overall effort and is anchored by DT's #57 Davon Godchaux (6040/293) and #91 Christian LaCouture (6050/307), both returning starters from a year ago.

Godchaux has 26 total tackles, 6 tackles for loss, and 3 sacks, while LaCouture has registered 19 tackles, 1 pass breakup, and 1 QB hurry. The Tigers are better on the edges this year with LE #92 Lewis Neal (6020/264) and RE #49 Arden Key (6060/231). Neal dominated a poor offensive tackle for Florida with 3 sacks and now has 32tt, 8tfl's, 7 sacks, 4pbu's, and 7 QB hurries on the season. He primarily aligns in a three-point stance and plays with outstanding hustle. Key is a true freshman who will flash as a pass rusher, but does not have tremendous girth or strength at the point of attack. He has 19tt, 2.0tfl's, and

1.5 sacks and will share time with #46 Tashawn Bower (6050/240), who is in the regular rotation at both end spots. He missed the Eastern Michigan and South Carolina games, but has chipped in 12tt, 3tfl's, and 1 sack.

Linebackers: IB #52 Kendell Beckwith (6020/252) started seven games in 2014 and is tied with WB #45 Deion Jones (6010/227) for the team lead in tackles with 51. Both stay on the field in all defensive packages and are active against the run and pass. Jones is the only full-time senior starter on this side of the football and has also intercepted two passes. SB #11 Lamar Louis (5110/232) plays in their Base 4-3, but he has not seen substantial play-time thus far.

Secondary: SS #33 Jamal Adams (6010/211) is the emotional leader of the LSU defense and a real tempo-setter for the Tigers. He is almost like an extra linebacker because of his aggressive nature and has logged 34tt, 2tfl's, 3pbu's, and 3int's during his sophomore season. #18 Tre'Davious White (5110/191) wears this prestigious honorary number recognizing his efforts on and off the field as a team representative, but more importantly, is the right corner with 22tt and 3pbu's. He is a long-limbed defender that can press and play 1-on-1 outside.

FS #29 Rickey Jefferson (6000/207) has 29tt and 3pbu's while filling in for expected starter #28 Jalen Mills (6000/196), who just returned against Florida from a training-camp leg injury. #13 Dwayne Thomas (6000/186) is the Star in their Nickel package and the starting left cornerback when they are in Regular. He is super quick and has registered 30tt and 6pbu's. True freshman #2 Kevin Toliver II (6020/197) is the left corner in Sub and has contributed 22tt, 1pbu, and 1int, but has all the measurables to be a future star in the SEC. As a group, this is the best collection of athletes Alabama's offense has faced all season long.

SCHEME

Although the 4-3 is their Base defense, Steele has opted to stay in his 4-2 Nickel against most every personnel grouping. Being new to the program and recognizing this as his best package of players, he has limited their subs and adjusted it to whatever the offense shows. One of the biggest questions in the Alabama game will be their approach to Silver (12 personnel) because of the Crimson Tide's ability to expand and contract their formations.

In simple terms, they play Under in Base, Over/Over G in Nickel, and Odd in 3-2 Dime. Their coverages include all variations of Quarters (C-7), two forms of C-2 (standard and cut), multiple ways of playing Man Free (C-1), and traditional Three-Deep (C-3 Buzz and C-6). When they pressure, it's usually with a "popping" linebacker combined with a line stunt. They also like to Fire-Zone from the field with the Star blitzing and the weak-side DE dropping off or Corner Cat from the boundary.

In short yardage and goal-line, they go to a 5-4 Double Sink with both safeties remaining in the game.

WHERE IS THE YARDAGE?

Steele will likely rely on a six-man "box" to contain RB Derrick Henry with line movements up front and then quick support from one of the safeties to get to the oversized runner before he gets started.

Therefore, play-action fakes toward SS #33 Adams and actual runs away from him might be in order, because FS #29 Jefferson is not as "nosey" from depth nor as good a tackler, and that same remark can be made about #28 Mills as well.

"Tempo" has a place in the game plan because it likely limits some of the Tigers' checks and the Tide can monitor #33 Adams.

Runs from Trey can possibly get Henry to a secondary player due to the numbers advantage on the short side.

"Switch" routes and 2nd man through route concepts have given LSU some problems because they are new to Steele's zone-match philosophy.

Be patient, both teams are going to try and limit the opposing RB's and then see if the quarterback can consistently beat them on a "long" field.

SPECIAL TEAMS OVERVIEW

Bradley Dale Peveto is in the second year of his second tour of duty under Miles, but statistically speaking, the Tigers have struggled through their first seven games in 2015 and have allowed kickoff and punt-return touchdowns in the same season for the first time since 1999. #14 Trent Domingue is the placekicker, but has shared kickoff duties with #36 Cameron Gamble. Domingue has 7 touchbacks on 31 kickoffs (23%) with 2 going out-of-bounds, while Gamble has 5 touchbacks on 19 kickoffs (26%) with one traveling OB.

As a team, the Tigers rank 100th in KO Coverage by giving up 23.1 yards per return, including a 96-yard TD runback vs. South Carolina. On Kickoff Returns, LSU stands 110th in the country at 18.3 yards per attempt with true freshman #1 Donte Jackson (5110/167) hauling back 8 for a 20.5-yard average. However, vs. Florida, #5 Guice and #34 Williams were deep because they bring more size to the table. Surprisingly, LSU is 119th in the country in Net Punting at 33.1 yards per exchange. #38 Jamie Keehn is a 26-year-old Australian who is in his 3rd season as the starter. He is averaging only 39.7 yards on 32 punts with 2 touchbacks, 13 fair catches, and 12 landing inside the -20. Against UF, the Gators had a 72-yard punt return for a score, so the coverage problems are still recent. #18 White has been their primary punt returner, and he has 9 attempts for an 11.4-yard average with a 69-yard TD vs. Kentucky, but #1 Jackson handled those duties in the WKU game, and Miles recently stated publicly that he would likely continue vs. Alabama. Jackson has reportedly been clocked at 4.24 in the forty. As a unit, they rank 42nd in the NCAA with a 10.7-yard average. Domingue has had a "perfect" season thus far by making all 35 of his PAT attempts and going 9 for 9 on field goals with a long of 45 yards, plus he caught the game-winning TD pass against the Gators on a much-publicized fake FG. Because of Miles's history with trick plays, every LSU opponent must be alert and ready to "play" all four downs.

RADIO BROADCAST NOTES

TAILGATE SHOW/CHRIS
- annual "Game of the Century" (10th year both ranked)
- mirror images on offense and defense (RB's and D)
- who can push the "game" on to the other QB's shoulders?

GAME PLAN/KEYS TO WIN
- offense: ball security and 3rd downs (avoid #33 Adams)
- defense: stack the box and defend the shots!
- ST's: win "hidden yardage" and keep rabbit in hat!

PREGAME SHOW/ELI

- 80th meeting/Bama goes for 50th win in series
- high stakes rivalry defined=SECW, SEC, BCS, and CFP!
- O and D cancel out=ball security and special teams!

STAR TO WATCH

LSU: A Robinson

2015 NCAA STATISTICS

Offense		Defense
41st (199.5)	Rushing	3rd (78.5)
57th (233.4)	Passing	38th (197.3)
49th (432.9)	Total	4th (275.8)
43rd (33.5pts)	Scoring	10th (16.4pts)
111th (33.6%)	3rd Downs	17th (31.3%)
53rd (85.7%)	RZ	t-61st (83.3%)
41st (13 total)	Sacks	6th (27 total)

Penalties   80th (6.8 per
                  game)
TO Margin   .t-38th (+3)

BAMA NOTES (AP #8/COACHES #8)

- 1892/857-326-43 (Bryant-Denny 101,821)
- 49-25-5 vs. LSU/7-8 in Tuscaloosa/6-7 for team leading at half
- since 2008, only last 3 games of '10 season/no implications
- going for 8th consecutive 10+win season in 2015
- 124th consecutive week in AP poll (leads nation)
- #1 in seven straight seasons (18-7 on ESPN *GameDay*)
- NS, 98-18, 9th season (189-60-1 overall) (4 BCS titles)
    117th game as UA coach/12-1 in SEC openers
    54-7 at home/30-6 on road/57 straight over unranked
- most wins since '08 (91) (most in SEC history over 6-yr span)
- 35-13 vs. Top 25/19-7 vs. Top 10/9-2 in rematches after loss
- 73-4 when 140+yds rush since '08 (AU13, UM/OSU14, UM15)
- 90-6 when leading at half (LSU '07/'10, AU '10/'13, UM '14)
- 38 nonoffensive touchdowns since 2007 (16int/4fr/5kor/9pr/4blks)
- only turned ball over 124 times in last 102 games (since '08)
- 105 turnovers in 89 games (since '09) int/57.3 and fumble/144.7
- 191 consecutive games scoring (longest in school history)
- 7 players in 2015 NFL Draft (48 in last 7yrs, incl 17 Rd1)
- Players of Week:
    O: Kelly, Ridley, A Stewart
    D: Anderson, Ragland, Reed
    ST: Griffith, JK Scott

BAMA OFFENSE (5 RETURNING STARTERS)

- Lane Kiffin/OC (scored 1st half 111 straight games)
- game-plan approach

- QB: Jake Coker, 63.8%-1623yds-7td-6int
- RB: Derrick Henry, rush TD/13 straight, 180att/1044yds/5.8/14td
    Kenyan Drake, 265rush/181rec/232KR
- TE: O. J. Howard, 26rec/290yds/11.2avg
- WR: Calvin Ridley-45/A Stewart-31/Mullaney-24
- OL: Joe Moore Award Honor Roll (toughness, effort, team-
    work, physicality, tone setting, and finish)

BAMA DEFENSE (7 RETURNING STARTERS)

- Kirby Smart/DC (16 shutouts since '08)
- 3rd nationally/6.3 three-and-outs per game
- only allowed 132 total TD's since '09 (LSU 3rd with 172)
- less than 300 total yards in 71 of 116 games/-200=33x
- 10 points or less 54 times since 2007 (116 total games)
- allowed only 59 rushing td's since 2007 (OSU/93)
- DL: leads nation in pbu's (17), Dalvin Tomlinson (6)
- LB: Reggie Ragland, 71tt
- DB: Minkah Fitzpatrick, 2 pick-sixes; Eddie Jackson, 5int, 2 for
    scores

BAMA SPECIAL TEAMS

- PK: Adam Griffith, 51KO/24TB, 10-16FG, 32-32PAT
- PT: JK Scott, 43.3avg/6TB/9FC/11 -20
- PR/KOR: Cyrus Jones, 23pr/8.5avg

LSU (#2 CFP)

- Tiger Stadium (102,321)
- 3-time national champions (1958, 2003, and 2007)/SEC 11x
- Les Miles/11th year (Michigan '76)
    110-29/60-24 in SEC/7-4 after Bye/24 4th-qtr wins

16-16 vs. Top Ten/59-9 when winning turnover margin

61-0 when rush 100+ and hold opp below 100+ rushing

- Offense (Cam Cameron)

    head coach Indiana/Miami Dolphins

    5th rush/116th pass/28th total/14th scoring

    QB: #6 Brandon Harris

    RB: #7 Leonard Fournette

    TE/FB: #85 Dillon Gordon (inj) and #44 JD Moore

    WR: #83 Travin Dural, 24rec; #15 Malachi Dupre, 21rec

    OL: #74 Alexander, #65 Hawkins, #77 Pocic (94 starts)

- Defense (Kevin Steele)

    4-3/4-2 Nickel or 3-2 Dime

    DL: #92 Lewis Neal, 32tt/8tfl/7sks/7qh

    LB: #52 Kendell Beckwith, 51tt; #45 Deion Jones, 51tt

    DB: #33 Jamal Adams (DBU)

- Special Teams

    PK: #14 Trent Domingue, 9-9FG/35-35PAT

    PT: #38 Jamie Keehn, 39.7avg/33.1net/3-yr starter

    KOR/PR: #1 Donte Jackson (4.24); #18 T White (UK td)

- Tigers, Bayou Bengals, Chinese Bandits, #GeauxTigers, Billy Cannon, Charles Alexander (the Great), Dalton-James Gang, Mad Hatter

WESTERN KENTUCKY UNIVERSITY, 2016

Head Coach: Jeff Brohm/3rd year (21-7)

OC: Brohm (Bobby Petrino at Louisville)

DC: Nick Holt/4th year (DC at USC and Washington)

ST: Tony Levine/1st year (former UH head coach, '12–'14)

2015 Record: 12-2/8-0, Conference USA Champions

Top Players Lost: QB Brandon Doughty, TE Tyler Higbee, IB
Nick Holt, CB Wonderful Terry, CB Prince Charles
Iworah

2016 Record: 1-0/0-0 (Rice 46–14 W)

Returning Starters: 8 offense/4 defense/1 specialist

Best Players: RB #20 Anthony Wales, WR #2 Taywan Taylor,
WR #15 Nicholas Norris, LT #76 Forrest Lamp, OC #70
Max Halpin, DE #72 Derik Overstreet, ILB #6 TJ McCol-
lum, #8 SS Marcus Ward, #31 FS Branden Leston

Tapes Viewed: 2015—VU, Indiana, LSU, Marshall, USM;
2016—did not see Rice

2015 NCAA STATISTICAL RANKINGS

Rushing Offense	89th (154.1)	Rushing Defense	59th (165.6)
Passing Offense	4th (372.2)	Passing Defense	86th (239.6)
Total Offense	9th (526.4)	Total Defense	72nd (405.2)
Scoring Offense	3rd (44.3)	Scoring Defense	53rd (25.9)
Turnover Margin	4th (+14—31 gained, 17 lost)		
3rd Down Offense	11th (47.8%)	3rd Down Defense	33rd (35.2%)
Red Zone Offense	33rd (87.7%)	Red Zone Defense	24th (77.6%)
Sacks Allowed	19th (16)	Sacks For	64th (26)
Penalties	59th (5.9 per game)		
KOR	65th (21.1)	KOC	25th (19.1)
PR	72nd (7.6)	Net Punt	65th (37.2)

Upcoming Schedule: @ Miami-Ohio, VU, Houston Baptist

GENERAL COMMENTS

Western Kentucky enjoyed their most successful season in school history last year when they finished 12-2, won the Conference USA title, defeated South Florida in the Miami Beach Bowl, and ended the campaign at #24 in the Associated Press final rankings. Since moving up from the old Division 1-AA (FCS) level in 2009, they have drastically improved from one of the worst programs in the country to a top-tier contender in the Group of Five conferences.

Head coach Jeff Brohm arrived in Bowling Green as the offensive coordinator with Bobby Petrino, who only stayed for one season in 2013. After being promoted, in two years Brohm has posted a 21-7 record and put together a prolific offensive attack. In 2016, they return eight starters, but lose record-setting QB Brandon Doughty.

Nick Holt runs the defense, and they made tremendous strides in 2015, but only return four starters for this season.

Despite outscoring the Hilltoppers 76–7 in two previous meetings (2008 and 2012), the Crimson Tide will face a far greater challenge because of this team's accomplished schemes and several legitimate players.

OFFENSIVE OVERVIEW

Brohm lost former offensive coordinator Tyson Helton to Southern California in the off-season and replaced him with Garrick McGee, his onetime boss at UAB. After spending parts of seven seasons in the NFL as a quarterback, Brohm embarked on his coaching career and gained extensive experience with the Bobby Petrino style of offense at Louisville from 2003 to 2008. The Hilltoppers are returning the entire offensive line, both tailbacks, and their top wide receiver from a year ago, so replacing the 6th-year senior QB Doughty is their major concern.

PERSONNEL

Quarterbacks: Senior #9 Nelson Fishback suffered a pectoral tear over the summer, so South Florida transfer #14 Mike White (6040/215) won the job and then had a record-setting debut against Rice. He completed 25 of 31 passes for 517 yards and 3 touchdowns. At USF, White lost all five of his starts as a true freshman in 2013 and then played in 11 of 12 games in 2014 before sitting out last year. In 17 total appearances for the Bulls, this redshirt junior completed 215 of 417 passes (51.6%) for 2722 yards, 11 touchdowns, and 16 interceptions. Regardless, the QB is always productive in this scheme, going back to Doug Nussmeier at Idaho (in the early 90's), Stefan LeFors at Louisville (in the early 2000's), and Doughty most recently at WKU.

Running Backs: #20 Anthony Wales (5100/195) and #9 D'Andre Ferby (6010/240) combined for over 1,700 yards and scored 20 touchdowns after #33 Leon Allen went down with a knee injury last

September. Wales is athletic and has quickness as a runner and receiver. He added 27 receptions for 225 yards (8.3avg) and 2 more scores in 2016, while Ferby is the bigger piece of the backfield committee and chipped in an additional 9 receptions for 33 yards a year ago. Allen was granted a 5th year of eligibility and had a 1542-yard rushing season in 2014 to go along with 79 career receptions; however, it appears that he will not be 100% by the Alabama game. In the Rice game, Wales had 15 carries for 58 yards and scored twice, while #3 Quinton Baker (5100/195) contributed 9 runs for 42 yards. Ferby had only one carry and Allen did not play.

Tight Ends: Tyler Higbee, when healthy, was extremely productive in 2015 with 38 receptions and 8 touchdowns in only 9 games. He was drafted by the Los Angeles Rams and will likely be replaced by two seniors, #18 Shaq Johnson and #89 Desmond Maxwell, neither of whom caught a single pass last year. Vs. Rice, Johnson had one catch for 35 yards on a trick play.

Wide Receivers: #2 Taywan Taylor (6010/195) is arguably their best player, who is coming off a sensational 2015 campaign with 86 receptions for 1467 yards (17.1avg) and 17 touchdowns. A very skilled performer, he will align outside, in the slot or motion from the backfield. He will double-move on the perimeter and has capable hands in a crowd. He may be the top NFL prospect in the entire Conference USA. In the Rice game, he had 5 receptions for 165 yards.

#15 Nicholas Norris (5090/175) primarily aligns as the slot, where they can easily get the football to him. He tallied 63 receptions for 971 yards (15.4avg) and 6 touchdowns last season. He has make-miss ability in space and can be dangerous as a runner after the catch. Against the Owls, he grabbed 7 passes for 147 yards and 2 touchdowns. #1 Nacarius Fant (5090/195) is a multipurpose athlete who caught 5 passes for 44 yards and a touchdown in the opener, and he is capable of throwing the football as evidenced by his 2 completions for touchdowns in 2015.

Offensive Line: #76 Forrest Lamp (6040/300) is the left tackle, but projects to guard in the NFL. He is better in pass protection than as a run blocker, but lacks the length to stay outside as a pro. #70 Max Halpin (6030/295) looks competent in the pivot and has made 25 starts in his career.

SCHEME

Overall, this offense is a QB-friendly system that is characterized by multiple personnel groupings, a variety of formations, misdirection runs and passes, and an involved screen game. They are primarily a Blue and Silver team with a dose of Red, Green, and Purple. The QB will play from under center, in the Pistol, and from the Gun. The offensive tackles align in two-point stances, while the guards utilize three-point stances that are "readable" in terms of bird/rabbit (run/pass) plays. Their runs include an outside Stretch play, a classic Zone between the tackles handoff, a typical Power O, and a Toss Crack. The passing attack revolves around all forms of Screens, an adjustable Double-Seam (Seattle), and shallow Mesh concepts.

ANTICIPATED GAME PLAN

Brohm will run their offense, which means they will play up-tempo, mix personnel, and give Alabama multiple formation looks. With White as the QB, they will try to get the football out of his hand quickly or move the pocket to keep him from being a stationary target. Their counter actions in both the run and pass will be utilized to try and take advantage of Alabama's aggressive speed on defense.

DEFENSIVE OVERVIEW

Holt is a veteran coordinator with major-school experience at Washington and USC. The Hilltoppers made huge strides in 2015, but lost seven starters and will rely on several key returnees to continue that improvement. Plus, they added two Louisville transfers that should help them with depth in their front seven.

PERSONNEL

Defensive Line: DE #72 Derik Overstreet (6020/255) is the only re-turner up front, and he is just an ordinary player. A duck-footed ath-lete, he is not real "edgy" as a rusher and recorded 48tt, 9tfl's, and 2 sacks last year. Two inside DT's, #9 Omarius Bryant (6030/310) and #3 Chris Johnson (6020/290), were part of the rotation last year, and both bring some size and athletic quickness to the interior. Johnson is typ-ically the Nose, while Bryant aligns as the 3-tech.

Linebackers: #6 T. J. McCollum (6030/240) transferred from UAB and led the team with 106tt in 2015. He is an active defender in terms of finding the football, but is not particularly explosive in a short area or fast to the perimeter. He had 12tt in the Hilltoppers' win over Rice. #2 Keith Brown (6010/240) is a graduate transfer from Louisville and will partner up with McCollum to give them competent linebacker play. He added 6tt in his first start for WKU.

Secondary: Both starting safeties return in #8 Marcus Ward (6020/210) and #31 Branden Leston (6030/205). Ward is a three-year starter at strong safety and totaled 57 tackles with 17 pass contacts and an interception as a junior. His coverage quickness and speed is questionable downfield, but with his solid frame, he is adequate in run support. Leston is the free safety and he finished 2015 with 96tt, 7pbu's, and a single pick. He will tackle high when the runner is already stacked up, but he has a number of low misses out in space. Both cornerbacks are new to the lineup, with #23 De'Andre Sim-mons (5110/195) lining up on the left and #7 Joe Brown (5100/195) on the right.

SCHEME

Holt begins in an adjustable 4-3 and has shown the willingness to play it vs. any three-WR groupings. Against four-wides, he will go to their Nickel 3-3 package, as he does in most 3rd down passing situations. In Base, they can slide and stay Even (13/31) with four-down linemen, go Odd with the boundary DE standing up, or align in Double Sink. In Nickel, it's primarily Odd with a dose of Even thrown in. Coverage-wise, the 'Toppers are a heavy C-3/C-6 team; obviously Holt was influenced during his time with Pete Carroll at USC, with C-7 being their split-safety look.

WHERE IS THE YARDAGE?

Initially, the invitation to attack the perimeter will be there for the Tide because of the lack of quality outside pass rushers and cornerbacks on this WKU team. The two defensive tackles are active, but can be worn down over the course of a full game. Throw and run to the edges to get a lead, pound and punish between the hash marks to finish the job.

SPECIAL TEAMS OVERVIEW

After three years as the University of Houston head coach (2012–14), Tony Levine was relieved of his duties and he sat out the 2015 season. He returns to the sidelines in 2016 as the WKU special teams' coordinator and tight ends coach. He has extensive experience coaching the kicking units at Louisiana Tech, Louisville, with the Carolina Panthers as a staff assistant, and at Houston under Kevin Sumlin. Last year, the Hilltoppers were 25th in the nation on Kickoff Coverage at 21.1 yards per return. #37 Ryan Nuss handled the kickoffs for the first nine games of the campaign before being injured. He had 8 touchbacks on 64 kickoffs (12.5%). In the first game of 2016, #39 Alex Rinella was the primary kickoff man with six attempts and two touchbacks. #49 Jake Collins was the starting punter for the final 11 games in 2015 and averaged 41.7 on 37 attempts. Vs. Rice, he averaged 47.5yds on 2 punts. As a team, WKU ranked 65th in Net Punting at 37.2 yards per exchange last season. #81 Kylen Towner (5080/175) was their main kick- and punt-return specialist in 2015. On KOR's, he averaged 23.7 yards on 32 runbacks with a 98-yard TD vs. Louisiana Tech. He also had a 94-yard touchdown against Old Dominion in 2014. The 'Toppers were 65th in the country on KOR's with an average of 21.1 yards per return. On punts, Towner averaged 7.1 yards on 14 efforts. Overall, this unit was 72nd nationally with a 7.6-yard average. Towner returned kickoffs vs. Rice, but Fant was the punt returner. Devoid of experience on field goals and extra points, WKU has had a three-man battle for that job. Against Rice, Nuss made 2 of 3 field goals with a long of 31 yards, while #88 Skyler Simcox (a transfer from Emory and Henry College) made his only attempt, from 29 yards away.

RADIO BROADCAST NOTES

TAILGATE SHOW/CHRIS
- home opener
- emotional maturity: 52-6 to inferior opponent
- improvement for each individual makes for better team

GAME PLAN FOR BAMA TO WIN
- offense: attack the edges, limited pass rush, new corners
- defense: alignment/assignment, contain Taywan Taylor
- ST's: control field position, make WKU go long field

PREGAME SHOW/ELI

- WKU is no joke, especially the offense
- QB scenario will continue to play itself out
- overall improvement from game #1 to #2

STAR TO WATCH:

WKU: Anthony Averett

2015 NCAA STATISTICS

Offense		Defense
32nd (199.9)	Rushing	1st (75.7)
62nd (227.1)	Passing	30th (200.6)
45th (427.1)	Total	3rd (276.3)
30th (35.1pts)	Scoring	3rd (15.1pts)
86th (37.4%)	3rd Downs	7th (28.6%)
82nd (82.3%)	RZ	t-62nd (83.3%)
45th (25 total)	Sacks	3rd (53 total)
Penalties	60th (5.9 per game)	
TO Margin	21st (+10)	

Net 77th, PR 20th, KOC 22nd, KOR 49th

BAMA NOTES: (#1 AP/AMWAY COACHES)

- 1892/865-326-43 (Bryant-Denny 101,821)
- 75-11-2 in home openers/9-0 under Saban
- 2-0 vs. WKU
- 16 national titles/25 SEC championships/35-28 in 63 bowls
- since 2008, only last 3 of '10 season/no implications (99/102)
- 8th straight 10+win/19th 11-win campaign/9th 12-win season
- 131st consecutive week in AP poll (leads nation)
- #1 in nine straight seasons (8 straight title games)
- NS (106-18)/10th season (197-60-1 overall) (5 BCS titles)
    - 125th game as UA coach/10-0 in openers (7-0 inside)
    - 56-7 at home/25-2 at Top 25/60 straight vs. unranked
- most wins since '08 (99) (most in SEC history over 6-yr span)
- 40-12 vs. Top 25/22-6 vs. Top 10/9-2 in rematches after loss
- 81-4 when 140+yds rush since '08 (AU '13, UM/OSU '14, UM '15)
- 96-6 when leading at half (LSU '07/'10, AU '10/'13, UM '14)
- 47 nonoffensive touchdowns since 2007 (20int/4fr/6kr/13pr/4blks)

- POW:

    O: D Harris, C Robinson, A Stewart, Jonah Williams

    D: J Allen, R Foster, M Humphrey

    ST: M Fitzpatrick, A Griffith, JK Scott

- only turned ball over 129 times in last 110 games (since '08)
- 110 turnovers in 97 games (since '09), int/58.2 and fumble/ 144.8
- 199 consecutive games scoring (longest in school history)
- 7 players in 2016 NFL Draft (44 in last 6yrs, incl 15 Rd1)
- 9 graduates on roster

BAMA OFFENSE (5 RETURNING STARTERS)

- Lane Kiffin/OC (scored 1st half 119 straight games)
- game-plan approach/lateral passes and vertical runs
- QB: Jalen Hurts/Blake Barnett
- RB: Bo Scarbrough (18att/104yds)/Damian Harris (9/138)
- TE: O. J. Howard, 72 career rec
- WR: Calvin Ridley (89rec/7td), Arderius Stewart (113/2), Robert Foster (inj), Gehrig Dieter (BGSU transfer)
- OL: Bradley Bozeman/Ross Pierschbacher OC/RG

BAMA DEFENSE (6 RETURNING STARTERS)

- Jeremy Pruitt/DC (seamless transition, 3 new on defense)
- Karl Dunbar/DL and Derrick Ansley/DB
- only allowed 142 total TD's since '09 (UF 2nd with 185)
- less than 300 total yards in 77 of 124 games/-200=37x
- 10 points or less 58 times since 2007 (124 total games)
- allowed only 62 rushing td's since 2007 (OSU, 96)
- DL: Jonathan Allen (12sk)/Dalvin Tomlinson (5pd)/D Hand
- ILB: Reuben Foster (73tt)/SD Hamilton/Rashaan Evans
- OLB: Tim Williams (9.5sk)/R Anderson (6.0sk)
- DB: Eddie Jackson (46tt/6int)/M Fitzpatrick (45/10/2)

BAMA SPECIAL TEAMS

- PK: Adam Griffith, 9KO/4TB/23-32FG/62-62PAT
- PT: JK Scott, 44.2avg/18FC/25 -20/1Blk/21-50+(47.0)
- PR/KOR: Ridley/Trevon Diggs

WKU

- 97th season/8th year as FBS program/bowl eligible 5 straight
- 0-2 all-time vs. UA/13 consecutive C-USA wins
- one of seven Group of Five teams to win 7+ in 5 consecutive yrs (WKU, Cin, NIU, Toledo, BSU, SDSU, Ark State)
- Jeff Brohm/2nd season (21-7)
- Offense (Brohm) (5 rec's with 30+ receptions in 2016)
    West Coast scheme/multiple groupings/formations
    QB: #14 Mike White, 25-31-517/11td-16int at USF
    RB: #20 Anthony Wales, 6th straight/1091/9td
    WR: #2 Taywan Taylor, 86/1467/17td; #15 Nicholas Norris, 87yd TD vs. Rice
    OL: #76 Forrest Lamp, 38th start/NFL
- Defense (Nick Holt, former DC at USC and Washington)
    DL: #42 Derik Overstreet, 23rd start
    LB: #6 TJ McCollum, 12tt vs. Rice/106 last year
    DB: #8 Marcus Ward, 134tt in career; #31 Branden Leston, 96tt in 2016
- Special Teams
    PK: #37 Ryan Nuss, 2/3 FG
    PT: #49 Jake Collins
    Ret: #81 Kylen Towner, 3rec/111yds; #1 Nacarius Fant
- WKU, Hilltoppers, The Hill, 'Toppers, Brandon Doughty, Romeo Crennel, Jimmy Feix Field

INDEX